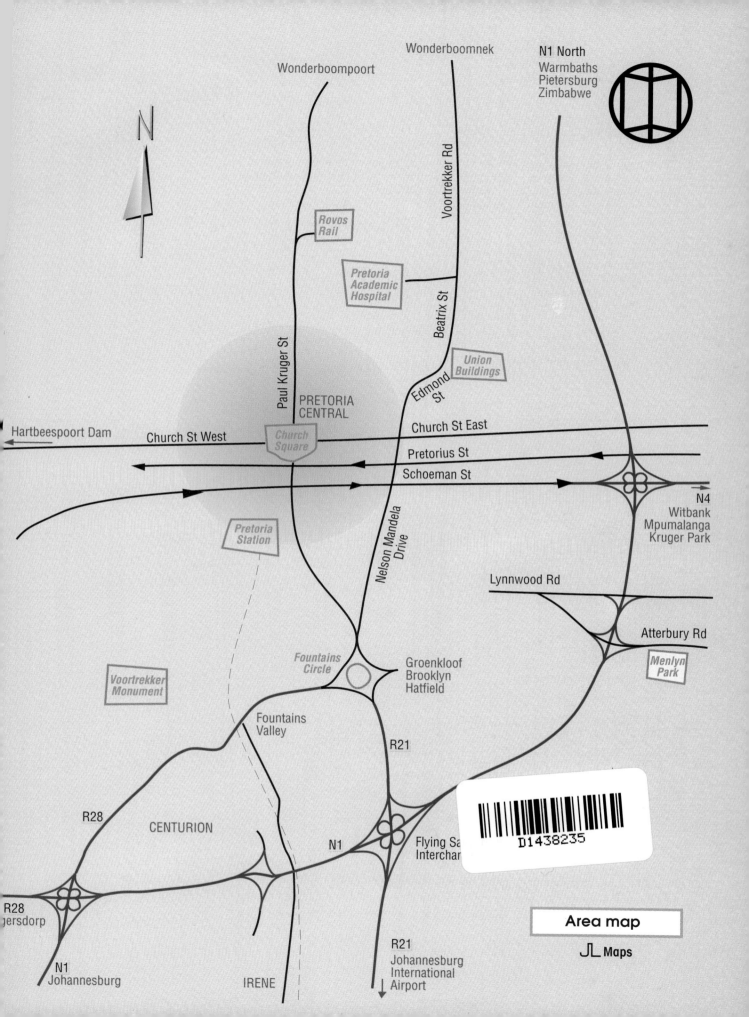

Published by J L van Schaik Publishers
1064 Arcadia Street, Hatfield, Pretoria

First edition 1999
ISBN 0 627 02447 5

Editing & layout by Joan Lötter
Cover design by Brightmark
Cover photos by Walter Knirr
All photos in text by Abrie Swiegers

Typesetting in 11,5 on 16 pt Weiss by A1 Graphics, Pretoria
Printed and bound by NBD,
Drukkery Street, Goodwood, Western Cape

Acknowledgements

The publication of this guide was made possible by the generous
contribution of several sponsors. The authors and publisher wish to
convey their sincere thanks and appreciation to:

Army Surplus Stores

Bouwer Broers

Chagall's Restaurant

Charnan Medical Group

Coquis Mansuitrusters

Die Werf

Engadini Landscaping

Espada Ranch

Hein Scheffer Furnishers

Hyper Paint

Kitty Hawk Lodge

Konica Business Systems

Le Man 2000

Ludwig's Roses

Lynnwood Domestic Services

Marié Vermeulen-Breedt

Multi-Net Systems

Ocean Basket

Phil Minnaar Sculptor

Plan Photo Repro cc

Pre Rand Motors

Pro Lab, Sunnyside

Sammy Marks Square

Shere View Accommodation
and Entertainment

Silverton Houthandelaars

Sinodale Sentrum

South-East Japanese
Restaurant

Supreme Framers

Uitkykvleismark

*The information contained in this book has been confirmed as far as possible up to the
time of going to press. As the nature of the contents is such that it fluctuates on a
daily basis, neither the authors nor the publisher can be held responsible for any
changes in particulars.*

Discover Pretoria

Heinie Heydenrych

Abrie Swiegers

J L van Schaik
1999

Foreword

Over the past hundred and fifty years Pretoria has grown among beautiful hills and valleys to a mature city, worthy of its status as administrative capital of South Africa.

Unlike Johannesburg and towns such as Cullinan and those on the Rand, no major economic discovery boosted the development of Pretoria. Yet the city has succeeded to interest and charm both citzens and visitors throughout her history.

On the other hand Pretoria has often been the focus of international attention. Many great moments in the history of South Africa have taken place in this city. One of the best-known events was the inauguration of President Nelson Mandela.

Over the last three decades a truly cosmopolitan aura has developed in Pretoria. Many foreign embassies are situated here, while trade missions also opened offices. The city has absorbed these influences and gracefully applies them to the best advantage.

The highest educational standards are maintained as is proved by the fact that the two largest universities in the country – those of South Africa and Pretoria – are firmly established. In the field of science and technology also, Pretoria has significantly contributed to South Africa's achievements.

Popularly nick-named Jacaranda City, Pretoria pulls her weight in all aspects. With her interesting features and fascinating history, this city has much to offer the visitor.

It is our hope that this publication will guide and enhance your discovery of Pretoria's delightful secrets.

The Publisher

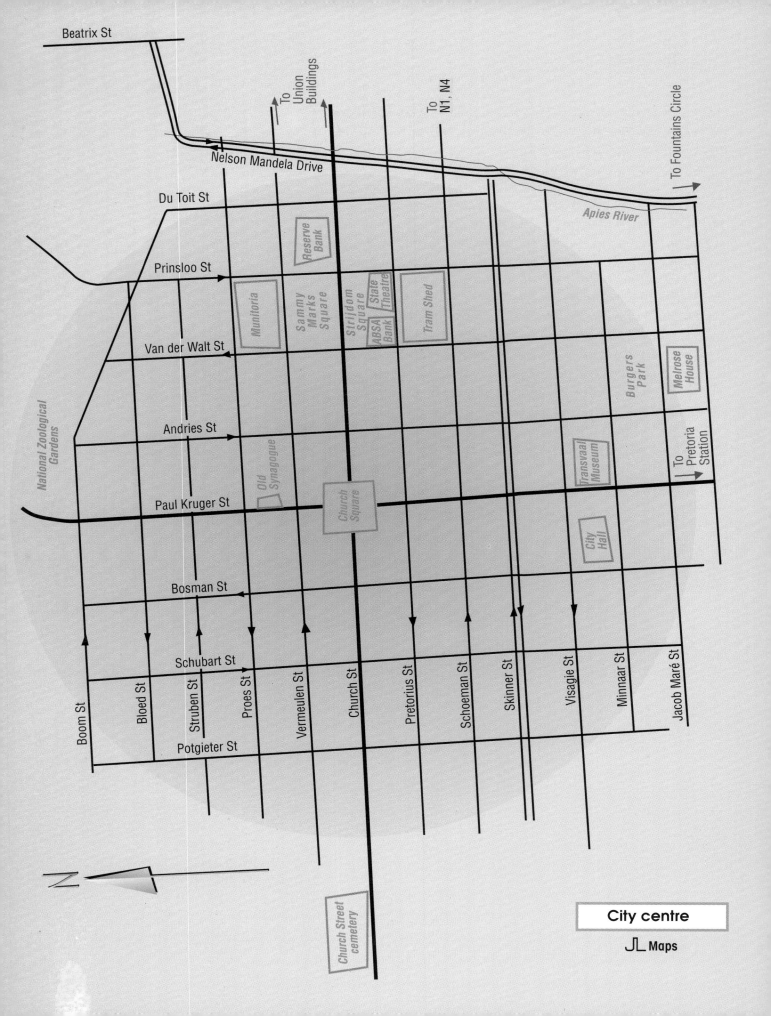

Contents

Fountains Circle's water feature was installed for Pretoria's centenary in 1955 to commemorate the life-giving water from Fountains Valley close by. Unisa is in the background.

Facts and figures

1

Topography and geomorphology

The topography of Pretoria is dominated by the three quartzite ridges which are the result of millions of years of erosion and still protrude above the surrounding landscape in an east-west direction forming two parallel troughs in which the city is situated.

The northernmost ridge is the Magaliesberg which starts northwest of Rustenburg in the Northwest Province and runs more or less west-east from the Hartbeestpoort Dam through Pretoria and then curves in a south-eastern direction through the eastern suburbs of the city. South of the Magaliesberg and parallel to it is a second ridge consisting of the Waterberg or Daspoortrant, the Silverton Ridge and the Bronberge (literally translated: source mountains). The valley between these two ridges is known as the 'Moot', the Dutch word for 'moat', signifying a valley or, originally, a water-filled trench around a medieval castle. The valley to the south of the second ridge is again bounded on the south by a third quartzite protrusion consisting of the Skurweberg, Kwaggasrant, Langeberge, Skanskop, Klapperkop and Waterkloof Ridge. In this southern valley the town originally developed. It still contains the city centre and, among other things, the densely populated Sunnyside which abounds

Location: City centre (approximately)	25' 45' S by 28' 15' E
Altitude:	1370 m or 4494 feet
Founding date:	16 November 1855
Population (1992 census):	849 230
Municipal area:	632 square km or 244 square miles
Average annual rainfall:	700 mm or 27,5 inches
Average day temperature:	Summer – 15 to 28° C
	Winter – 6 to 23° C

Status: Administrative capital of the Republic of South Africa (Cape Town is the legislative capital)

Road distances

To Johannesburg International Airport:	48 km	or	30 miles
To Johannesburg:	58 km	or	36 miles
To Durban:	646 km	or	404 miles
To Cape Town:	1460 km	or	913 miles
To Bloemfontein:	456 km	or	285 miles
To Maseru (Lesotho):	488 km	or	305 miles
To Mbabane (Swaziland):	372 km	or	233 miles
To Windhoek (Namibia):	1859 km	or	1162 miles
To Gaborone (Botswana):	350 km	or	219 miles
To Maputo (Mozambique):	583 km	or	364 miles
To Kruger National Park (Numbi Gate):	386 km	or	241 miles

with flats (apartments). The city of Pretoria sprawls over the two valleys, while suburbs like Pretoria North, Sinoville, Annlin, Montana and Wonderboom in the north and Monument Park, Valhalla and Centurion in the south spill over onto the plains beyond the ridges. (Centurion is a separate municipality.)

Although the three ridges form natural barriers, they are not impenetrable. Folding of the earth's crust and geological faults have shaped neks or poorts over or through which the different parts of the city are connected. Examples are Derdepoort (meaning 'third gateway'), through which the N1 freeway runs; Wonderboompoort through which the Apies River has carved a passage over millions of years; and the Elandspoort between Skanskop and Klapperkop containing the Fountains Valley and allowing the roads from Johannesburg and Kempton Park and the railway line from the south to reach the city. Further faults to the west of the city in the Magaliesberg range mark well-known sites such as the Hartebeespoort through which the Crocodile River flows and across which the wall of the Hartbeespoort Dam was built.

The three ridges mentioned offer spectacular vistas of the city. Johann Rissik Drive on the southernmost ridge affords a view of the other two ridges and the intervening valleys as well as the Union Buildings, one of the landmarks of the city. From the Union Buildings on Meintjeskop an excellent view may be had over the central part of the city, with the Voortrekker Monument, another landmark, in the distance.

Geological activity of the granite to the south of Pretoria to form the Johannesburg igneous dome has resulted in the exposure of dolomite rock in the area south of where the city developed. These processes have caused water trapped underneath the dolomite to reach the surface and form springs. The best known of these are those in the Fountains Valley. These springs are the source of the Apies River and provided sustenance to the early inhabitants of the area. The water sources played a crucial role in the early history of the city and to mark this fact a large dolomite rock was put on display in front of Munitoria, built to house the offices of the city administration. The west wing was destroyed in a fire a few years ago and subsequently imploded.

Climate

The climate in general is moderate, day temperatures ranging from 15 to over 30°C in summer and between 6 and 23°C in winter. The city has an exceptionally large municipal area: Church Street is 26 km in length from west to east, and the north-south distance of Greater

Pretoria, from Soshanguve in the north to the border of Centurion in the south, is about the same distance. Considerable variations in both temperature and rainfall occur. Average temperatures are appreciably lower in the south. Subtropical plants which would perish in the cooler climate of the south, grow north of the Magaliesberg.

Winter nights can be cold, the mercury dropping to below freez-

Pretoria's sunshine draws one out, whether for coffee, to catch a balloon, to be pushed, to take to the road any which way, or to fly away!

ing at times. Frost occurs in parts of Pretoria in winter, but the days (April to September) are usually very pleasant. In summer (October to March) the days can be hot, temperatures rising to over 30°C on occasion, but the nights usually cool down considerably. The average annual rainfall is 700 mm or 27,5 inches occurring mainly in the form of thundershowers which cool down the warm summer afternoons or evenings.

The lush vegetation of Fontains Valley is still there to enjoy, and the Apies River still provides its vital water.

Earliest inhabitants

Evidence has been found that Homo sapiens – modern man as we know him – and his predecessors had lived in the area of the present city of Pretoria since the latter part of early stone age, some 200 000 years ago. The Middle Stone Age (120 000 to 40 000 years ago) is better represented in the form of stone implements. Although evidence from the

History

Late Stone Age (40 000 to 10 000 years ago) is scarce, artefacts from this period have been discovered in the mountains near the city. The First Iron Age people arrived in the area between the Limpopo and Vaal Rivers about 1800 years ago. Although not well represented in the Pretoria area, one of the earliest Iron Age settlements is to be found some 40 km west of Pretoria at Broederstroom, south of the Hartbeespoort Dam. The earliest Iron Age settlement found in the Pretoria municipal area dates from about AD 1200.

Pottery found in the Groenkloof Reserve near the Fountains Valley is associated with early Tswana (Western Sotho)-speaking societies. These people were later followed by other Tswana and Ndebele speakers who settled west and north of Pretoria.

Black inhabitants 1800–1839

Introduction

According to oral tradition the parent tribe of the Ndebele in the area where Pretoria was later established was that of a chief called Msi (or Musi) who lived three or four centuries ago. The river which runs through the city was called after one of Msi's sons, Tshwane, which

The ruins of Lucas Bronkhorst's farm house

means 'little monkey' or 'little baboon'. When the first whites arrived they took over the name and called it the Apies (Monkey or Monkeys) River. Another theory is that they called it the Apies after the blue vervet monkeys which inhabited its banks.

The Difaqane and Mzilikazi

Around 1820 the *Difaqane* or *Mfecane* started, the black migration process which set into motion a period of unequalled disruption and dislocation among the black inhabitants of the highveld plateau of the interior. It was the result of a chain reaction of attacks set in motion by several Nguni groups across the Drakensberg from the present Kwazulu-Natal in order to escape Zulu expansion. The most important event during the *Difaqane* was the migration of Mzilikazi, a subservient chief of King Shaka of the Zulus, to the highveld. After roaming about in the eastern part of the highveld for some time he and his followers moved to an area north and north-west of present-day Pretoria. The main settlement seems to have been some distance north of Pretoria, although some researchers claim that Mzilikazi's capital was within the northern part of the present municipal territory. There are today still reminders of Mzilikazi's sojourn in the vicinity of Pretoria. One of these is the name Silkaatsnek for an area in the Magaliesberg west of Pretoria just north of the Hartbeespoort Dam. 'Silkaats' is a corruption by the Voortrekkers of the name Mzilikazi.

A typical farm building from the 1850s

During 1832 a military force sent by Dingane, king of the Zulu, attacked Mzilikazi and the Matabele, as his followers were called, and they moved to the valley of the Marico River further west in the present Northwest Province. Here clashes occurred between them and the Voortrekkers when the vanguard of the latter moved into the interior. Late in 1837 the Voortrekkers launched a reprisal attack on the Matabele. With the help of Griqua and Tswana allies they finally destroyed the Ndebele power north of the Vaal. Mzilikazi, with the remainder of his followers, thereupon fled across the Limpopo and established his new seat at Bulawayo in the present Zimbabwe.

Arrival of the first whites 1839–1850

After Mzilikazi had vacated the Pretoria area the earlier inhabitants, the Tswana, returned from the middle 1830s. Although the Apies River was sought after as a water source, there is no evidence of a particularly large concentration of blacks on the spot where the city later developed. Almost simultaneously with the Tswana the first whites moved in. They settled mainly along water sources such as the Apies River. The brothers Lucas and Gert Bronkhorst were the first whites to receive farms on land where Pretoria is situated today, although other farms were awarded in the district of Pretoria at the same time.

The Bronkhorst family had left the Cape Colony with the Great Trek party of A H Potgieter in 1836 and had taken part in the battle of

Vegkop in the Free State against Mzilikazi's war machine. After that they followed the Voortrekker leader Piet Retief to Natal. After the death of Retief and his men at the hands of Dingane they returned to the highveld with Potgieter. They settled along the Mooi River at Potchefstroom but finally chose in 1839/40 to set up a permanent home near the Fountains in Pretoria. In 1841 Lucas and Gert Bronkhorst were respectively awarded the farms Groenkloof and Elandspoort. Groenkloof included inter alia the present Fountains Valley, and the sites of forts Schanskop and Klapperkop. Elandspoort became the later central city between Elandspoortrant in the south and Daspoortrant in the north and from Pretoria West in the west to Hatfield and Brooklyn in the east. After 160 years the foundations of Lucas Bronkhorst's modest homestead can still be seen in the Fountains Valley.

After having changed hands several times a portion of the farm Groenkloof was transferred to the government. Finally in 1895 hunting was prohibited in this area making it the second proclaimed game sanctuary in South Africa, in fact on the African continent. This portion consists of the present Groenkloof Reserve and the Fountains Valley.

Other white settlers followed the Bronkhorsts into the fertile and well-watered area of the present Pretoria. By the 1850s Pretoria had become a white settlement, drawing not only Afrikaners but an increasing number of English-speaking inhabitants.

The founding and early years of Pretoria 1850–1902

The early development of Pretoria was closely associated with the political and constitutional development of the Voortrekker state north of the Vaal River. After recognition by the British authorities of the independence of the Voortrekkers north of the Vaal River in 1852, the South African Republic, as the state became known, remained deeply divided. It consisted of three largely independent communities under their own leaders. In the south-west Andries Pretorius and his followers were settled around Potchefstroom and Rustenburg; in the far north a group under A H Potgieter lived in the Soutpansberg with Schoemansdal as their town; and in the east there was another group under W F Joubert's leadership spread over Ohrigstad and Lydenburg. There was in fact a fourth small group in the south-east along the Buffels River who chose the name Utrecht for their community.

A capital for the South African Republic

When M W Pretorius took over the leadership of the western group from his late father, Andries Pretorius, in 1853, he decided to do something

about this divided state of affairs. In 1853 he bought parts of the farms Elandspoort and Daspoort along the Apies River for the purpose of establishing a centrally situated capital. The town was established in 1855, the actual founding date being 16 November. (This happened to be the same day on which Livingstone discovered the Victoria Falls, and on 16 November 1869 the Suez Canal was inaugurated.)

Although the town was not immediately recognized as the capital of the Republic, it was properly surveyed and the first town map is dated 1857. The surveying was done by A F du Toit, the first magistrate. Although Du Toit had no training in this regard and performed his task with only a chain and a pair of ship's binoculars, he did a remarkably good job: sixteen years later a qualified land surveyor declared that he could not improve on it.

Pretoria was recognized as capital only in 1860. From that year the Volksraad, the legislative council of the South African Republic, met there regularly. M W Pretorius, the first state president, called the town after his father Andries Pretorius. Andries Pretorius had acquired great leadership status when he led the Voortrekkers to victory in the decisive battle of Blood River (in the north of the present Kwazulu-Natal) on 16 December 1838 against the army of Dingane; subsequently he led his followers across the Drakensberg onto the highveld. Today two statues (erected for Pretoria's centenary in 1955) in front of the town hall commemorate the founder of Pretoria and the man after whom it was called.

Even after the official recognition of Pretoria as capital a state of civil war existed from 1860 to 1864 between the legal authorities in Pretoria and a rebel group. Only after opposing armies had confronted each other several times and the respective leaders had fled more than once was peace and order restored. At least one of the streets in Pretoria owes its name to this period of conflict. Bloed Street was so named when shots were fired there at a son of A F du Toit, the first magistrate. According to popular belief the younger Du Toit was visiting the house of the rebel leader Stephanus Schoeman when this happened. It is not clear whether he was killed or just wounded. Some say that his horse was shot. Nevertheless blood flowed and hence the name of the street.

The NZASM railway to Maputo is commemorated by this part of the original bridge at the Fountains entrance to the city

Paul Kruger in the history of Pretoria

One of the personalities most closely associated with the history of Pretoria was Paul Kruger, president of the South African Republic from 1883 to the end of the Anglo-Boer War in 1902. As a boy Kruger had taken part in the Great Trek from the Cape Colony. During the early stormy years of the South African Republic, especially the period of civil war (1860–1864), he emerged as a strong figure who tried to restore order and respect for the legal authorities, and as a military leader and mediator.

In 1877 Sir Theophilus Shepstone annexed the South African Republic for Britain and in 1881 its independence was restored after the short First Transvaal

Kruger statue on Church Square

Paul Kruger's house on Church Street

Pretoria railway station

War of Independence (December 1880 – February 1881). Kruger helped as member of a triumvirate to steer the state through this difficult post-war phase. In May 1883 he was elected president and remained head of state nominally until the end of the Anglo-Boer War in 1902. During these almost two decades his name became synonymous with Afrikaner nationalism and he jealously guarded the independence of the republic. One of his greatest achievements was the completion of the railway line to Delagoa Bay (Maputo) in Mozambique at the beginning of 1895, making the republic independent of the colonial harbours.

This was a period of great change brought about by the discovery of gold on the Witwatersrand in 1886. With it came the revival of British

Steam trains can still be seen around Pretoria

imperial interest in the interior and the influx of thousands of fortune seekers, the Uitlanders (Foreigners), as they were called. To Kruger the foreigners seemed to threaten the moral values and independence of the republic and its predominantly rural population. The diplomatic pressure from Britain backing the constitutional demands of the Uitlanders eventually led to the Anglo-Boer War of 1899–1902. When the tide of the war turned against the two Boer republics by mid-1900 Kruger and his government moved to Waterval-Onder in the eastern Transvaal (Mpumalanga Province). When it was eventually decided that the president should leave the country in voluntary exile to prevent his capture by the British forces, he left Delagoa Bay (Maputo) by ship (the Gelderland, made available by Queen Wilhelmina of the Netherlands), never to return to his beloved country. After his death in Switzerland in 1904 his body was returned to South Africa and he was buried amid great public mourning in the cemetery in Church Street West. His presidential home in Church Street is a national monument. The modest house also reflects the SA Republican way of life in the latter part of the 19th century.

Development of the status of Pretoria

Pretoria has retained its status as capital city ever since 1860. When Sir Theophilus Shepstone annexed the South African Republic for Britain in 1877 it remained the capital. For some months after the start of the revolt against annexation the Boers used Heidelberg as their provisional seat of government, but after they had regained their independence in 1881 this status reverted on a permanent basis to Pretoria. After the Anglo-Boer War of 1899–1902 it remained the capital of the Transvaal

This building, dating from 1913 and situated on the corner of Mitchell and Von Wielligh Streets, still serves as a hotel.

Houses, Waterkloof

colony (1902–1910). When the Union of South Africa was founded in 1910 consisting of the four colonies of the Cape, Natal, Transvaal and the Orange River Colony (the latter two the former Boer republics), Pretoria became the administrative capital with Cape Town designated as the legislative capital and seat of parliament. When South Africa became a republic outside the Commonwealth in 1961 the city retained the status of administrative capital. That was also the case when the Government of National Unity took over after the first universal democratic election in 1994.

Pretoria acquired municipal status in 1903 and city status in 1931.

Because of its status as administrative capital Pretoria has witnessed historically important events. It was here that the first state president was sworn in after South Africa had become a republic in 1961 and here also President Nelson Mandela was sworn in as president after the elections of 1994.

Opposite:
Pretoria power station

Subsidised housing (originally for whites) in Pretoria West

17

Physical development of the city

Early development of a white city

Because Pretoria is an administrative capital it has since 1910 housed the headquarters of many government departments, of the South African National Defence Force and the South African Police Service, of a large number of statutory councils and educational, research and commercial institutions as well as industries. The city therefore steadily grew in size as residential areas developed in response to the demand for land to house the growing number of employees of these institutions. New townships and suburbs were therefore proclaimed from time to time.

Most of these townships were white. That was because the professional and skilled employees of these institutions were almost exclusively white, even though there were many non-professional and unskilled employees such as messengers, cleaners, etc, in government departments. The work force of industries was also largely black and that is still the case. From the earliest years there were black residential areas in Pretoria, such as Schoolplaats, Marabastad and Bantule, which had their origin in the days of the South African Republic before 1902. While most white areas or townships developed in an orderly way and were provided with basic services such as roads, running water, sewerage, refuse removal and electricity, most of the black areas developed in a more haphazard way

Freeways around Pretoria

Church Street from the east in jacaranda time

and were poorly serviced. This was because the constitution of the South African Republic excluded people of colour from citizenship and the right to own land, except in demarcated black areas traditionally occupied by blacks – therefore not in towns established by whites. Today the Asiatic Bazaar, the popular black shopping area along Boom Street north-west of the city centre, is the only remaining one of these 19th century residential areas which is still black, although today it is a trading area and not a residential one. However, it is equally true that certain white

Family outing

areas adjoining the municipal borders and called peri-urban townships, also did not have sewerage or tarred roads. These were incorporated into Greater Pretoria in the 1960s.

Segregated black townships

In the twentieth century blacks were still regarded as temporary inhabitants of 'white' cities such as Pretoria. This principle was embodied in an Act of 1923. Local authorities were allowed to set aside 'locations' for blacks but the latter could not obtain property rights. Atteridgeville was the first black township established by the municipality of Pretoria since 1910. It was proclaimed in 1939 and named after a lady town councillor. Here houses were built by the municipality and leased to the inhabitants. By 1967 some 10 000 houses had been built. Sanitary services, running water, electricity and refuse removal were provided. By 1992 Atteridgeville had grown to more than 110 000 inhabitants and it has long been regarded as a model black township.

In 1945 the farm Vlakfontein north-east of the city was bought to establish another black township. It was proclaimed in 1953 and later it was named Mamelodi. It is a Tswana word meaning, among other things, 'place of joy'. A theory about the origin of the name is that the township

Mamelodi township

was called after President Paul Kruger who was referred to by this name meaning 'father of whistling' or 'man who can imitate birds'.

A unique black residential area in Pretoria was Lady Selborne, northwest of the city where the present township of Suiderberg is situated. It was proclaimed in 1905 and called after the wife of the then high commissioner, Lord Selborne. Lady Selborne was the only urban area in Pretoria at the time where blacks could own land. Due to subletting the area became very overcrowded.

Group areas reinforce the segregated pattern

In 1958 a new era dawned when group areas were declared for the various races in terms of the Group Areas Act passed the previous year. Atteridgeville and Mamelodi were declared black but Lady Selborne was designated a white area. By the late 1960s all the blacks in Lady Selborne had been removed to Atteridgeville and elsewhere. Coloureds

Silverlakes private development east of the city, an up-market golfing estate

were removed to Eersterust which was designated a coloured area. Likewise Indians were moved to Laudium which was designated an Indian area.

Abolition of the pass laws and the influx of blacks

A new era dawned with the abolition of the pass laws and influx control in 1986. Many blacks streamed to the cities from the black homelands in search of work. This caused a great increase in the number of black people in the towns and cities. Many of these newcomers to the city found shelter in informal settlements in the form of squatter camps.

Multiracial city government since 1994

Mamelodi and Atteridgeville were both initially administered directly by the municipality and eventually by their own town councils, while Eersterust and Laudium were administered by semi-independent management committees. Following the changes at national government level after the universal democratic elections of April 1994, all four these bodies and the original Pretoria City Council were drawn together in the Pretoria Metropolitan Substructure in December 1994. This body served all residents of greater Pretoria in the interim period until the local government elections of November 1995. Since the local elections of November 1995 the inhabitants of Pretoria, like their counterparts in other South African towns, were represented for the first time by a democratically constituted local council. For the first time also Pretoria has a black mayor. The Pretoria Metropolitan Substructure, together with a Northern Pretoria Metropolitan Substructure (representing Akasia and Soshanguve), and the Centurion City Council in the south, form the Greater Pretoria Metropolitan Council.

Ethnic elegance

Pretoria has an attractive natural environment. This environment can be explored by visiting the parks, nature reserves, bird sanctuary, botanical garden and the zoo, by walking the nature trails, and driving the jacaranda routes listed below. Further information may be obtained from either the *Tourist Rendezvous* at tel. 308 8909 or at the Pretoria City Council's *Department of Culture and Recreation* at tel. 308 8833 or 308 8840.

The natural environment

Parks and public gardens

Burgers Park

Burgers Park, five blocks south-east of Church Square, is also mentioned in passing in the section on **Architecture**. This park, a few street blocks from the city centre, could easily have become for Pretoria what the Company Garden is for Cape Town: a tranquil haven almost in the heart of the city. It is perhaps only a block or two too far away for that. However, it is still a beautiful park worth a visit.

The park, bordered in the west and east by Andries and Van der Walt Streets and in the south and north by Jacob Maré and Burgers Park Streets respectively, was called after T F Burgers, who was President of the South African Republic from 1872 to 1877. He requested that a piece of land be set aside for use as a botanical garden. However, it was only in 1890–92 that a park was laid out. The contract was awarded to George Heys, the owner of Melrose House across the park in Jacob Maré Street. A number of commemorative trees were planted in the garden, among them the Queen Wilhelmina tree planted in 1898 on the occasion of the birthday of the Dutch Queen. The Victorian style kiosk, which today houses a restaurant, and the bandstand add an old-world charm to the park.

*Autumn leaves
in the suburbs*

*Winter fruit
at the farmer's market*

Summer butterfly

Spring flowers

Pretoria: a place for all seasons

Anytime airshow at Waterkloof airport. Everybody is enchanted by the 'flying cheetah'. The cheetah is the superfast squad's mascot.

The bandstand in Burgers Park. The florarium is in the background.

An interesting feature of the park is the so-called florarium, a building erected in the 1960s to display a variety of exotic plants in four carefully controlled environments. The building contains ferns, orchids, fuschias, etc in one section, succulents in others, and tropical plants in another.

The park also contains the statue of President T F Burgers and the memorial for members of the South African Scottish Regiment who fell during the First World War. Both are discussed under **Statues and public sculptures** and **Monuments and memorials** respectively.

Hours: 06:00–22:00 daily in summer and 06:00–18:00 in winter
Admission: Free

Venning Park, Arcadia

This formal park in Arcadia near the United States Embassy, bounded by Pretorius and Schoeman Streets in the north and south and by Farenden and Eastwood Streets in the west and east, is a delightful place to visit. The central feature is a rose garden which is immaculately kept and a joy to behold. The roses are at their best in October and November, but the garden is always worth visiting and the park also contains a tearoom, Café Rose, where refreshments can be enjoyed in the open air in a relaxed atmosphere and beautiful surroundings.

Hours: All day throughout the year

Springbok Park, Hatfield

This is an informal garden containing only indigenous plants. It is six street blocks east of Venning Park, also between Pretorius and Schoeman Streets, and bounded in the west and east by Hilda and Grosvenor Streets. It contains about 100 white stinkwood trees (*Celtis africana*), which are also to be seen in Fountains Valley and along some of Pretoria's streets, as well as other indigenous trees. There is a pond and waterfall connected with a lower pond which houses a group of waterfowl. There is a wide variety of perennials and bulbous plants, watsonia and gladiolus lilies, as well as the stately long-stemmed agapanthus with its mauve-blue flowers, which are a delight to behold in spring and summer. Namaqualand daisies and other annuals are sown at the beginning of winter and provide splashes of colour in spring (August and September).

Hours: All day throughout the year
Admission: Free

The kiosk in Burgers Park where you can enjoy a cup of tea

29

Jan Celliers Park, Groenkloof

This 4,5 hectare park is situated in Groenkloof between Van Wouw and Wenning Streets to the south and north and Wangemann and Broderick Streets in the west and east. There are many *Proteaceae* (protea plants) and other striking plants such as aloes and agapanthus. The dominating feature of the garden is a stream containing 14 miniature waterfalls connecting two ponds, with a large variety of plants along the border of the stream. The rest of the park consists of large lawns broken up by rockeries and groups of trees and shrubs. All the plants are indigenous.

The proteas are at their best in winter and spring (June–August and September–October), while the aloes make a spectacular show in late winter. In spring the different indigenous wild flowers such as gazanias, Namaqualand daisies and portulacas provide a show of colour.

Hours: All day throughout the year. Guided walks by arrangement with the municipality, tel: 313 8820.

Admission: Free

Tranquility in Jan Celliers Park, Groenkloof

Strelitzia, an elegant
indigenous flower

Duck in anywhere!
A quiet spot at the
Pioneer Museum, Silverton

Music in Magnolia Dell on Art Market Saturday

Magnolia Dell, Muckleneuk

This well-frequented park at the northern end of Queen Wilhelmina Drive, where it meets Walker Street and University Road, owes its name to the magnolias planted in the 1950s and 1960s. Some ten different varieties of magnolia occur, among them the *Magnolia grandiflora* along Queen Wilhelmina Avenue. Willows and spacious lawns adorn the banks of the Walker Spruit which runs through the garden. Several indigenous tree species such as acacias (*Acacia caffra*, the common hook-thorn, and *Acacia karoo*, the sweet thorn) and the evergreen karee (*Rhus lancea*) also occur in the park.

There is a tearoom and restaurant situated in the park.

An art and craft market is held on the lawns on the first Saturday of every month. Occasionally a Friday evening moonlight market is also held.

An interesting feature of University Road which runs from Magnolia Dell past Pretoria Boys High and the University of Pretoria to Burnett Street, is the double row of date palms next to it. They were planted to commemorate the discovery of Tutankhamen's tomb (1922) and have since been declared a national monument.

Hours: All day throughout the year.
Admission: Free

32

Palm trees to commemorate the discovery of Tutankhamen's tomb on 26 November 1922

Art in the park: Magnolia Dell

Union Buildings gardens, Meintjeskop

The grounds around the Union Buildings cover no less than 118 hectares. Behind the famous building by Sir Herbert Baker natural vegetation occupies 87 hectares of the koppie (hill), but the part that is seen most by visitors and passers-by is the formal garden in front of the building which is intensively cultivated. The large lawns sweeping up towards the buildings and the flower-bedecked terraces in front of the buildings comprise the country's best-known formal garden. The equestrian statue of Louis Botha, first Prime Minister of the Union of South Africa, on the lawn has witnessed many momentous occasions. The flower beds on the terraces display many different colours at different times of the year.

Hours: Open all day throughout the year
Admission: Free

University of South Africa garden, Muckleneuk Ridge

The large headquarters of Unisa, as the name of this correspondence university is usually abbreviated, catch the eye as one enters the city from the south. Around this striking building is a garden of almost 23 hectares with lots of indigenous vegetation. It contains no fewer than 180 plant species, among which are a large number of indigenous trees and shrubs. A trail enables the visitor to view the plants from close quarters. The university also has a cycad garden where a variety of African cycads can be seen. The cycads are protected plants which are the almost extinct remainder of a group of plants that formed the dominant vegetation type some 300 million years ago. Individual specimens may become hundreds or even thousands of years old. In the cycad garden are also to be seen other typical indigenous plants such as the *Cussonia*, known commonly as the cabbage tree because its shape and the colour of the leaves resemble a cabbage. In addition there is a water garden.

Hours: Open throughout the year Monday to Friday 07:45–16:00 by arrangement with Unisa's Department of Public Relations at tel: 429 2624. Guided walks by arrangement.
Admission: Free

Pretoria National Botanical Garden

The Pretoria National Botanical Garden, only 10 km from the city centre, serves as a 'window' for the tourist on the flora of the southern African subcontinent. Although only 76 ha in size, it contains 500 of

South Africa's approximately 1000 indigenous tree species and more than half the 1700 flowering plants that occur in the Pretoria district. (This is equal to the total for the British Isles which are one hundred times the size.) It also houses a world-famous herbarium, the Mary Gunn Library, and associated laboratories.

What makes the garden particularly interesting is the fact that it lies at an altitude of 1300 to 1400 m (about 3225 to 3550 feet) on the divide between the highveld plateau and the lowveld, i.e. the coastal plain where among others the Kruger National Park is situated. Consequently it has plant species from both regions. In addition the garden has frost-free north-facing aspects as well as frosty south-facing ones, making it suitable for a very large variety of plants.

Although the garden is not meant to be a game reserve, it is home to a variety of small game. Dassies (rock-rabbits) can often be seen in the rocky parts sunning themselves, and flocks of guinea-fowl roam the open spaces, while no fewer than 185 species of birds have been sighted there. Small buck are also seen from time to time. The garden was declared a national monument in 1979.

A network of footpaths several kilometres long takes the visitor through most parts of the garden. In the central part is a 30 m high waterfall close to which is a tea garden where traditional South African meals as well as scones and other refreshments can be enjoyed.

Hours: 08:00–18:00 every day of the week. For guided tours phone between 08:00 and 09:00 and between 15:00 and 16:30 on weekdays.

Admission: Charged

Tel: 804 3200

Animal life

Austin Roberts Bird Sanctuary

For the nature and bird lover Pretoria provides in quite a novel way by means of a bird sanctuary where many bird species can be seen in their natural surroundings. The sanctuary is a fenced piece of veld 11 hectares in extent right in the middle of the city's eastern suburbs. One cannot enter the sanctuary but it can be viewed from four sides, while a hide in the north-western corner allows one to observe at close quarters the waders which frequent the dam next to which it is situated. The blue crane, the national bird of South Africa which appears on the 5 cent coin, can often be seen from the surrounding roads next to the fence. A tea garden and restaurant next to the sanctuary is also quite appropriately called The Blue Crane.

The sanctuary, which provides a safe haven for thousands of birds, was called after the famous south African ornithologist, Dr Austin Roberts, as was the impressive bird hall in the Transvaal Museum in Paul Kruger Street. Roberts is also the author of the standard book on South African birds *Roberts' birds of southern Africa*, first published in 1940. Four further editions have appeared since.

Hours: The hide is open every day including weekends and public holidays 07:00–17:00
Admission: Free

Blue Crane Restaurant,
Austin Roberts Bird Sanctuary

Flamingoes, Pretoria Zoo

Grey lourie, garden visitor, originates from the much warmer Bushveld

Coucal (vlei lourie), garden visitor

Indian elephants, Pretoria Zoo

Pretoria National Zoological Gardens and aquarium and reptile park

Although the zoo and its accompanying aquarium and reptile park contain specimens that do not form part of the natural environment of Pretoria and therefore should not, strictly speaking, be discussed under this heading, much of their content comes from the larger South African environment and their discussion here is therefore warranted.

Zoo

The zoo in Pretoria is the best in South Africa and one of the ten best in the world. It boasts not only animals from all over the world but also many South African species, including the 'Big Five' – the lion, leopard, elephant, rhinoceros and buffalo. The zoo attracts one million visitors per year. However, it is geared not only towards entertainment and education, but attention is also given to the breeding of endangered species.

The zoo is attractively laid out and the pens and cages conform to international standards. The setting is extremely picturesque and kilometres of footpaths wind through park-like surroundings with large open lawns, flower beds and many trees, while picnic spots and braai (barbeque) facilities are provided. There is also a kiosk and restaurant.

Apart from normal daytime visits the zoo offers regular night tours. These night tours incorporate a video and a visit to the enclosures of nocturnal animals. The zoo also has a farmyard where children can come face to face with domesticated animals.

An overhead cable-way affords visitors an unspoilt view of large parts of the zoo and the city.

Inside the zoo grounds is a fountain which was donated to the people of the South African Republic (Transvaal Republic) by Sammy Marks, the well-known early entrepreneur and industrialist and confidant of President Kruger (see box on Sammy Marks under **Museums**). It stood on Church Square until 1954 when the statue of Kruger finally found its resting place there.

Hours:	Open daily, including public holidays: 08:00–18:00 in summer and 08:00–17:30 in winter
Admission:	Charged
Further information:	Tel: 328 3265/328 6020

Aquarium and reptile park

Next to the zoo in Boom Street is the aquarium and reptile park. It incorporates the largest inland salt water aquarium in South Africa and a freshwater section with some 180 species.

Both the aquarium and the reptile park house specimens from all over the world – including some endangered species – and both have active breeding programmes.

Location:	Boom Street, cnr Paul Kruger Street, next to the zoo
Hours:	Open daily, including public holidays: 08:00–18:00 in summer and 08:00–17:30 in winter
Admission:	Charged
Tel:	328 3265/328 6020

Nature reserves and trails

Wonderboom Nature Reserve

Some 15 minutes' drive to the north of the city centre is a nature reserve which contains a remarkable tree. This is the Wonderboom (wonder tree or miracle tree) which is a national monument and is therefore discussed under **Monuments** as well. A 450 ha nature reserve has been declared around the wild fig tree to protect it and today it is one of the foremost reserves within the city limits. Apart from the miracle tree the reserve is also home to some small game such as small antelope, dassies (rock-rabbits), vervet monkeys, and a number of bird species.

But the reserve also protects several historical sites. On top of the ridge that forms part of the reserve are the remains of Fort Wonderboompoort. It is a fairly steep climb from the south of the tree up to the fort, but it is worth while in terms of the fort as well as the view over the city. The fort is one of four built during the 1890s to defend Pretoria against foreign attack (see box on the Jameson Raid and the forts under **Military traces of the past**). Although the forts were never used during war-time, Fort Wonderboompoort is an interesting relic of a century ago and the German know-how used in its construction. It was designed by two engineers of the German engineering firm of Krupp, and was built by a German contractor. This was also the case with Fort Klapperkop and Fort Schanskop on the other side of town.

On the western side of the ridge where it is penetrated by the Apies River to form the Wonderboompoort (gateway), there is a cave which is thought to have been the dwelling place of prehistoric hunters of some 50 000 years ago. An archaeological site which yielded a large number of stone implements such as cleavers, hand-axes and choppers, was discovered when a road was built through the poort decades ago. The cave can be reached via a path which starts to the west of the tree.

Another feature of the Wonderboompoort is the man-made waterfall on the eastern wall. The water is pumped up from the Apies River below and it is a lovely surprise to see it falling. It was installed for Pretoria's 100th birthday in 1955.

Facilities: Picnic and braai/barbeque facilities with ablution blocks. Footpaths lead to the fort and the cave, while others are merely meant to enable the visitor to explore the reserve.

Hours: The reserve is open every day from sunrise to sunset.

Admission: Charged

Spring splendour in a Schoeman Street park

Fountains Valley

The Fountains Valley has been called 'Pretoria's spring of life'. That is because of the underground spring in the valley which attracted the first white settlers and supplied the pioneer town with water (see the discussion of the first white homestead there and the arrival of the first white settlers under **Monuments** and **History** respectively).

One of the first farms awarded to settlers in 1839/40 was Groenkloof. That farm included inter alia the present Fountains Valley. After the farm had changed hands several times a portion of it was transferred to the government. In 1895 hunting was prohibited there, making it one of the first proclaimed game sanctuaries in South Africa – and on the African continent. This portion consists of the present Fountains Valley and the Groenkloof Reserve.

The recreation resort that has been developed in the Fountains Valley contains a large caravan park, picnic and braai (barbeque) sites, a swimming pool, tennis courts, lawns and flower beds, and a miniature railway worked by a steam locomotive on which visitors can have a ride (usually on weekends).

The reserve is not separate from the recreation resort. It consists of a richly wooded valley with mainly white stinkwood (*Celtis africana*) trees which has earned it the name of 'valley of a thousand trees'. A two-day hiking trail over a distance of 15 km (9,4 miles) starts at the recreation resort. On the first day 10,5 km (6,5 miles) is covered and on the second day 4,5 km (2,8 miles).

At the traffic circle called 'Fountains Circle' situated next to the Fountains Valley the group of fountains were installed for Pretoria's 100th birthday to commemorate the life-giving water of the valley.

Fountains picnic

Hours: Mon–Sun, including public holidays: 07:00–24:00. Gates close for entry at 20:00 on Saturdays and 18:00 on Sundays.
Admission: Charged
Tel: General: 44 7131
Hiking trail: 313 8833/313 8820

Rietvlei Nature Reserve and Trail

The Rietvlei Nature Reserve resulted from the establishment of the Rietvlei Water Scheme. This scheme was built when it became clear that the springs in the Fountains Valley could no longer supply sufficient water for the town's needs. The Rietvlei Dam was completed in 1934. In 1937 the area east of the dam was declared a nature reserve.

The nature reserve, on the shore of the Rietvlei Dam, covers 3400 ha and is home to a large variety of grasses, indigenous trees typical of the highveld, and some 1500 head of game. Because Rietvlei is situated on the highveld (the central plateau) it has species that do not occur in the low-lying Kruger National Park in Mpumalanga. The inhabitants include a variety of antelope, zebra, brown hyena, jackal, small game such as genets, meerkats, otters, hares, mongoose, hedgehogs, antbears, and porcupines. Rietvlei also has a variety of bird life including the fish eagle, secretary bird and numerous water birds. The dam offers angling and yachting (only for members of the yacht club). Historical sites in the reserve include the old farm homestead, a stacked stone entrenchment dating back to the Anglo-Boer War, and Voortrekker graves. There is a hiking trail of 20 km (12,5 miles) with two overnight huts.

Admission:	Charged
Hours:	Game viewing Sundays and public holidays: 09:00–17:00
Facilities:	30 km tarred roads for game viewing. Picnic and braai/barbeque facilities. Hiking trail with overnight accommodation by prior arrangement. Trophy hunting (by prior arrangement). Angling by permit obtainable at the gate.
Tel:	313 8820/345 2274

Roodeplaat Dam Nature Reserve

The Roodeplaat Dam, situated some 20 km north-east of Pretoria, is a larger expanse of water than the Rietvlei Dam. It is formed by the damming of the Hartebeest Spruit and the Pienaars River. Unlike Rietvlei Dam, Roodeplaat is not a water supply dam for the city of Pretoria, but an irrigation dam, which has become a favourite recreation spot for city dwellers. Along the shore is a caravan park and camping

All aboard! The miniature train at Fountains Valley is ready to go.

site often frequented by anglers, while the dam itself is used for water-skiing and power-boating. Many of the picnic sites are right on the edge of the dam and good roads lead to these sites.

Facilities: Barbeque/braai facilities and ablution blocks
Admission: Charged

Derdepoort Recreation Resort

This resort just north-east of the city offers visitors the opportunity to experience a farm atmosphere in true bushveld surroundings. The resort has lots of shaded picnic and braai/barbeque facilites. A swimming pool with hot showers and an adventure park next to the picnic area provide recreation for young and old alike, while cold drinks and light refreshments can be bought from a kiosk. A miniature train next to the playground is very popular. In addition there are two covered entertainment areas with barbeque facilities and a kitchen for hire. A restaurant and tea garden is housed in a restored old farmhouse which forms part of the resort.

Hours: Daily 07:00–20:00
Tel: 808 0828/9
Admission: Charged

Moreleta Spruit Hiking and Nature Trail

The Moreleta Spruit is a stream running through the eastern suburbs of Pretoria which has been left relatively unspoilt by the urban development around it. The stream rises south-east of Pretoria, near the Rietvlei Nature Reserve. It then flows through the suburbs of Moreleta Park,

Moreleta Trail runs through unspoilt nature

Moreleta Trail through the suburbs

Plumbago tea garden on Moreleta Trail

Have a break, have a picnic! Pretoria has many attractive picnic sites, like this one at the Pioneer Museum, Silverton.

Faerie Glen, Garsfontein, Lynnwood Glen, Lynnwood Manor, Murray-field and Silverton. Eventually it converges with another stream and discharges into the Roodeplaat Dam, north-east of the city. Along this course it traverses a variety of landscapes with differing vegetation.

The trail follows the stream closely. It makes for a very pleasant walk and is often used by bird lovers and watchers. It is at present possible to hike from Moreleta Kloof in Rubenstein Drive, Moreleta Park, to Silverton, but the trail can also be done in sections. The easiest starting point is probably the one in Menlyn Drive. However, there are starting points in Jacqueline Drive in Garsfontein, Manitoba Drive in Faerie Glen, Louis Botha Drive in Lynnwood Glen, or Lynnwood Road in Lynnwood Ridge. From Manitoba Drive to Louis Botha Drive the stream runs through the Faerie Glen Nature Reserve. The trail ends at the Pioneer Museum in Silverton.

Hikers should take care to do the trail in groups as vagrants have been known to molest people along the route.

Hours: Open at all times
Facilities: Tea garden at Louis Botha Drive starting point at the Faerie Glen Nature Reserve
Tel: 313 8820

Faerie Glen Nature Reserve and trail

The Faerie Glen Nature Reserve is the jewel of the Moreleta stream. It is the largest area along the stream of more or less undisturbed natural habitat with diverse geology, soils, micro-climates and vegetation. The diverse habitats cater for a variety of birds and small mammals. The Moreleta Spruit hiking trail follows the stream through the reserve, but there are two other trails and it is possible to scale the Bronberg which forms part of the reserve. From the top there is a good view of some of the eastern suburbs and part of the stream.

Admission:	No charge
Facilities:	A private tea garden, Plumbago Tea Garden, where information on the hiking trails can be obtained.
Tel:	313 8820 or 348 7773

Jacaranda splendour

Although the jacaranda tree is not indigenous to South Africa, it has become synomous with Pretoria so that the city is often referred to as the Jacaranda City. The large number of jacarandas along the streets of Pretoria and in parks and gardens burst into lilac every October turning the city into a spectacle that defies description. The jacaranda is to Pretoria what the oak is to Stellenbosch, and there is a legend that if a jacaranda bloom falls on a student's head – university and technicon exams begin in October when the jacarandas are in bloom – he or she will pass their exams even though they may not have prepared well.

Typical Pretoria street in jacaranda time

The story of Pretoria's jacarandas

The jacaranda is a native of South America, specifically Argentina. Today they also occur in Brazil, southern California, the West Indies and Australia. The botanical name is *Jacaranda mimosifolia* of the family Bignoniaceae. The tree has adapted well to the warmer parts of southern Africa and today the main concentrations are in Pretoria and Johannesburg.

In 1888 J D (Japie) Celliers ordered two jacaranda seedlings from Brazil. They were planted in the garden of his home 'Myrtle Lodge' in Sunnyside. Today these original trees can be seen in the grounds of Sunnyside School in Leyds Street. In 1898 a nurseryman was granted a concession by the government of the South African Republic to plant trees in Groenkloof, Pretoria. James Clark, Pretoria seed merchant and nurseryman, ordered seeds from Australia. Among the eucalyptus seeds which reached Clark from Australia for planting in Groenkloof, there was a packet of jacaranda seeds.

Eight years later, on 16 November 1906, the 51st anniversary of the

founding of Pretoria, Clark presented 200 jacaranda trees to the city council of Pretoria. These trees were planted along Bosman (then Koch) Street and in Arcadia Park where the Pretoria Art Museum was opened in 1964. Clark was nicknamed 'Jacaranda Jim' and died in January 1956 at the age of 92.

However, the large-scale planting of jacarandas was due to the other 'Jacaranda Jim', Frank Walton Jameson. When Jameson became a member of the town council in 1909 he felt strongly that the town, as the proposed administrative capital of the to-be-formed Union of South Africa, should be beautified to suit its new status. He suggested that jacarandas be planted along all the streets. When it appeared that little money was set aside for that purpose he saw to it that a nursery for propagating trees was established in Prince's Park, where the bus terminus is today situated opposite the cemetery in Church Street West.

When Jameson retired from the council in 1920 some 6000 trees had been planted. The nursery was moved but the policy of planting jacarandas was continued. By 1939 the number of trees had increased to 17 000. When Jameson died at the age of 82 in 1956 – some two months after James Clark's death – he was buried in Rebecca Street Cemetery in Pretoria West where some of the finest jacaranda avenues in the city can be seen. Thanks mainly to F W Jameson Pretoria today has some 70 000 jacarandas and is known as the 'Jacaranda City'.

The white jacarandas in Herbert Baker Street in Groenkloof originated in Peru. The tree was discovered in the jungle of that country and some cuttings were taken to California. The only cutting that survived was grafted onto an established mauve jacaranda tree and in 1957 the first white flowers appeared in Los Angeles. In November 1961 Pretoria's director of Parks, Mr Harri Bruins-Lich, received from Dr William Steward, director of the Arnold Arboretum and Botanical Gardens in Los Angeles, a specimen of the white jacaranda. It was presented to the city council and accepted by the mayor at the time, Mr L R Bester. Another specimen was presented to the state president, Mr C R Swart.

Before leaving for South Africa Dr Steward had the saplings sent here. Since it was winter in California the little trees were bare of leaves. The trees were therefore planted in Kirstenbosch Botanical Garden in Cape Town. By the time they were handed over in November, they had grown leaves.

Two years later the first white flowers appeared on Pretoria's tree. Since the propagation of white jacarandas from seeds proved impossible they were grafted onto ordinary mauve jacarandas. Today there are still only about one hundred white jacarandas, mainly confined to Herbert Baker Street in Groenkloof. ■

White jacarandas in Herbert Baker Street, Groenkloof

Jacaranda routes

Three routes along jacaranda-lined streets have been identified which display the splendour of these trees to the best advantage. All three start at the Tourist Rendezvous on the corner of Vermeulen and Prinsloo Streets.

Route 1 (±11 km)

Drive eastward along Vermeulen Street, across Beatrix Street, and up to where Vermeulen Street is joined by Church Street next to the gardens of the Union Buildings on the left. Turn left into Church Street and almost immediately right into Wessels Street. Cross Pretorius and Schoeman Streets and pass the Pretoria Art Museum on your left. Turn left into Park Street and pass Johann, Beckett, Farenden, Eastwood and Orient Streets. Turn left into Hill Street and right again into Schoeman Street. Cross Festival and Hilda Streets and turn left into Grosvenor Street and left again into Pretorius Street. Pass Hilda, Festival, Hill, Orient, and Eastwood Streets and turn right into Farenden Street, right again into Church Street and left into Eastwood Street. Pass Thomas, Harcourt, Merton and George Streets and turn left into Government Avenue. Travel along Government Avenue past the Union Buildings and up to Hamilton Street beyond. Turn left into Hamilton Street and then right into Proes Street,

crossing Beatrix and Ockerse Streets, Nelson Mandela Drive, and Du Toit Street, turn left into Prinsloo Street and drive up to Vermeulen Street where the route started.

Route 2 (±17 km)

From the Tourist Rendezvous drive up Prinsloo Street, crossing Church, Pretorius, Schoeman, Skinner and Visagie Streets, then turn left into Jacob Maré Street. Cross Nelson Mandela Drive, Gerard Moerdijk, Joubert, Mears, Troye and Celliers Streets and turn left into Leyds Street. The Sunnyside School is on your left. It was at this school that the first jacarandas were planted in 1888. The original two trees can be seen from the school gate. Cross Jorissen, Kotze, Esselen Streets, pass De Rapper and Wyland Streets and turn right into Park Street. Cross Wessels Street and pass the Pretoria Art Museum on your left. Pass Beckett Street and cross Farenden Street and turn right into Kirkness Street. Pass Minolta Loftus Rugby Ground on your left and turn left into Lynnwood Road. Cross University Road and pass the University of Pretoria on your left. Pass Roper Street and turn left into Tindall Road and then right into Duxbury Road. Turn right into Duncan Street and cross Lunnon and Lynnwood Roads, Brooks and Anderson Streets before turning right into Murray Street. Turn left where

Roper Street forms a T-junction with it.

Travel along Roper Street crossing Mackenzie, Marais, Charles, Nicholson and Nixon Streets before you reach Boshoff Street. You are now at the Austin Roberts Bird Sanctuary. Turn left into Boshoff Street and right into Dey Street. Pass Muckleneuk Street and turn right into Middel Street. Turn right at the next traffic light into Queen Wilhelmina Avenue. Pass Muckleneuk, Boshoff, Mackie, Totius, and Sibelius Streets and pass Magnolia Dell on your right. Turn right into University Road. Cross Charles Street and turn left into Walton Jameson Avenue, called after the town engineer who first planted jacarandas along Pretoria's streets. Cross Jorissen Street and travel up to the T-junction with Minni Street where you turn right. Turn left at the next T-junction into Park Street. Pass the intersection with Hamilton Street and turn right into Beatrix Street. Cross Pretorius, Church and Vermeulen Streets and turn left into Proes Street. Pass Ockerse, Nelson Mandela Drive, and Du Toit Street and turn left into Prinsloo Street. Drive up to Vermeulen Street where the route started.

Route 3 (±24 km)

From the Tourist Rendezvous, drive along Vermeulen Street and turn left into Du Toit Street and then left again into Proes Street. Cross Prinsloo and Van der Walt

Streets and turn left into Andries Street. Cross Vermeulen, Church, Pretorius, Schoeman, Skinner and Visagie Streets and pass Burgers Park on your left. Cross Jacob Maré and Scheiding Streets and follow the signs to Johannesburg International Airport passing the University of South Africa on your left.

Continue up to the Fountains Circle and take Nelson Mandela Drive towards Kempton Park and the airport from there. About one km from the Fountains Circle, turn left into Johann Rissik Drive.

Continue along this road for several kilometres until you reach Rigel Avenue North. Turn left into Rigel Ave North which becomes Queen Wilhelmina Ave. Turn left at the first traffic light into Wenning Street, and left again into Broderick Street. Turn right into Van Wouw Street, then left into Wangemann Street and right again into Herbert Baker Street where Pretoria's white jacarandas grow. Travel along Herbert Baker Street and turn right into Baines Street. At the bottom of Baines Street past the Groenkloof Plaza, turn left

into George Storrar Drive. Turn right at the next traffic light into Leyds Street. The South African Bureau of Standards is on your right. Turn right into Sibelius Street. Pass Arnoldi and Lingbeek Streets and and turn left into Lente Street, and left again into Ormonde Street. Turn left again into Berea Street and continue along this street until it becomes Mears Street. Turn right into Ridge Street and then right into Elandspoort Road which becomes Mears Street. Turn left into Walker Street and continue along this street until it turns to the right and becomes Van der Walt Street. Cross Scheiding, Jacob Maré, Visagie, Skinner, Schoeman, Pretorius and Church Streets and turn left into Vermeulen Street. The route began at the next intersection with Prinsloo Street.

General

At the height of jacaranda season (October–November) the view over the city bowl from high places such as the Union Buildings, Muckleneuk and Johann Rissik Drive is worth your while.

Jacarandas grow anywhere, but these at the corner of Celliers and Walker Streets are only 50 metres from the original pair.

More white jacarandas in Herbert Baker Street under Klapperkop

Jacarandas downtown, Skinner Street

There are a number of relics of the military history of the South African Republic (Transvaal Republic) and South Africa at large, in and around Pretoria. These are mainly in the form of buildings ranging from formal military structures, such as the interesting and well-preserved forts on the hills around the city, to houses for military officers, barracks, stables for horses, and cemeteries.

Military traces of the past

Church Street Cemetery, with its graves of British and Boer soldiers from the Anglo-Boer War of 1899–1902, is discussed separately, while military memorials are dealt with under **Monuments and Memorials**.

The forts around Pretoria

Four well-built forts occur on the hills surrounding Pretoria. South of the city are Fort Schanskop, on the hill next to and east of the Voortrekker Monument, and some two kilometres further east, Fort Klapperkop (named after the fruit of an indigenous shrub) on the Waterkloof Ridge near Johann Rissik Drive. Fort Wonderboom Poort is on the Magaliesberg above Wonderboom Nature Reserve north of the city, and Fort Daspoortrand west of the city on the Daspoort Ridge (also called the Witwatersberg).

The building of these forts resulted from the Jameson raid of December 1895–January 1896 (see box). The raid dramatically underlined the possibility of an attack from outside and the importance of being prepared for such an eventuality. Measures were therefore immediately taken to prepare for an attack, specifically on Pretoria, the seat of the government. A defence plan for Pretoria was drawn up by a former

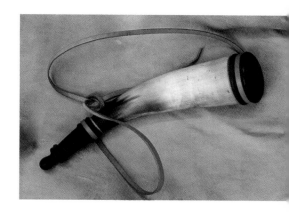

Powder-horn

The citizens of the old South African Republic were proud of their coat of arms.

French artillery officer, Capt. Leon Grunberg, but this was later replaced by one for which two German engineers, Heinrich C Werner and Otto A A von Dewitz of the German engineering firm Krupp were responsible.

Great importance was attached to guarding the road from Johannesburg to Pretoria and warding off a possible threat from that direction. Two forts were therefore approved on either side of the poort through which this road passed. These were Fort Schanskop and Fort Klapperkop. Fort Wonderboom would guard the northern entrance to the city. These three forts were built by the architect/draftsman Christiaan Kunz.

Fort Daspoortrand, also known as Wesfort (Western Fort), differs from the other three in that it was built in the French style by the firm of Scheider, Grunberg & Leon. The engineer Edgar Cassen was in charge of the construction. It is a hexagonal structure as opposed to the other three which are pentagonal.

The four forts were handed over to the government between April 1897 and November 1898. All four forts had loopholes in the walls and contained various rooms such as officers' and soldiers' rooms, kitchens, hospitals, machine and telegraph rooms, ammunition magazines and storerooms for provisions. In the case of Fort Daspoortrand the magazines were underground and connected by passages with the inner court.

All four forts were equipped with different artillery pieces which were, however, removed after the outbreak of the Anglo-Boer War when they were needed on the front.

The forts were never used in an offensive fashion during the war and were in fact unmanned after the outbreak of war. After the occupation of Pretoria on 5 June 1900 the British occupied the forts and also built a series of blockhouses around Pretoria, one of which was a few hundred metres from Fort Daspoortrand.

Fort Klapperkop was turned into a military museum which was opened in 1966. In 1978 Fort Schanskop was also opened as a museum. Klapperkop and Schanskop were both declared national monuments in 1938. Fort Wonderboom Poort's ruins were excavated in 1986 and declared a national monument in 1987. Fort Daspoortrand was at the time of writing in a state of decay, but there has been talk of a cultural organization undertaking to restore it.

Fort Klapperkop is open to the public and is being restored as an Anglo-Boer War museum. It affords an interesting insight into the military architecture of a century ago.

Hours: 08:00–16:00
Entrance: Charged

The Jameson raid

This event took place against the background of the mining revolution on the Witwatersrand, following the discovery of the gold-bearing reef in 1886 which led to the influx of thousands of foreigners, 'Uitlanders' as they were called. The government of the South African Republic guarded its independence jealously and made it very difficult for these people to acquire citizenship. A residence of five years was initially required. But in an attempt to satisfy the political demands of the Uitlanders and at the same time safeguard the independence of the Republic a Second Volksraad was instituted in 1890 to which the Uitlanders could elect representatives. This second house of parliament had limited powers. The original house, the First Volksraad, was responsible for all matters of policy and for the independence of the state. The resolutions of the Second Volksraad were subject to the approval of the First Volksraad. Moreover, it had jurisdiction only over lesser matters such as mining, roads, postal, telegraphic and telephonic services, patents and copyright, samples and trade marks, infectious diseases, company matters, insolvency, civil and criminal procedure, and any matters which the First Volksraad chose to refer to it. All citizens over the age of sixteen, including foreigners who had been naturalized for two years, could vote for members of the Second Volksraad. However, to be able to vote for the First Volksraad an Uitlander needed to have been in the Republic for fourteen years.

The institution of a Second Volksraad did not solve the grievances of the Uitlanders. Soon an organized Uitlander movement resulted which insisted on an equal enfranchisement for all inhabitants of the Republic. The Uitlanders became increasingly vociferous in their demands. They were egged on by mining magnates who wanted to gain their own economic and political ends, and supported by the British High Commissioner in South Africa and by the Cape Prime Minister, arch imperialist Cecil John Rhodes, who saw Kruger as the chief stumbling block in the way of a united South Africa under the Union Jack. In addition the conditions for stronger British imperial activity in South Africa improved in 1895 when the Unionist government of Lord Salisbury came to power and the outspoken imperialist Joseph Chamberlain became Secretary of State for the Colonies.

Under these circumstances Cecil John Rhodes decided that the time had come for direct intervention in Transvaal affairs. The idea was that an Uitlander uprising in Johannesburg would coincide with a raid into the Transvaal from the Bechuanaland (now Botswana) border by Dr Leander Starr Jameson, the administrator of Rhodes' British South Africa Company in Southern Rhodesia (now Zimbabwe). Although Chamberlain distanced himself officially from the raid, he knew about the conspiracy and even advised Rhodes about a suitable date.

But the Jameson raid ended in a fiasco. Rhodes and the Uitlander leaders disagreed about aspects of the plan and the Cape prime minister therefore decided not to go through with it. However, by that time Jameson had already crossed the Transvaal border at Pitsani. Kruger's government was also prepared for them: in an attempt to sabotage the telegraphic communication with Pretoria Jameson's men cut the wrong telegraph wires on the night of 29 December 1895. Consequently the Transvaal government troops were waiting for them and on 2 January 1896 Jameson and his henchmen were captured at Doornkop near Krugersdorp.

Magnanimously Jameson and his men were handed over to the British government, but the Uitlander leaders in Johannesburg were arrested and charged. The ringleaders were sentenced to death, but their sentences were commuted to fines of £25 000. In Britain a commission of enquiry cleared Chamberlain from complicity in the plot. However, it was dubbed 'The Commission of no Inquiry' by the opposition and there is today little doubt that it was a huge cover-up. ■

Fort Klapperkop

Thaba Tshwane (Voortrekkerhoogte)

The military complex on the hills south-west of Pretoria, known until recently as Voortrekkerhoogte (Voortrekker Heights) and currently as Thaba Tshwane, was originally called Roberts Heights. It was named after Lord Frederick Sleigh Roberts, the Commander-in-Chief of the British forces in South Africa from 1899 to 1900 during the Anglo-Boer War. In June 1900 Roberts occupied Pretoria with his forces. During the course of 1900 he moved his camp from the town proper to the healthier high-lying area which would allow him and his men more space. In 1938, the year of the centenary of the Great Trek, the name was changed to Voortrekkerhoogte and in 1997 to Thaba Tshwane.

Some wood-and-corrugated-iron structures erected by Lord Roberts remain to this day. The building known as 'Die Vesting' (the stronghold or fortress) in Gen Johannes de Kock Road is one of the original ones. This building with its large stoep (veranda) and attractive bay windows on the northern side served as the residence of Sir Pierre van Ryneveld, Chief of the Defence Force from 1926 to 1949. East of the house the original stables have been preserved. The house is today the official residence of the Chief of the Navy.

The 'blockhouse' to the south-east of Die Vesting in Johannes de Kock Road gave the house its name. It has walls of double corrugated iron with the cavity filled with stones.

Another wood-and-iron building from 1900 is the house at 17 Ben Viljoen Road which was originally built as an officers' mess. It also boasts an attractive veranda. It was one of several similar buildings along this road. Other remaining wood-and-iron buildings are in Piet Retief Road and Jacobus Naudé Road. These served as homes for junior officers.

The building serving as headquarters of Northern Transvaal Command in the centre of Thaba Tshwane is another wood-and-iron structure dating from 1902–1904. The off-white building with its red roof and three gables with a veranda has no specific style characteristics but it is a good example of the prefabricated office buildings of the time.

There are also several historic brick-and-mortar buildings at Thaba Tshwane. The South African Air Force Officers' Club Building in the south-eastern corner of Thaba Tshwane was designed in 1902 by Sir Herbert Baker (see box under Historical Buildings) as home for the commanding officer of the British forces. The Military College building towards the north-western part of Thaba Tshwane has a corner-stone laid by Lord Kitchener in June 1902 when it was erected as a club building for use by British troops still stationed here. With its two storeys this was one of the most imposing buildings to be erected at that time. It was the first building at Thaba Tshwane to be declared a national monument.

Defence headquarters

The buildings at defence headquarters west of Potgieter Street predate those at Thaba Tshwane. The first building erected here as barracks for the State Artillery of the South African Republic was handed over in September 1898. With its two storeys, raised corner pavilions and central dome this building was particularly imposing for that time. Behind the barracks is another preserved building from the same time, the stables. It was built in 1897 to accommodate 268 horses as well as artillery sheds. A feature is the attractive sandstone gables. Unfortunately the present defence headquarters were erected during the twenties in front of the old barracks, partly obscuring the façade.

North of the barracks' forecourt is the machine room building, also built in 1897, used today as an officers' mess.

During the 1890s fifteen officers' houses were built along Artillery Road. These have all survived and are still in use.

Every Boer naturally carried his pocket knife with him always, whether it be peace or war. Knives bearing the coat of arms of the Republic were popular. This one also has the Free State coat of arms at the top.

Diamond Hill Battlefield cemetery

After the occupation of Pretoria during the Anglo-Boer War by Lord Roberts on 5 June 1900 the Boer forces under the command of Gen Louis Botha took up a position with some 4000 men about 25 km east of the capital at Diamond Hill, also known as Donkerhoek. This position would enable him to defend the Delagoa Bay (Maputo) railway line, along which President Paul Kruger and his government were retreating eastwards towards Mozambique, and also to reorganize his badly demoralized troops.

On 11 June Roberts attacked the Boer line. After some strong resistance Botha realized that a Boer victory was no longer possible and he quietly evacuated the hill during the night. Although the battle was fairly inconclusive Botha then withdrew eastwards along the railway line.

The Boers had about 30 casualties compared to the 175 of the British. A cemetery at Diamond Hill contains the remains of the fallen British. The battle was decisive. If Botha had been successful in defending his position he might have been able to launch an attack on Pretoria and possibly recaptured the capital. As it turned out it was the start of the gradual retreat of the Boer forces towards the east.

Getting there: Travel east along the N4 freeway (Schoeman Street) to Bronkhorstspruit/Witbank for about 25 km from Church Square and take the Boschkop/Donkerhoek turn-off. At the top of the off-ramp turn left towards Donkerhoek. After 150 m turn right at the T-junction towards Bronkhorstspruit. After 1,5 km turn right again at the Rhenosterfontein signpost. Travel 5,6 km along this dirt road and left at the National Monument sign. The dirt track of about 200 m takes one to the neatly paved Diamond Hill cemetery site. Soldiers from a number of regiments, including some from Australia and New Zealand, are buried here, while others who fell in later battles are also commemorated.

A neat thatched shelter provides shade but no running water or other facilities. The site offers a beautiful view over the surrounding countryside.

Rooihuiskraal battle site, 1881

After the annexation of the South African Republic for Britain by Sir Theophilus Shepstone in 1877 a resistance movement developed among the Transvaal Boers. This movement reached a climax in December 1880 when thousands of Boers resolved at a mass meeting to restore the Boer government. On 16 December 1880 the first shots in the First Transvaal War of Independence were fired at Potchefstroom. The war was short-lived and came to an end after the Battle of Amajuba on the border between Natal and the Transvaal on 27 February 1881.

Soon after the start of hostilities Pretoria with its British garrison was besieged by the Boers. A number of laagers or fortified encampments were set up by the Boers at an average distance of about 15 km from Pretoria. One of these was at Rooihuiskraal (literally the red house and kraal/farm, belonging to F Erasmus) south-west of the town in the present Centurion municipality. As the situation deteriorated in the town the British undertook sorties in different directions. The first unsuccessful attack on Rooihuiskraal took place on 29 December 1880 and a second one on 12 February 1881. The latter encounter ended with the numerically superior British suffering ten casualties with none on the side of the Boers.

A farm outbuilding has been preserved and the area surrounding the building is a picturesque and tranquil picnic ground with ablution and other facilities where tame reindeer roam about.

Getting there: Travel along the Ben Schoeman Freeway towards Johannesburg. Pass the Lyttelton/Voortrekkerhoogte turn-off and that to Krugersdorp/Pretoria East/Pietersburg. Take the turn-off marked Old Johannesburg Road. Turn left at the T-junction and cross the bridge over the freeway. (You are now going back the way you have come, but on a different road.) Pass the first traffic light sign-posted Rooihuiskraal/The Reeds to the left and turn left into Panorama Road at the second traffic light. Travel 2 km along this road to a traffic light and turn right into Rooihuiskraal Road. The Rooihuiskraal picnic site is on the right after 1,3 km.

Irene Concentration Camp cemetery

The concentration camp at Irene, south of Pretoria, was established during the Anglo-Boer War in accordance with the policy devised by the British military commander-in-chief in South Africa during the second half of 1900 (see box on concentration camp policy).

The camp was started in December 1900 and it existed until after the conclusion of peace on 31 May 1902. In March 1902 a second camp was established when it was decided to move the camp at Nylstroom to

The concentration camp policy

By the middle of 1900 the tide had apparently turned in the Anglo-Boer War. On 13 March of that year the Free State capital, Bloemfontein, was occupied by the British forces and on 5 June it was the turn of Pretoria, capital of the South African Republic. But, contrary to the expectations of the British military commanders, the Boer leaders did not sue for peace and the war dragged on.

As the Boer forces retreated and the war entered its guerilla warfare stage, the British commander-in-chief, Lord Roberts, in September 1900 approved the establishment of so-called refugee camps. Three months later he gave orders that all non-combatants in certain areas be removed to these camps. By the end of the war there were more than 40 camps which housed some 116 000 whites, while another 60 camps contained 115 000 blacks.

Most of the inhabitants of the camps were in fact not refugees but civilians who were displaced or otherwise affected during the British military drives in pursuit of bands of Boer guerillas. However, there were additional motives for the establishment of the camps for whites, although these were not publicly stated. Firstly the British military hoped that the internment of the Boer families in the camps would persuade the Boer fighters in the field to surrender, and secondly it was done to prevent help in the form of food supplies and shelter being rendered to these fighters by civilians on the farms. Blacks were also cleared from the land to prevent Boer commandos obtaining supplies. Subsequently black men were employed as labourers in the British war effort while their families remained in the camps. There can be little doubt therefore that the concentration camps were devised and used as a measure aimed at ending the resistance of the fighting Boers.

The numbers of the camp inhabitants were swelled by the 'scorched earth' policy of burning farms and harvests applied by the British troops from the middle of 1900. Hundreds of farm homesteads were burned down leading to an outcry in the British House of Commons. Orders were issued late in 1900 that there had to be sound reasons and that the burning of homesteads could not simply take place as a matter of course, but it still happened, even if on a smaller scale than before. In any case a 'scorched earth' policy was applied because the British army stripped the veld of all food supplies that could aid the Boer forces.

During the last months of 1901 conditions improved in the camps, largely through the pressure brought to bear in official circles by Emily Hobhouse. But by then the harm had been done. A total of 27 927 Boers died in the camps of whom 26 251 were women and children. More than 14 000 blacks died in their camps. ■

Irene Concentration Camp cemetery

Irene. For a few months therefore there were two camps at Irene. The present cemetery is situated on part of the site of the original camp.

The camp population varied between 4000 and 4700 at different times. A total of between 1100 and 1200 inmates died in the original camp. A variety of diseases caused these deaths, including enteric fever, diarrhoea, measles, dysentery, pneumonia, whooping cough, malaria, and even scurvy – due to a lack of fresh fruit and vegetables in the diet. One of the camp doctors was also ill for a week and in June 1902 the camp matron contracted double pneumonia and died a week later.

The camp conditions may be blamed for the numerous diseases and extremely high mortality. There was overcrowding in the tents housing the inmates. This, coupled with the extreme summer and winter temperatures and severe fluctuations between day and night temperatures together with the poor clothing possessed by the inmates, contributed enormously to the high incidence of respiratory ailments such as bronchitis, whooping cough and pneumonia. The poor circulation and insufficient fresh air in the tents further created ideal conditions for diseases to spread. Another contributing factor was the poor health condition of persons entering the camp. Poor personal hygiene resulted from the lack of basic facilities and entirely inadequate health care facilities provided by the camp authorities. Hospital accommodation was in fact absent at first and inadequate since 1901. The inmates mistrusted hospital care and were reluctant to allow seriously ill children and others to be hospitalized because very few if any survived hospitalization. The camp diet was almost devoid of fresh milk, meat and vegetables.

Today the cemetery is one of the best-kept war cemeteries with lawns and a memorial wall honouring the dead. Members of the youth movement, the Voortrekkers (local version of Girl Guides and Boy Scouts), care for the cemetery.

Entry: Free

A young Winston Churchill in South Africa a century ago. He wore the uniform of the South African Light Horse, and was war correspondent of the Morning Post.

Voortrekker Monument

The solid shape of the Voortrekker Monument on a koppie (hill) outside the city dominates the skyline towards the south-west. The monument is a tribute to the Voortrekkers who carried western civilization to the interior of South Africa during the Great Trek.

The Great Trek was one of the dominant events of 19th century

Monuments and memorials

South African history. It started in 1835/36 and eventually some 6000 whites – mainly stock farmers and their families – left for the interior with all their possessions. These pioneers were of Dutch, German and French descent as well as some of the 1820 Settlers from Britain. All were subjects of the British colonial governors at Cape Town. One of the main reasons for their decision to trek, was the insecurity of their existence along the frontier. Repeated clashes had occurred with the black people along the frontier, who were also cattle herders, over a period of more than 50 years. Many cattle farmers lost their lives and others all their property in the process. During the 1770s the advance guard of the cattle farmers had come into contact with the blacks in the vicinity of the Great Fish River, some 800 km from Cape Town. Successive attempts by the governors of the Dutch East India Company at Cape Town and by the British governors after Britain's take-over of the colony in 1806 to regulate relations along the frontier by means of territorial segregation, had failed. The last straw was that after the abolition of slavery in 1834, slave owners were required to fetch their compensation promised by the British government, in London!

The subsequent Great Trek represents a heroic phase in the history of the Afrikaners and the inevitable clashes with the indigenous groups in

the interior laid the foundation for future race relations. The dramatic events during the Trek, which culminated in the establishment of two independent states in the interior in 1852 and 1854, and the way of life of the Trekkers, are depicted in the frieze in the main hall of the monument.

The foundation stone was laid in 1938 during the centenary celebrations of the Great Trek and the monument was inaugurated on 16 December 1949. The architect was Gerard Moerdijk. The monument was a giant cooperative effort by Afrikaner artists, sculptors and builders.

Apart from the frieze in the Hall of Heroes, the main features of the monument are the cenotaph in the basement of the monument inscribed with the words 'Ons vir jou Suid-Afrika' (We for thee, South Africa), and a flame symbolizing the light of civilization. The monument is designed in such a way that on 16 December every year – the date of the Battle of Blood River in 1838 – a ray of sunlight falls through a hole in the domed roof onto the cenotaph at 12:00 noon. The flame was lit by a torch borne by members of the Voortrekker youth movement in relays from Cape Town during the inauguration celebrations in 1949.

The symbolism is explained in a brochure obtainable at the monument.

Voortrekker Monument

Hours: Mon–Sat
09:00–16:45
Sun 11:00–16:45
Entrance: Charged

Strijdom monument

The J G Strijdom head beneath a triangular dome on Strijdom Square (cnr Church & Van der Walt Streets) was unveiled in 1972 in honour of J G Strijdom, Prime Minister of South Africa from 1954 to 1958. Coert Steynberg was the sculptor.

The group of horses on a marble column was sculpted by Danie de Jager.

Monument for victims of terrorism

This monument in front of Munitoria, the municipal offices building, was originally erected in memory of those members of the public who had lost their lives in acts of terrorism against apartheid mainly during the 1980s. Today it honours all victims of terrorism irrespective of what side they were on. (The western block of Munitoria has been destroyed by fire and imploded, but the monument still stands.)

Dolomite rock

A piece of dolomite rock is a reminder of the water sources found in the springs in the Fountains Valley.

The dolomite rock was exposed through upsurging of the granite formation to the south of Pretoria to form the Johannesburg dome. The water in these rocks wells up to the surface in the shape of the springs which feed the Apies River at the Fountains Valley.

Monument to J G Strijdom on Strijdom Square

Bronkhorst house ruins in Fountains Valley

Foundations of Bronkhorst homestead

These foundations in the Fountains Valley recreation resort are the remains of the first white homestead built in Pretoria in 1839/41. The farm Groenkloof was registered in the name of L C Bronkhorst in August 1841 and it was here that he built his modest homestead. Bronkhorst had left the Cape Colony with the Great Trek in 1836 and, having shared the dramatic experiences of the Trekkers in the Free State and Natal, he returned to the highveld

plateau. After having lived at Potchefstroom in the western Transvaal, today the Northwest Province, the group to which he and his brother Gert belonged, were on their way with their ox-wagons past the present Pretoria to the eastern Transvaal, today Mpumalanga. The Bronkhorst brothers and some other Voortrekkers decided to stay and here, near the spring known as today as The Fountains, Lucas Bronkhorst built his home.

Monument for fallen soldiers in border wars

A considerable number of South African soldiers died during the border wars fought between 1975 – when the former Portuguese colonies of Angola and Mozambique became independent – and 1985. The monument is in the form of a charging soldier with a rifle with fixed bayonet and was erected in the grounds of Fort Klapperkop. Around the pedestal of the monument the names of all the fallen for the different years can be seen on plaques.

The main theatre of war was at the border of South West Africa (Namibia) and Angola.

Hours: 08:00–16:00

Monument for fallen soldiers in border wars, erected at Fort Klapperkop

Monument for Scottish SA Regiment 1914—1918

Memorial for South African Scottish Regiment, 1914–1918

On the northern side of the picturesque Burgers Park which is bounded by Burgers Park Ave, Andries, Jacob Maré and Van der Walt Streets, is a memorial to the soldiers of the Scottish Regiment of the South African Defence Force who fell during World War I, 1914–1918.

Memorial for Pretorians who fell in the two World Wars and Korean War

This memorial in front of the Union Buildings below the Delville Wood Memorial is in the form of a cross-wall with a symbolic pill-box at each end, with a roof in the shape of a military 'tin hat' worn by soldiers of the time, and a sarcophagus lower down. The rolls of honour appear on bronze plaques. The monument was designed by Gordon Leith.

Police memorial

This memorial on the extreme left below the lower terrace in front of the Union Buildings was unveiled in 1983 to commemorate the 70th anniversary of the founding of the South African Police Service.

The two-metre high solid wall represents the task of protection, and the second higher wall around a curved row of pillars represents the various branches of the police service.

A wreath is laid annually at the memorial by the Minister of Safety and Security to honour policemen who have died in the performance of their duties.

Delville Wood War Memorial, World War I

This monument on the lower terrace in front of the Union Buildings is a replica of one on the battlefield in France. It shows two life-sized male figures on either side of a horse. It commemorates the battle in July 1916 when some 2 500 South African troops lost their lives in one of the fiercest battles of the war at the Delville forest near Longueval along the Somme River.

The original monument in France was designed by Sir Herbert Baker.

Delville Wood Memorial

Cenotaph for members of Native Corps

This memorial in Atteridgeville honours some 700 members of the so-called Native Corps, a corps of black soldiers, who lost their lives during World War I. These soldiers died when the troop ship on which they were travelling, the *SS Mendi*, struck a mine in the English Channel in February 1917.

NZASM railway coach

On the main platform of Pretoria railway station is a directors' or guests' railway coach. It was ordered from Europe by the NZASM – Nederlandsch Zuid-Afrikaansche Spoorweg Maatschappij (Netherlands South African Railway Company) – established in 1887 which built the railway line from Pretoria to Delagoa Bay (Maputo) as well as a number of other lines in the South African Republic.

South African Air Force Memorial

For a country as young as South Africa with a formal defence force not yet a century old, there are ample traces of an illustrious military past. One of these is the South African Air Force Memorial near Thaba Tshwane. The striking structure consisting of a combination of triangular shapes used at different angles to create the impression of an aircraft, commemorates the men of the South African Air Force who have lost their lives in war over the different periods: 1920–1939; 1939–1945; and since 1945. The latter period also includes the Korean War of 1950–1953 and the border wars in which South Africans were involved. It was designed by Morgenstern and Morgenstern architects.

Three plaques inside the memorial honour the men who paid the highest price in the different periods. There is also a tiny chapel which can seat about 15 people.

Hollanders in Transvaal

In the Tram Shed shopping centre is a memorial to the role played by Dutchmen and their descendants in the Transvaal, i.e. the area north of the Vaal River which constituted one of the four provinces of South Africa until the new political dispensation of 1994.

In 1852 the independence of the Voortrekkers in this area was recognized. Thus came into existence the first independent republic resulting from the Great Trek – named in Dutch the Zuid-Afrikaansche Republiek (South African Republic). The spoken language of the white inhabitants was a mixture of Dutch and Afrikaans, the official language was Dutch, the first private newspaper appeared in Dutch and the constitution of the republic was written in Dutch. Dutch school teachers were often used as private tutors, as administrators in the education department and as civil servants in the public service of a pioneering community in the interior where formally educated people were scarce. When the state decided in the 1880s that it should have its own railway line to a non-British port, the task of surveying, building and administering it was entrusted to a Dutch company.

Some of the Dutchmen who contributed to public and cultural life returned to the Netherlands but many accepted citizenship of their adopted state and their descendants have contributed in many ways to the national life of the Transvaal and South Africa. This memorial contains concentric circles on the paving with names of Dutch families. The circles are divided into segments representing the various areas of public life where the different families made contributions.

Fountain to commemorate Dutch settlers in the Transvaal

Pretoria's connection with Vincent van Gogh

On the wall of the Hervormde Kerk (Reformed Church) in Du Toit Street between Church and Vermeulen Streets is a plaque bearing the names of Dutch citizens and ex-Dutchmen who lost their lives on the side of the Boer forces during the Anglo-Boer War of 1899–1902. On it appears the name of Cornelis Vincent (Cor) van Gogh. He was the youngest brother of the famous painter Vincent van Gogh. Vincent van Gogh's close relationship with his brother Theo, to whom he wrote many letters, is well known, but hardly anything is known about his three sisters and the young Cor. The fact that the name Vincent appears so often in the Van Gogh family can probably be ascribed to the fact that their grandfather as well as one of the uncles – a wealthy art dealer – also bore this name.

Cor came to the Transvaal in 1889 at the age of 22. Initially he worked at a mine near Germiston, but he later entered the service of the NZASM (Netherlands South African Railway Company) as a draftsman. He got married in South Africa, but his wife apparently left him, although the marriage was never formally dissolved.

At the outbreak of the Anglo-Boer War Cor joined the Boer forces. Towards the end of March 1900 he was captured by the British, probably in the vicinity of Brandfort in the Free State. While he was held as a prisoner-of-war he became ill and was transferred to a military hospital at Brandfort. He died there on 14 April 1900 at the age of 33. Although, according to a statement of the Transvaal section of the Red Cross, Cor van Gogh accidentally shot himself, it is generally accepted that he actually committed suicide, like his famous brother. He was buried in an unidentified grave at Brandfort. ■

Sir Pierre van Ryneveld

This small and unobtrusive memorial next to the N4 East freeway commemorates General Sir Pierre van Ryneveld's pioneering flight from 4 February to 20 March 1920 from England over Africa to Cape Town. He was accompanied by Sir Quintin Brand. It was a difficult and dangerous enterprise during which two aircraft were written off. Van Ryneveld and Brand were both knighted for their achievement. In 1927 Van Ryneveld undertook the first non-stop flight from Pretoria to Cape Town and in the same year he became the first person to undertake a parachute jump from an aircraft in South Africa. Van Ryneveld was Chief of the South African Defence Force from 1926 to 1949.

A memorial to mark the event is to be seen on the University of Pretoria's experimental farm to the left of the N4 into Pretoria, next to the two rows of pine trees flanking a dirt road running at right angles to the N4.

Plaque with names of the Dutch who died in the Anglo-Boer War

Solomon Mahlangu Square

Solomon Mahlangu was a young man of Mamelodi who died following the civil unrest of the 1980s in the black townships of South Africa. A square in Mamelodi was named in his honour and a memorial erected.

Stanza Bopape Memorial

This memorial is in Mandela Village Squatter Camp (Stanza Bopape Village), Mamelodi. Stanza Bopape was killed by security police after having been arrested for undermining activities.

The Wonderboom

This wild fig (*Ficus*) tree, belonging to the *Moraceae* family, has been declared a national monument. It is several centuries old – possibly more than 1000 years – and the name Wonderboom (miracle tree) was given to it by a party of Voortrekkers in 1836. It is the largest example of the species. The central trunk is about four metres in circumference, but over the years new roots and trunks were formed where the spreading branches touched the ground. Consequently the tree today has the appearance of twelve trees whose branches spread over a circle 50 metres in diameter.

The tree was regarded as sacred by indigenous people after a chief was buried there. The wild figs it bears are edible and loved by birds and baboons.

Visiting hours: Mon–Thurs 10:00–17:00
Fri–Sun 09:00–17:00
Entrance: Charged

The Wonderboom

Pretoria station building

Church Square

Southern façade of the Square

The **Standard Bank Building** on the eastern corner of Paul Kruger Street south of Church Square was built between 1931 and 1934. It was designed by William Henry Stucke. It is typical of bank buildings in the neo-classical art deco style of the period and reminiscent of

Architecture: Historical buildings

Sir Herbert Baker's South Africa House on Trafalgar Square in London.

The **Old Raadsaal** (legislative council chamber) to the south of the Kruger statue, on the western corner of Paul Kruger Street, was the parliament building of the South African Republic (Transvaal Republic). It is the best example of a public building in the architectural style of the last quarter of the 19th century and shows the typical influence of French and German Baroque.

The building was designed by Sytze Wierda, Chief Architect of the Department of Public Works. Wierda came to the Transvaal from the Netherlands and the contemporary European trends in public building design can clearly be seen in the building. The style can be described as early Renaissance or Italian. The timber was imported from Norway, the roof tiles from Scotland, and the sandstone came from north of Pretoria. The corner-stone was laid by President Paul Kruger in 1889 and the building was completed the following year.

The statue of a woman wearing a helmet and representing freedom on top of the cupola has given rise to several myths. One of these is that President Paul Kruger remarked that it would be unfitting for a woman to appear bareheaded in public.

Western façade of the Square

The western façade of Church Square consists of three buildings to the south-west of the Square: the Old Netherlands Bank building, the Law Chambers and the Café Riche building. But partly hidden by these buildings and hemmed in between the Netherlands Bank Building and the modern (late 1950s, architects Meiring & Naudé and Moerdijk &

Church Square from the north-west with Tudor Chambers on the far left

Paul Kruger's statue on Church Square

Café Riche on the western façade of Church Square

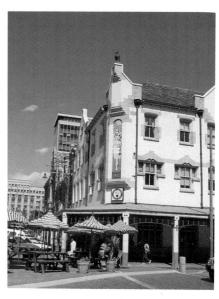

History of Church Square

The square now known as Church Square formed the hub of the town of Pretoria since it was founded in 1855. It served as both a market and a church square. Since the 1860s farmers from the surrounding districts converged on the Square with their tented ox-wagons to sell their produce and to attend the three-monthly Holy Communion service held in the church on the Square. The first church was built in 1856 and consecrated the following year. It was a simple structure of stone and mud with a thatched roof. This church building was struck by lightning in 1882 and subsequently demolished. A second church was built in 1884–1885 which was demolished in 1904–1905. Today there is a Church Square without a church! However, Church *Street* does have a church: the 'Dopper' Church attended by Pres Kruger.

Church Square has been the scene of important events in the history of South Africa and the South African Republic. Here the first church was inaugurated in 1857 and the Vierkleur (literally Fourcolour, the flag of the South African Republic) was hoisted for the first time; the proclamation was read by which Sir Theophilus Shepstone annexed the South African Republic for Britain in 1877; Paul Kruger took the oath as President of the South African Republic in 1883 (portrayed in one of the panels on the base of the Kruger statue); Kruger was introduced to his people from the balcony of the Old Raadsaal after winning the presidential elections of 1893 and 1898; here Queen Victoria's diamond jubilee was celebrated in 1897; on 11 October 1899 in the adjacent council chamber of the First Volksraad (upper house of parliament) of the South African Republic the reply of Great Britain to the ultimatum of the Republic – which led to the outbreak of the Anglo-Boer War of 1899–1902 – was awaited; the Union Jack was hoisted on the Old Raadsaal after the occupation of Pretoria by the British troops in June 1900; the memorial service for President Kruger was held in the half-broken-down church in 1904; the proclamation of the Union of South Africa – which brought together the four colonies – was read on 31 May 1910; and the inauguration of the first state president of the Republic of South Africa took place after the Union of South Africa had become a republic in 1961. Here also many a rousing patriotic and political gathering has taken place.

Originally the Square was in the centre of the town, but over the last years business activity has shifted eastward, while residential development has been doing so since the 1950s. Today the downtown business centre of gravity is around Strijdom Square rather than Church Square. Decentralization has also led to the development of new shopping and office complexes in the suburbs.

In 1974 plans were announced by the provincial administration to demolish the Old Netherlands Bank building, the Law Chambers and the Café Riche building as well as the Pretoria post office to make way for modern office blocks. A strong protest was mounted by the citizens of Pretoria and a mass meeting in July 1975 was attended by about 10 000 people. A petition with more than 6900 signatures for the retention of the buildings was taken to the highest authority and the historical buildings were saved.

Lately plans have been afoot to give the Square a new lease on life. Because it has been used for many years as a terminus for bus routes to and from all parts of the city and was closed to ordinary traffic, the Square lost much of its soul. It became a space hurriedly crossed by pedestrians and bus commuters whose value was only recognized by patriotic Afrikaners from time to time and by tourist guides showing their charges the Kruger statue and the historic buildings around it. However, the buses have now been removed, cars are once more allowed on the Square and parking is available. A scheme has been put into place to make the Square part of a cultural space stretching for three street blocks up to the State Theatre – the whole length of the pedestrianized part of Church Street. The idea is that artists should utilize this space, and that there should be 24 hour activity with film festivals, buskers, open-air performance platforms, a skating ramp, a basket ball court and even a street soccer field. The many foreign embassies in the city have also been invited to make a contribution to the revitalization of the Square and the whole cultural precinct and to making it tourist friendly.

As part of the plan to revitalize Church Square, a Christmas concert was held in the Capitol Theatre just off the Square in December 1998 (see *Western façade of the Square*). To bring the Square itself to life the coffee shop on the western side, Café Riche, has started serving a stylish Sunday breakfast or brunch on the lawn right under President Kruger's stern countenance, the food fare being supplemented by cultural performances such as Zulu dances.

With all the envisaged actions and developments Church Square, with its pigeons and tranquility amongst the bustle of city life, may well become for Pretoria a mixture of what the Company Garden is for Cape Town, Trafalgar Square and Hyde Park for London, and many of the inner city squares for countless European cities. ■

Watson) Provincial Administration Building, is the old **Capitol Theatre**. It was one of the elegant theatres of the 1930s with artificial stars in the high domed ceiling. It was opened in 1931 but the façade was altered in the early sixties to complement the adjacent Provincial Administration Building. Since 1974 the theatre has been used as a parking garage.

The **Old Netherlands Bank** was built in 1896–1897 and was designed in the Flemish Renaissance style by Willem de Zwaan. De Zwaan was also co-responsible for the design of Church Square which was laid out as it is today in 1912. The Netherlands Bank, founded in the Netherlands in 1887 (now called Nedbank), did business here until 1953 but today the building houses offices. The stepped gable, brickwork and excellent proportions make it particularly impressive. The beautiful decorative cast iron gates and ballustrade were manufactured in Delft, Holland.

The **Law Chambers** is the oldest building on the western façade. It was designed by William M Philip and was built in 1890–1891. With its three graceful gables and perfect proportions it forms a harmonious link between the two buildings on either side. The building was restored in 1988.

The **Café Riche Building**, on the corner of Church Street West and the Square, was built in 1905 and was designed by the Dutch-born architect Frans Soff in the art nouveau style. The original name was the Reserve Investment Building but the Café Riche Lounge Bar on the ground floor became so popular that the building came to be known by its name. It contains a basement from where one can see through safety glass windows the pedestrians walking by on the pavement above. A sense of light-heartedness is given to the exterior of the building by the owl on top of the corner gable. The relief of Mercury, messenger of the gods, on the corner panel below the gable, with the word 'Commerce' below it, is the work of Van Wouw. Soff and Van Wouw also cooperated in connection with the Women's Memorial in Bloemfontein, Soff being responsible for the design and Van Wouw for the woman's statue which forms part of the memorial.

The **General Post Office building,** on the north-western corner of Church Street West and the Square, was designed by William Hawke of the Cape Colony, a pupil of Sir Herbert Baker (see box on Baker). The corner-stone was laid in 1910. The design represents formal aspects of art nouveau and art deco, but there is a more classical aura represented by the Doric columns and ornamental relief work on the façade. The building was restored in 1986 and is still being used as the Pretoria post office.

The **National Bank, Government Mint and annexe** appear in that order next to the post office. They were probably erected in 1903. The

National Bank Building was the home of the first Transvaal Bank founded to administer the government funds of the South African Republic. The National Bank and mint were established in 1891, the mint being the first in the Southern Hemisphere. Frank Emley and Frank Scott teamed up in designing the building. The tall and narrow annexe to the right of the building was erected at the turn of the century to provide additional office space for the bank and mint. In 1892 the first gold sovereigns were minted on three imported German coining presses.

In 1899 President Kruger gave the industrialist Sammy Marks permission to use the mint for a day in gratitude for his presentation of the Kruger statue, which had by then not been erected. On that day 215 gold tickeys (threepenny pieces) were minted. Today these tickeys are extremely valuable collectors' pieces.

The building was renovated and restored in 1986.

The **Bank of Africa Building**, also known as the Kirkness Building after its builder J J Kirkness, in Palace Lane in the north-western corner of the Square (now part of the post office) was erected in 1906. It was designed by T A Sladdin. It is in the British neo-Renaissance style which replaced the dominating Dutch, Belgian and German influence after the Anglo-Boer War. This style is particularly noticeable in the Doric columns and the pediment.

The northern side of the Square

The **Palace of Justice** on the northern side of the Square, which housed the supreme court of South Africa, is in the Italian Renaissance style. Like the Old Raadsaal opposite, it was designed by Sytze Wierda, Chief Architect of the Department of Public Works of the South African Republic. Building work started in 1897. During the Anglo-Boer War of 1899–1902 the uncompleted building was used as a military hospital for British troops. It was completed in 1902 and contains many admirable features such as a glass dome, a huge chandelier, graceful columns, beautiful ballustrades and striking red and black floor tiles. The building was being restored since 1994 and on the Vermeulen Street side of the building later additions were removed during 1996–1997 to reveal a typically Renaissance double staircase and other features. At the time of writing this work was not completed. The supreme court has moved to its new building across the street in Vermeulen Street.

The **Reserve Bank Building** on the northern side of the Square east of Paul Kruger Street is one of Sir Herbert Baker's last and most imposing buildings in South Africa. Baker is best known for the design of the Union Buildings overlooking the central city where inter alia the offices of the President are housed (see box for a discussion of Baker's work).

The **Old Mutual building** on the northern side of the Square is, like the adjacent Reserve Bank building, in the post-World War I neo-classical style. It was designed by Fred M Glennie and built in 1929. It is built mainly of sandstone with plaster in parts. In the fifties part of the building was taken over by the Reserve Bank and the whole building was bought by the bank in the early seventies.

The eastern side of the Square

Ons Eerste Volksbank building (Our First People's Bank building) in Mutual Lane in the north-eastern corner of the Square is an example of Cape architecture which embodies the pursuit of a national identity. Ons Eerste Volksbank was founded in the late twenties to give the Afrikaner a foothold in the economy and was replaced in 1934 by Volkskas (now ABSA) Bank, one of the largest commercial banks today.

First National Bank building, on the corner of Church Street East and the Square, was completed in 1939 and was designed by Gordon Leith who was known as one of the masters of traditional style architecture in South Africa. First National Bank was previously known as Barclays Bank.

Tudor Chambers on the south-eastern corner of the Square and Church Street East was designed in the neo-Gothic style by John Ellis (1874–1929) for businesman George Heys, the owner of Melrose House which is discussed elsewhere. The building was completed in 1904. In about 1960 the Tudor Chambers lost its cupola and a bronze dragon which served as a weather vane.

The Raadsaal on the southern façade of Church Square

Sir Herbert Baker, architect

Sir Herbert Baker had a profound influence on the architecture of public buildings in South Africa. Baker was born in Cobham, Kent, England in 1862. After being attached to a prominent firm of architects in London he left for the Cape colony in 1892. He hoped to be able to assist his brother Lionel as a fruit farmer and to find better career opportunities than those existing in England.

At the Cape Baker met Cecil John Rhodes, Cape prime minister, who asked him to restore his house Groote Schuur, which had been burned down. This building subsequently became the official Cape residence of the South African head of state. The two men became great friends. They both hoped to be able to create a typical South African architecture and the great bulk of Baker's work over the next ten years was devoted to this ideal. Hoping to use Baker to win fame by means of architecture, Rhodes sent him on a study tour of Greece, Sicily, Italy and Egypt.

After Rhodes's death in 1902 Baker was invited by Lord Alfred Milner, governor of the Transvaal and Orange River Colony after the Anglo-Boer War of 1899–1902, to help with his reconstruction plans. In Johannesburg he built a home for himself from stone found in the local koppies (hills).

The development and reconstruction of South Africa after the war brought Baker commissions from all over the country. He imported or trained artisans to do the work in the projects he undertook and preferred the pure and attractive local building materials to the often inferior imported materials which were in vogue at that time.

During a period of general eclecticism in architecture Baker developed his own architectural style. For every region he chose an overseas style which suited the local climate and general milieu rather than following European fashions slavishly. For the first time climatic conditions were consciously taken into account by an architect in South Africa. The churches he designed were derived from English, French and Bizantyne examples, often built in stone from the local environment. His houses are a mixture of motifs from the Cape Dutch buildings he admired.

Baker's best known building in Pretoria – and South Africa as a whole – is the Union Buildings on Meintjeskop overlooking the eastern and southern suburbs and the central city. It is the symbolic seat of government in Pretoria and today houses the offices of the President and the Minister of Foreign Affairs. In Pretoria he also designed the railway station and the Old Reserve Bank Building on Church Square.

After a stay of twenty years in South Africa Baker left for India in 1913 to work on the design of the new administrative building for the government in New Delhi. Shortly before the First World War started he returned to England where he was inter alia responsible for the design of South Africa House which houses the South African embassy on Trafalgar Square in London.

All over South Africa today are to be found cathedrals, chapels, churches, public buildings, schools, housing schemes, private homes, office buildings, banks, and memorials designed by Baker. Outside Pretoria the already mentioned Groote Schuur in Cape Town and the Rhodes Memorial against Lion's Head just above the University of Cape Town are his best-known creations.

Baker died in England in 1946. ■

Overleaf:
Union Buildings at night

Union Buildings and gardens

Union Buildings detail

The Union Buildings

This imposing building on Meintjeskop overlooking the central city is one of Pretoria's landmarks. The Union Buildings represent the climax of architect Sir Herbert Baker's achievements in South Africa (see box for discussion of Baker's work). The building was meant to be the symbolic seat of government after the unionization of the four colonies of the Transvaal, Orange River Colony (Orange Free State), Cape Colony and Natal to form the Union of South Africa in 1910.

Baker utilized a plateau on top of the hill split by a depression such as the Greeks would have chosen for an amphitheatre. He designed two wings containing offices, connected by a semi-circular building with a colonnade enclosing an amphitheatre. The

classical features and the imposing locality gives the sandstone complex a particularly dignified and stately appearance.

At the time of the formation of the Union of South Africa (1910) there was a dire need for reconciling the Afrikaans and English speaking sections of the white population following the wounds left by the Anglo-Boer War (1899–1902). The two wings or office blocks therefore symbolized these two groups linked as reconciled equals by the colonnade. It is ironical that although the symbolism did not take black South Africans into account, today the building houses the offices of the first black president of the country.

The Union Buildings was originally intended to house a large number of civil servants. The basement level contained the state archives. Today the building is home only to the offices of the President and the Minister of Foreign Affairs. The amphitheatre has been the venue for important state occasions such as funerals of statesmen and the inauguration of President Mandela in 1994 and President Mbeki in 1999.

The statues on the building, on the lower terrace and in the spacious garden in front of the complex add to the general aura of stateliness. The various statues are discussed under 'Statues and public sculptures'. They include the following: the Mercury figure on the small dome in the amphitheatre, the two Atlas figures on top of the domes on the side wings, the statues of Louis Botha and J B M Hertzog, former prime ministers, in the garden and on the lawn respectively, and the bust of J C Smuts, former prime minister, on the western lawn. The memorial honouring soldiers who fell at Delville Wood in World War I on the lower terrace, and the War Memorial dedicated to the Pretoria soldiers who fell in the First and Second World Wars and the Korean War, are discussed under 'Monuments and memorials'.

For guided tours of the Union Building and its gardens contact the Expeditionary Force, at tel 667 2833. A private tour called 'The Baker's Dozen' is offered by appointment. Telephone Leoné Jackson at 344 3197.

Leendert te Groen Building

This building next to the *Pretoria News* building in Vermeulen Street was, as indicated on the façade, at one stage the Eureka Cigarette Factory. The building was erected in 1903–1905. The third tenant, Leendert te Groen, started his cigarette factory there, making cigarettes from locally produced Transvaal tobacco. The building is a typical example of an apartment on top of a shop, which was popular at the time. It is a national monument and until recently served as a museum for work of the artist J H Pierneef.

Sammy Marks building on Church Street with the Reserve Bank behind

Sammy Marks and Kynoch buildings

The Sammy Marks Building with its many triangular gables and the adjacent Kynoch Building were both designed by Willem de Zwaan, the Dutch-born architect who was also responsible for the Old Netherlands Bank Building on Church Square. The Sammy Marks Building was erected for Samuel Marks, philanthropist, industrialist and pioneer in scientific farming. The building has three storeys with shops on the ground floor and office space on top. The Sammy Marks Building is considered the best-proportioned of the historical city buildings, particularly the placing of the windows on the north side.

The Kynoch Building, interesting for its flat roof, was probably erected between 1876 and 1884 for the firm of Kynochs, manufacturers of ammunition and dynamite, and is now the oldest existing building in Pretoria.

Lion Bridge and Wierda Bridge

Although bridges are not buildings, they are nevertheless structures – in these two cases designed by an architect. It is perhaps fitting to mention them here. Before the discovery of gold on the Witwatersrand there were no proper bridges in the Republic. During the 1890s an extensive road and bridge building programme was undertaken by the government of the South African Republic.

The Lion Bridge, with statues of lions at either end, spans the Apies River shortly after its confluence with Walker Spruit. The spot was known as Leeuwdrif – lion ford – when the dirt road crossed the stream here, because in the pioneering days of Pretoria marauding lions often attacked

Sytze Wierda, architect

Together with the British architect Sir Herbert Baker the Dutch-born Sytze Wopkes Wierda had the greatest early influence on public architecture in South Africa. But whereas Baker's work can be seen from Cape Town to Mpumalanga, Wierda's is confined to Pretoria and Johannesburg and other towns north of the Vaal River. Wierda's merit lies in the introduction of the neo-Renaissance architectural style in the South African Republic and the use of local building stone in his designs.

Wierda was born in Friesland in the Netherlands in 1839. After qualifying as an architect he entered the service of the Dutch State Railways in 1866 where his duties entailed the design of station and other buildings. He also designed a large number of churches in the Netherlands. In 1887 he accepted the post of government engineer and architect of the South African Republic. Under his guidance the Department of Public Works of the republic was formed.

The economic prosperity of the South African Republic after the discovery of gold on the Witwatersrand in 1886 and the great need for state buildings created the opportunity for him and others to apply the current French, Italian and Flemish-Dutch Neo-Renaissance architectural style in the Republic. In Pretoria he was responsible for inter alia the Old Raadsaal (1889–92), the Palace of Justice (1896–99), the Staats Meisjes School (1894), the Staats Model School (1897) (all discussed elsewhere), the Government Printing Works (1890) on the corner of Vermeulen and Bosman Streets, and the Compol Building (originally known as the Nieuwe Goewernements Gebouw, i.e. the New Government Building) on the corner of Pretorius Street and Volkstem Lane. He also designed the magistrates' offices in Klerksdorp and Krugersdorp (both 1890), the main post office of Johannesburg (1897) and the Johannesburg Fort (1899).

In addition to buildings Wierda was also responsible for the design of bridges of which the Lion Bridge in Church Street, Pretoria, and the bridge over the Sesmylspruit near Wierda Park in Centurion are the best known. Wierda also designed the Paardekraal Monument near Krugersdorp which commemorates the 1880 decision of the Transvaal burghers to take up arms and regain their independence from Britain.

In the Netherlands his ability was recognized when he was made a member of the Koninklijk Instituut van Ingenieurs (Royal Institute of Engineers). In 1894 he was nominated as an honorary member of the South African Association of Engineers and Architects.

Wierda died in Cape Town in 1911. ■

Typical Victorian house built early in the 20th century

grazing cattle in the vicinity. The first bridge in this position was called Arcadia Bridge because it linked the farm Arcadia with the town. The later bridge was designed by Sytze Wierda, government architect, who was also responsible for the Old Raadsaal and the Palace of Justice on Church Square. The lions were cast in Scotland and when the lions were placed, the bridge became known as Lion Bridge.

The other remaining bridge designed by Wierda is that over the Sesmylspruit – literally translated Six-mile Spruit or stream – near the Wierda Park residential township in the Centurion municipality.

Tram Shed

Today a bustling shopping centre, this building on the corner of Van der Walt & Schoeman Streets stood vacant for a number of years in the heart of Pretoria. As the name indicates, the building originally served as a shed for electric trams running between the city centre and various parts of Pretoria. The building was erected in 1912 and is built of the red Kirkness bricks which are still to be found in some older buildings in the city. It is a good example of the successful conversion of an industrial building to serve another purpose.

Staats Model School

This red brick building on the corner of Van der Walt & Skinner Streets which today houses the Gauteng Education Department Library, was designed by Sytze Wierda, chief architect of the Republic. It was completed in 1896.

During the Anglo-Boer War (1899–1902) the building served as a temporary prison for British officers. One of the best-known episodes in connection with the war was the escape from here of Winston Churchill, the later British prime minister, who was then a war correspondent. The building housed various schools over the years until it was turned into a library in 1951.

Staats Meisjes School

Like the *Staats Model School,* this building on the corner of Visagie & Prinsloo Streets was designed by state architect Wierda. During the

Pretoria City Hall with equestrian statue of Andries Pretorius in the foreground

Anglo-Boer War (1899–1902) the building served as a military hospital. It has housed different schools, at present the Hamilton Primary School.

City hall

The city hall was built in the 1930s during the Depression, partly to create jobs. The style is neo-Classic and it is very visible in Paul Kruger Street, opposite the Transvaal Museum. One of its features is a magnificant pipe-organ, the second largest in the southern hemisphere.

Structures in and around Burgers Park

Apart from the statue of President Burgers and the memorial to members of the Transvaal Scottish Regiment who fell during the First World War, discussed under 'Statues' and 'Monuments and memorials' respectively, there are also a number of interesting historical structures in the park. The *Victorian bandstand* or pavilion in the centre of the park is one of the pre-cast iron structures which could be ordered from catalogues around the turn of the century. It was manufactured by the firm of MacFarlane of Glasgow and erected in 1895. It was used in earlier days during civic occasions and official receptions. The kiosk in the park was used for the same purpose. The look-out floor at the top was meant to afford visitors to the park a view across the park. Today the building houses a restaurant.

The *Curator's house* was built in 1904. This building, with its turret and art nouveau detail, was meant to complement the decorative character of the park. Next to the house is a turret of a house in the vicinity that was demolished in the 1960s and erected on a brick base to preserve it and serve as a decoration and as a reminder of the fine Victorian architecture to be found in Pretoria earlier in the century. Another reminder is to be found in the two gates at the Jacob Maré Street entrance to the park: two gates with the words *Park* and *Zicht* on them. The gates used to belong to the manor house Parkzicht (Park View) which stood next to Melrose House.

Barton Keep in the same vicinity, at 212 Jacob Maré Street, was the property of Eddie Bourke, friend of George Heys and a fellow businessman. The plans for the building were drawn up in the Netherlands and many of the materials were imported. In 1887 the Bourkes started building the house with the help of Dutch craftsmen in the neo-Medieval style then in vogue. It is dominated by a large round turret and characterized by a multitude of portals, nooks and crannies.

Bourke was a popular figure who later became mayor of Pretoria (1903–1904). Bourke Street in Sunnyside was named after him. The house often served as venue for receptions and other social events. Since the forties it has housed the conservatoire of music of the Hervormde Church.

In Andries Street, between Skinner and Schoeman Streets, is a Victorian apartment building decorated with an abundance of cast-iron 'lace', Sher Court. It has been declared a national monument.

A bit further south-west is the railway station complex and also the Victoria Hotel. The **railway station,** at the southern end of Paul Kruger Street, is another of Sir Herbert Baker's designs. Like the Union Buildings, the erection of the building was one of a number of government projects undertaken at the time of the formation of the Union of South Africa in 1910 to strengthen sentiments of national unity. It was the first proper station building to be erected since the completion of the railway from Pretoria to Delagoa Bay (Maputo) in 1895. The old **NZASM building,** to the left as one faces the station, was built in 1891 to serve as a goods office for the NZASM (Netherlands South African Railway Company). This soundly built structure was restored and today serves as the offices of the railways electricity section. The high stoep used to serve as a train platform.

Opposite the railway station on the corner of Scheiding and Paul Kruger Streets is the **Victoria Hotel.** The building was erected in 1896 and originally it was known as the Hollandia Hotel. It was often frequented by Dutchmen connected with the NZASM which built the railway line from Pretoria to Delagoa Bay (Maputo). When the British forces under Lord Roberts occupied Pretoria in June 1900 the name was summarily changed to the Victoria Hotel. The building has unfortunately lost its decorative cast-iron work, but the turrets and gables and the verandas have remained and the interior still breathes the atmosphere of a century ago.

Railway houses, Salvokop. South-west of the Pretoria railway station is a group of houses built for staff members of the NZASM. The government of President Paul Kruger regarded such a railway line as important for the economic independence of the republic because the land-locked state was dependent for its contact with the coast on the railway lines of the Cape Colony and Natal. The NZASM was eventually responsible for a whole network of railways in the republic and a large staff of railway men from the Netherlands and other European states were imported to build and operate these railways. Station buildings and houses to accommodate the employees were built along the routes and the houses at Salvokop are representative of these structures. They are arranged in a semicircle around a common garden and were erected in the 1890s.

First University of Pretoria campus building

*Kya Rosa which first housed Transvaal University College
when it was founded in 1908*

University of Pretoria

The **Ou Letteregebou** (Old Arts Building) on the campus of the University of Pretoria forms the historical heart of the eastern campus of the University. It is situated at the eastern end of the inner square facing the faculty of Engineering office block at the University Road end. The building dates back to 1911 and was one of the first buildings of the young Pretoria University College (opened in 1908 with 32 students) to be completed.

In 1906 the Transvaal University College of Johannesburg grew out of the Transvaal Technical Institute. Two years later a branch of the University College was started in Pretoria. The two branches then developed separately. The Johannesburg branch was transformed in 1910 into the South African School of Mines and Technology which was to become the University of the Witwatersrand in 1922. The Pretoria branch had meanwhile developed its own identity concentrating on the human sciences. It became known as the Transvaal University College which eventually in 1930 became the autonomous University of Pretoria.

This stone building in the late French Renaissance style originally housed the whole of the university college, apart from two departments. In each stairwell a stained glass window contains the crest of the university college.

Behind the Ou Lettere Building rises the new 18 storeys tall Arts Building.

At the back of the Ou Lettere Building is the remainder of the Old Chemistry Building which was completed in the same year.

An extremely interesting building on the campus of the university is the **Old Merensky Library** which was completed in 1939. The architect was Gerhard Moerdijk, who was also responsible for the design of the Voortrekker Monument. There are obvious similarities. Like the monument it is built from granite and it conveys a definite monumental character. Moerdijk visited Egypt and the Middle East shortly before he embarked on the design and he described the library as a building in the Persian style with some African motifs. The zigzag design (sign for water) above the windows on the top floor reminds one of the Zimbabwe ruins. Today the building houses the Eduardo Villa Museum.

A third notable building on the campus is the replica of **Kya Rosa** near the entrance in Lynnwood Road. Kya Rosa was a private home belonging to the Jewish newspaperman Leo Weinthal which he called after his wife Rosa, Kya being the Xhosa and Zulu word for house. Weinthal became editor of a local newspaper in 1893. He was a personal confidant of President Paul Kruger and maintained a staunchly pro-Kruger stance in his editorials. In 1896 Weinthal clashed with Kruger's government over the sentencing of the Reform leaders who supported the Jameson Raid (see box under 'Military traces of the past'). In 1898 he started the newspaper the *Pretoria News* which still exists. After the Anglo-Boer War of 1899–1902 Weinthal became a supporter of the imperialistic ideals of Cecil John Rhodes.

Victoria Hotel, opposite the station

The Transvaal University College started in 1908 with a handful of students in this house which was situated in Skinner Street. The house has since had to make way for office blocks in the city. The alumni organization of the University of Pretoria decided to collect money to have a replica of Kya Rosa built and it was accurately and painstakingly reconstructed. The first sod was ceremoniously turned on 10 February 1983, exactly 75 years after the University College opened its doors to students. The 'new' Kya Rosa was officially opened in 1985. It serves as offices for the alumni organization.

Marabastad

Marabastad is the name given to an area north-west of the city centre which was set aside as a residential area for Indians, coloureds and blacks. Boom Street, which runs past the zoo further east, forms the main street of Marabastad. It is a predominantly Indian area containing many Indian-owned shops, still referred to as the Indian Bazaar. There is also a flea market with stalls where everything from food to clothes can be bought.

Marabastad contains a number of its original corrugated iron houses and a mosque. One of the interesting historical buildings is a Hindu temple, the **Meriammen Temple**. This temple was built in the thirties. The richly adorned façade is particularly attractive. It is a national monument.

The unique Gopirum of tiered precast concrete elements – Pretoria Meriammen Temple

Erasmus Castle

This castle-like house has earned for itself the name of the Ghost House. From a distance it looks like the mysterious type of building usually associated with scary films: larger than the average house, with one or two turrets and during a thunderstorm lightning illuminating the night sky around it. The unusual appearance stems partly from the fact that several late Victorian architectural styles were mixed, while art nouveau characteristics are also noticeable. The owner was J J P Erasmus.

The house is now situated on the property of Armscor, the arms and weapons manufacturing parastatal. Entrance is therefore limited to one or two specialized groups per year such as architectural students. The contact number for arranging visits is nevertheless given for groups of tourists with such interests: 428 3816.

Erasmus Castle, better known as the `Haunted House'

Heroes' Acre, Church Street cemetery

Cemeteries often tell fascinating stories about the history of the communities with which they are connected. Church Street cemetery in Pretoria is no exception. It is situated on the northern side of Church Street four and a half blocks west of Church Square, between Schubart Street and D F Malan Drive.

Close to the gate in Church Street is a section known as the Heroes'

Church Street cemetery

Acre. More than a century ago the decision was taken to reinter persons there who had played a prominent role in the history of the South African Republic. Andries Pretorius, Voortrekker leader after whom the town was named, was the first upon whom this honour was bestowed posthumously. The Voortrekker General A H Potgieter, after whom Potgieter Street in Pretoria and the town of Potchefstroom were called, was not reinterred but is honoured by a memorial.

Thomas François Burgers, progressive and controversial president of the South African Republic from 1872 to 1877, whose term of office ended with the annexation of the state by Sir Theophilus Shepstone for Britain, was also reinterred there. The legendary Paul Kruger, president from 1883 to 1902 (see discussion of his career under 'Statues') was not buried in the original Heroes' Acre but further east – which can be regarded as an extension of the Heroes' Acre and where a bust adorns his grave. Wreaths are laid on the grave on his birthday (10 October) every year.

Also buried in the extended Heroes' Acre is Dr H F Verwoerd, born in the Netherlands in 1901 and Prime Minister of South Africa from 1958 to 1966, who called a referendum which brought into existence the Republic of South Africa in 1961. He is generally regarded as the architect of the apartheid policy.

Two sections of the cemetery contain Boer and British graves, respectively, from the Anglo-Boer War of 1899–1902. The Boer fighters buried here are casualties from the Pretoria district, but they are not the only Pretoria casualties since many were buried at the battlefields as well as in gardens of remembrance elsewhere and in family graveyards on farms. Some of the tens of thousands of British soldiers who fell are buried in the British military section of the cemetery. Many soldiers died of enteric fever and other diseases and not in battle.

Buried in close proximity are two Australian soldiers who fought on the British side, H H Morant and P J Handcock, who were court-marshalled and executed for murdering Boer prisoners of war and civilians during the Anglo-Boer War.

Other well-known personalities buried here include E G Jansen, the first Afrikaans-speaking governor-general of South Africa (1951–1959); George Heys, the prominent businessman who had Melrose House built (see Melrose House under 'Museums'); A H Nelmapius, the first industrialist in the Transvaal Republic; J H M Struben, one of the English-speaking pioneers of the South African Republic and Pretoria, and State Attorney after whom Struben Street was named; R K Loveday, acting mayor of Pretoria after the Anglo-Boer War and a pioneer of wildlife conservation after whom Loveday Streets in Pretoria and Johannesburg were called; J R Lys, another English-speaking pioneer of Pretoria, magistrate from 1877 to 1880, and founder of the Anglican community in the town; and many others.

Breaker Morant and P J Handcock

Peter Joseph Handcock and Henry Harbord (Harry or Breaker) Morant were two Australians who volunteered for service on the British side in the Anglo-Boer War of 1899–1902 and who were executed in Pretoria by firing squad in 1902. Handcock was born in Australia where he became apprentice to an iron smith before volunteering for service in South Africa. Morant grew up in England but later emigrated to Australia where he became known as a horse trainer who knew how to break in wild horses. Hence the name 'Breaker'.

Both men served in the Bushveldt Carbineers, an irregular unit, which did service in the area north-east of Pietersburg, in the present Northern Province. A division of this unit under Morant was stationed at Strydpoort in that area. Early in 1901 this division, including both these men, was involved in an attack on a Boer homestead where Boer fighters were hiding. One of the men in the party, a certain Hunt, was killed in the attack. To take revenge one of the Boers taken prisoner was executed and a few days later another six.

A German missionary, Daniel Heese, came upon the bodies and threatened to report the killings. Shortly afterwards Heese was ambushed and shot dead. Thereupon the German consul protested to the British military authorities. Morant, Handcock and two other members of the Bushveldt Carbineers were brought before a military tribunal in Pietersburg and Pretoria and were found guilty of murder together with G W Witton. Witton's sentence was commuted to imprisonment, but Handcock and Morant were executed on 27 February 1902. ■

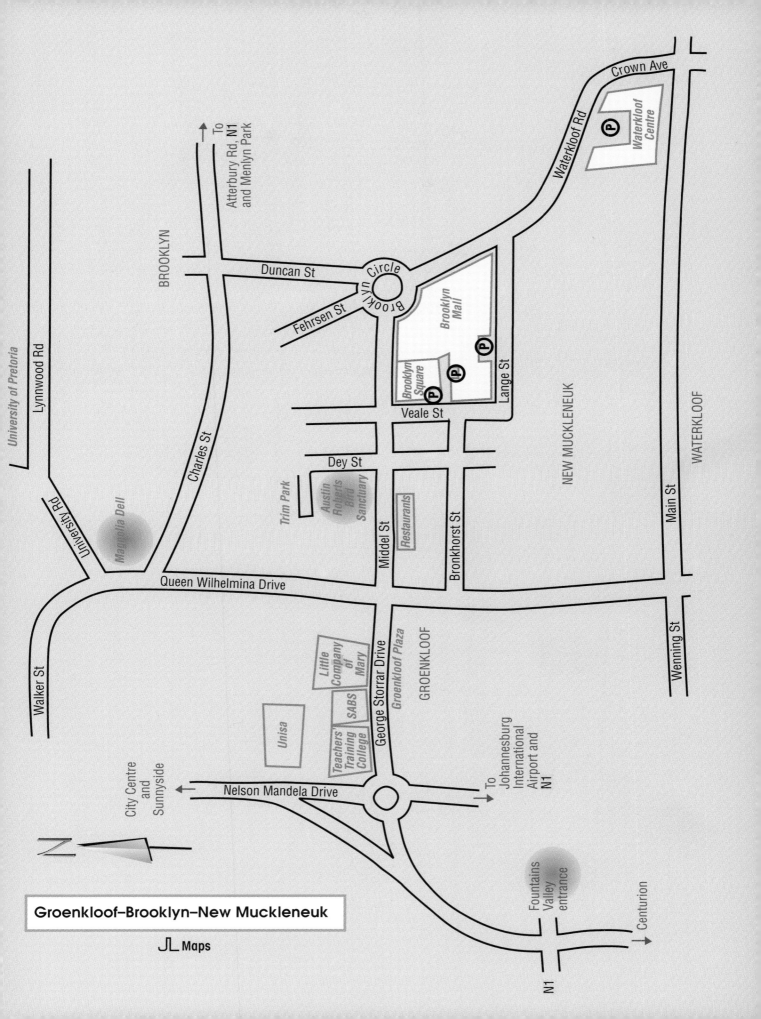

Groenkloof–Brooklyn–New Muckleneuk

JL Maps

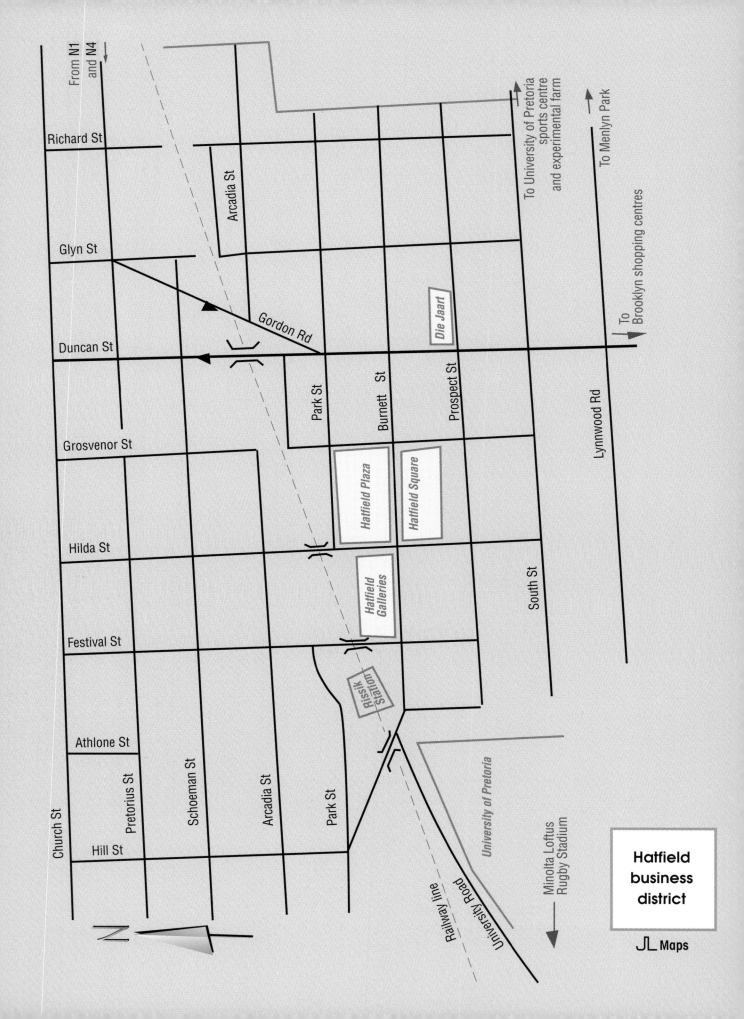

Hatfield
business
district

JL Maps

Although Pretoria does not have nearly as many modern and tall buildings as Johannesburg, its city core nevertheless contains a number of very modern shapes which dominate the skyline.

The 37-storey **South African Reserve Bank building** on the western side of the block between Vermeulen, Prinsloo, Church and Du Toit Streets, is the latest addition to Pretoria's modern architecture as well as

Architecture: Modern buildings

the tallest building in the city. This building with its reflective glass and black Rustenburg granite will be at home among the most modern in the world. The design is by Burg, Doherty, Bryant and Partners and received a merit award from the South African Institute of Architects.

A number of terraces, a fountain and an untitled abstract sculpture by Johan van Heerden were placed in the open space near the corner of Prinsloo and Church Streets to create a more relaxed atmosphere in contrast to the very formal character of the building.

Until the Reserve Bank building went up the **Volkskas** (now **ABSA Bank**) **building** on the corner of Pretorius and Van der Walt Streets was a landmark and the most prominent building in the city centre. The glass-enclosed elevator on the outside of the building's north side was a novelty. The architects were Pauw & Botha and the building was finished in 1978. Today this office block forms a natural link with Strijdom Square to the north and the **State Theatre** to the east, the two buildings and the square taking up the whole block between Pretorius, Van der Walt, Church and Prinsloo Streets. The formal nature of the two buildings is complemented by the informal atmosphere of the Square, which is further emphasized by the presence of trading stalls. The State Theatre on the eastern side of Strijdom Square rounds off the complex of structures

Downtown Pretoria with ABSA centre left and the Reserve Bank far right. The roofs of The Tram Shed can be seen in the bottom left corner.

which today occupy the former Market Square in the street block. This building housing five different theatres was completed in 1981 and at that time it was the largest centre of its kind in the Southern Hemisphere. The building was designed by Interplan Architects and Daneel Smit & Viljoen. The whole building is in concrete. Tapestries, sculptures, paintings and mosaics by South African artists adorn the interior. The square on the corner of Prinsloo and Church Streets forms an integral part of the building. The metal sculpture in this open space depicting two stylized hands raised upwards on a revolving pedestal, appropriately titled Applause, is the work of Danie de Jager.

The modern **Munitoria Building** in the block between Vermeulen, Van der Walt, Church and Prinsloo Streets houses the city government. This building was completed in 1969 and was designed by the firm of Burg Lodge & Doherty whose roots go back as far as 1904. A characteristic of this modern structure is the use of polished granite and mosaic covering large parts of the building, and the use of reflective glass windows. When the new shopping complex, Sammy Marks Square, was erected across Vermeulen Street, a raised passageway was constructed over the street to connect the two buildings and make Munitoria more accessible. The western wing of the building was gutted by fire in 1997 and has since been imploded.

In Pretorius Street, one block west from Church Square, is the building of the **Human Sciences Research Council**. It was built in the early 1980s and the architects received an award for their use of concrete in its construction. The colours on the street façade were added recently.

State Theatre

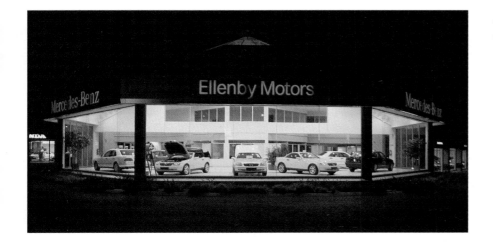

Motor showroom in the eastern suburbs

Suburban `motor city' southern suburbs

Overleaf: State Theatre and ABSA building at night

The African Window

The African Window is the title of an exhibition by the National Cultural History Museum. The exhibition consists of four parts.

The Rainbow Collection is a selection from the 3 750 000 objects comprising the total collection of the museum. The themes covered include tools, household articles, toys, artworks, jewellery, clothing, etc

Museums

from the various cultures comprising the South African nation. A computer provides easy access to the items.

The strikingly presented Access to Power exhibition deals with San (Bushman) rock art. Apart from the sheer simplistic beauty of this art form aspects illuminated include the San religion as expressed in art, the role of animals in this religion, supernatural energy, the healing of the sick and making rain.

People's Choice with the subtitle Making Music, is a collection of musical instruments from various cultures containing keyboard, percussion, wind and stringed instruments as well as exhibits on the mechanization of music, while the art of a group, the Vuma Wethu Dancers, is also displayed in photographs.

The fourth component is the exhibition Reach for the Stars. It deals with themes such as the utilization of space, threatening space, the seasons, cosmology, exploration of space, life in outer space i.e. UFO's, etc.

Apart from these permanent exhibitions there are also rotating photographic exhibitions on various themes such as Modjadji the African Rain Queen, and photographs as well as objects on Thulamela, the lost walled city in the far north east which had trade links with the Far East as long ago as 1200–1600 AD. The museum also has a film auditorium

Museum of Science and Technology in Skinner Street

Kruger House, Church Street

Transvaal Museum, Paul Kruger Street

Melrose House, Jacob Maré Street

where educational films are shown to visiting school and other groups and where film festivals are held.

Location:	Corner of Bosman and Visagie Streets
Visiting hours:	09:00–16:00
Entrance:	Charged
Tel:	324 6082

Voortrekker Monument Museum

The museum, housed in a building across the entrance courtyard from the Voortrekker Monument, focuses on the Great Trek period (1835/36–1854). A series of maps depict the most important migratory patterns in South African history in the nineteenth century. Other exhibits deal with the way of life of the Voortrekkers during this period: the oxwagon which served as home, birthplace, unit of defence in time of attack, etc; the Voortrekkers' clothing, food, medicine, hunting, weapons, religion, etc.

There is an à la carte restaurant next to the museum.

Location:	On a hill south of the city.
Visiting hours:	Monday to Saturday: 09:00–16:45
	Sunday: 11:00–16:45
Entrance:	Charged
Tel:	323 0682

Voortrekker wagon exhibited at the Monument Museum

Kruger House Museum

Kruger House Museum was the official residence of Paul Kruger, President of the South African Republic (Transvaal Republic), from 1883 until his voluntary exile in May 1900 during the Anglo-Boer War of 1899–1902. His wife stayed in the house until her death in July 1901. The residence is furnished with possessions of 'Oom Paul' (Uncle Paul), as the president was affectionately known, and Mrs Kruger. A presidential coach can be seen behind the house, while an exhibition hall contains a large number of tributes from the countries visited by Kruger after going into exile – the Netherlands, Germany, Belgium and France – as well as from Ireland, the United States and other countries which sympathized with the independence struggle of the Boers of the Transvaal and Free State. There are also orders, decorations and medals in honour of the President. The two marble lions in front of the house were presented to Kruger by Barney Barnato, the Johannesburg mining magnate.

Directly opposite the Kruger House Museum is the Gereformeerde Kerk (Reformed Church), 'Oom Paul's church' as it is still referred to. It is interesting that the clock in the steeple has no arms or inner works. This is because the Anglo-Boer War intervened before they could be ordered from overseas, and the congregation was too impoverished after the war to have them installed. The chairs used by the President and his wife can still be seen in front of the pulpit as they were placed when they attended services.

Location: Church Street, west of Church Square, in the block between Schubart and Potgieter Streets.
Visiting hours: Monday–Saturday: 08:30–16:00
Sunday: 11:00–16:00
Entrance: Charged
Tel: 326 9172

The life of Paul Kruger

S J P Kruger, or 'Oom Paul' (literally Uncle Paul) as he was affectionately known among fellow Afrikaners, was born in the eastern Cape Colony on 10 October 1825. When he was eleven years old his parents joined the Great Trek in 1836. He was an eye-witness of dramatic events such as the victory over the Matabele chief Mzilikazi's thousands at Vegkop in 1836, and the overrunning of the Voortrekker laagers by Dingane's Zulu warriors in February 1838. As a pioneer on trek he had only a basic literacy but he was an avid reader of the Bible and he drew a strong parallel between the history of Israel and that of his own people, later often referring to them as the chosen people or people of the Covenant. This belief had a strong influence on his political thinking.

Because of Kruger's leadership qualities he was elected assistant field cornet (assistant district military officer) at age seventeen and field cornet five years later in the fledgling Voortrekker republic north of the Vaal River. He was present during the negotiations with the British representatives which culminated in the Sand River Convention of 1852 recognizing the first independent Voortrekker state in the interior, subsequently named the South African Republic. It became the leit-motif of his career to maintain the independence of this new state.

As a young man Kruger distinguished himself during military operations, displaying exceptional bravery in 1854 when he recovered the body of Piet Potgieter from right in front of the cave where a bloody battle had taken place with chief Makapane's followers. When a state of civil war prevailed in the Transvaal from 1860 to 1864, with more than one coup taking place, he led a commando in the name of the legal state authority and eventually succeeded in restoring order.

When Sir Theophilus Shepstone annexed the Transvaal (South African Republic) for Britian in 1877 Kruger became one of the leaders of national resistance against the British annexation policy. He joined the protest delegation to Britain and impressed everybody with his natural gift for negotiation and mediation. When the rebellion against the annexation started in 1880 Kruger was elected a member of a rebel government and he attended the peace negotiations after the short successful war against Britain. In 1881 the Republic's independence was restored (and later confirmed by the London Convention of 1884). Kruger was a member of the triumvirate which acted as caretaker government and in 1883 he was elected President of the Republic. He was subsequently reelected three times and remained President nominally until 1902.

Kruger's greatest test as politician and statesman came with the discovery of the Witwatersrand gold-bearing reef in 1886. The Witwatersrand (literally reef or ridge of white waters) attracted thousands of fortune hunters. This worked wonders for the finances of the government, but it created enormous problems. The thousands of miners, traders, and others – Uitlanders (Foreigners), as they were called – threatened to outnumber the original conservative, farming-oriented population and clamoured for citizenship and the vote. It also created an economic problem because of a lack of facilities such as railway communication. The Uitlander problem threatened the very independence of the young republic which Kruger was determined to preserve. Kruger sought to resolve the problem by instituting a Second Volksraad (legislative assembly) who represented the Uitlanders. But this body had limited powers and did not satisfy the Uitlanders' political demands. Gradually the British authorities started taking up the cudgels on behalf of the Uitlanders. Also, because of the gold, the British government realized that it had been a mistake to withdraw from the interior of southern Africa through the conventions of the 1850s and the London Convention of 1884 and started reasserting itself. This process reached a climax under Joseph Chamberlain, Secretary of State for the Colonies since 1895, and Alfred Milner, British High Commissioner in South Africa since 1897. The resurgent British imperialism took the form of the encirclement of the South African Republic with British territory. Between 1885 and 1895 the British annexed a number of territories west, north and east of the Republic and cut it off from the sea.

One of Kruger's greatest achievements was the building of a railway line to a port outside the British sphere of influence. Largely on his insistence, a concession was approved in 1884 to build a railway line to Delagoa Bay (Maputo) in the Portuguese territory of Mozambique, and the tender awarded to a Dutch company. After many problems had been overcome the line was opened in January 1895. The Transvaal therefore had its 'own' railway, only two years after the railway line from the Cape Colony had reached Pretoria and after the Natal main line had been allowed over Transvaal soil. When the Anglo-Boer War finally broke out, the value of an own railway was proved by the fact that the company put its resources fully at the state's disposal.

It was the franchise question that finally led to the outbreak of the Anglo-Boer War in 1899. It is true that Kruger made concessions in this regard too late, but by 1899 the British were bent on war. That Kruger finally realized this is obvious from his desperate exclamation at a conference convened in 1899, in a last-minute attempt to avert war, that it was not the franchise that Milner wanted but his country. He decided that the Republic should take the initiative and issued an ultimatum to Britain on 9 October 1899 that British troops on the borders of the Republic be withdrawn, troop reinforcements at sea be recalled and all reinforcements to the British forces since the beginning of 1899 be removed within a reasonable time. The ultimatum was rejected and when it expired at 17:00 on 11 October 1899 war broke out between the South African Republic, supported by the Free State, and Britain.

The poorly equipped and badly trained Republican armies proved to be a much tougher nut than the British expected. But by the middle of 1900 the tide began to turn and the local leaders thought it better that the 75-year-old President should go into voluntary exile rather than fall to the enemy. Kruger travelled by train to Delagoa Bay where he boarded a Dutch vessel, the Gelderland, placed at his disposal by Queen Wilhelmina of the Netherlands.

Kruger was received enthusiastically in France, the Netherlands and Belgium. The German Kaiser declined to receive him officially. Despite the public display of sympathy for the Boer cause not a single European government lifted a finger to assist the republics. Kruger stayed temporarily on the French Riviera but spent the last two years of his life in Clarens on Lake Geneva, Switzerland. He died there on 14 July 1904.

His body was shipped back to South Africa and he was buried on 16 December 1904 in the Church Street cemetery amid massive public interest. The funeral had a stimulating influence on the reawakening of Afrikaner nationalism after the war.

Kruger was the personification of Afrikaner nationalism in its struggle against rampant British imperialism. His steadfastness, strength of character, approachability and the simplicity of his lifestyle made it easy for people to identify with him. He stood virtually alone in the way of British imperialist ideals and in the 1890s the British press waged a campaign against what it called 'Krugerism'. He is generally recognized as one of the greatest personalities Afrikanerdom has produced. After his death his example inspired Afrikaners for decades and it still does. ■

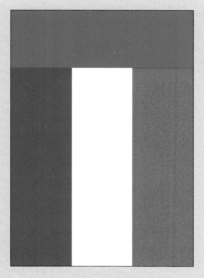

The flag of the ZAR: the Vierkleur

The Union Jack of Great Britain

Claude V Malan Museum

This centrally situated private museum is definitely worth a visit. It displays a mixture of old clocks, books, toys, china, antique jewellery and military memorabilia.

Location:	Polley's Arcade, between Pretorius and Schoeman Streets
Visiting hours:	Monday–Friday: 08:00–17:00
	Saturday: 09:00–13:00
Tel:	322 0544
Entrance:	Free

Melrose House Museum

This gracious late Victorian/ Edwardian homestead was built during the 1880s for prosperous Pretoria businessman George Heys. All the building materials, including the bricks, were imported from England and transported from the South African ports overland by ox-wagon to Pretoria. The furniture, carpets, porcelain and silver in the house all belonged to the original owners. The house therefore represents the lifestyle of the middle upper class society of Pretoria at the turn of the century.

Apart from the period objects in the house the dining room also contains the table where the peace treaty which ended the Anglo-Boer War of 1899–1902 was signed by Lord Kitchener and Lord Milner on behalf of Britain and 10 representatives of the two Boer Republics, the South African

Republic and the Orange Free State. A silver memorial plaque on the dining room table contains the engraved signatures of all the signatories.

Location:	275 Jacob Maré Street (parking from Scheiding Street at the back)
Visiting hours:	Tuesday–Sunday: 10:00–17:00
	Closed on Mondays and public holidays.
	Guided tours may be booked at the telephone numbers below.
Tea Garden:	The Prince of Wales Tea Garden is housed in the stable complex behind the house. Light meals, cakes, tea, coffee and cold drinks are served.
Tel:	322 2805/322 0420

Museum of Science and Technology

This museum aims to assist the public to acquire a better understanding of science and technology in an interesting and participatory way and to stimulate the interest of the youth in the physical sciences and technology. Visitors are encouraged to handle the models on display. Exhibits deal with nuclear energy, fuels, water conservation, space research, weather satellite receiving stations and holograms larger than one metre square. The Physicon, a physics encounter area, allows the visitor to get to know the laws of physics at first hand in a stimulating way.

Location:	Didacta Building, 211 Skinner Street
Visiting hours:	Monday–Friday: 08:00–16:00
	Sunday: 14:00–17:00
Entrance:	Charged
Tel:	322 6404

The renovated entrance to the Transvaal Museum

Transvaal Museum

The Transvaal Museum is a natural science museum which specializes in zoology and paleontology. Of major importance is the Austin Roberts bird hall which exhibits mounted specimens of all 875 indigenous bird species in reconstructed natural environments together with sound recordings of bird calls.

The museum is also in possession of the celebrated fossil skull dubbed 'Mrs Ples'. The skull was discovered in 1947 at the Sterkfontein caves near Krugersdorp, some 70 km southwest of Pretoria. It is estimated to be about 2.5 million years old and constitutes an extremely important link in the research around man's evolution. See the box below for a discussion of Mrs Ples.

There is a bookshop at the museum which sells books, videos, audiotapes, posters, games, casts of Mrs Ples and unusual curios relating to the following subjects: dinosaurs, birds, wildlife, mammals, insects, spiders, travel, early man, and plants and flowers.

There is also a convivial coffee shop.

Location: Paul Kruger Street between Visagie and Minnaar Streets. Mounted skeletons of a whale and several dinosauruses can be seen in front of the building.

Visiting hours: Mon–Sat 09:00–17:00
Sun 11:00–17:00

Entrance: Charged

Tel: 322 7632

Mrs Ples

The name *Mrs Ples* is derived from *Plesianthropus transvaalensis,* the name which the discoverer of the skull, Dr Robert Broom of the Transvaal Museum, chose for it. It is the most complete skull yet found of the species *Australopithecus africanus.* The original is in the custody of the museum and replicas can be seen there as well as at other scientific institutions world-wide.

Many scientists believe that *Australopithecus* is the genus from which all species belonging to the genus *Homo* evolved. But scientists have different opinions about the evolution of several species of *Homo,* and where the boundaries between these species occur, if such boundaries occur at all. One view is that *Australopithecus africanus* (including Mrs Ples) led to the species *Homo habilis* ('handy man', about 1.8 million years ago), which in turn led to *Homo erectus* ('man who walks upright', about one million years ago), leading to *Homo sapiens,* meaning 'wise man', a description derived from the successful way in which this being has coped with environmental changes. Homo sapiens is the only hominid species alive on earth today.

Scientists at museums and universities are currently engaged in research on Mrs Ples and other fossils, hoping to establish what they looked like, how they lived, and what they could do in terms of culture and technology. For instance, excavations in the Sterkfontein valley indicate quite clearly that our ancestors had the ability to control fire. Without the controlled use of fire it would have been impossible for modern man to develop rocket engines, and without rockets it would not have been possible to explore the moon or Mars and the rest of the universe. ■

Mrs Ples

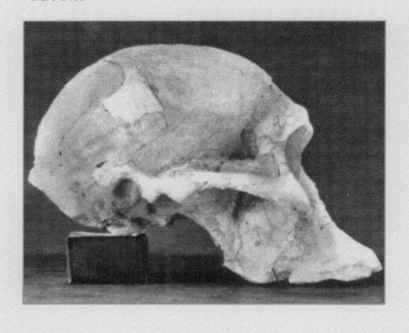

Geological Survey Museum

This museum adjoins the Transvaal Museum in the same building. It contains a display of examples of minerals and gemstones from southern Africa and other parts of the world.

Location:	Paul Kruger Street between Visagie and Minnaar Streets
Visiting hours:	Mon–Sat 09:00–17:00 Sun 11:00–17:00
Entrance:	Charged
Tel:	322 7632

Correctional Services Museum

This is the only museum of its kind in South Africa. The exhibits depict the development of the penal system in South Africa from the most barbaric methods to the modern penological system of today, as well as prisoners' hobbies and illegal activities.

Location:	Central Prison grounds, upper Potgieter Street
Visiting hours:	Tues–Fri 09:00–15:00
	Closed on public holidays
Entrance:	Free
Tel:	314 1766

Pioneer Museum

This museum in Silverton east of the city centre represents the pioneering phase in the settlement of whites in Pretoria. The house dates back to 1848 and the whole complex, consisting of the house, an outbuilding and a farmyard, is typical of the way of life of the white pioneers in the period immediately following the Great Trek. There are also stables, a water mill, a threshing floor and a herb garden. There are picnic facilities and gatherings and festivities are held there, for instance new year's day feasts when games and sport typical of the pioneers are played. Demonstrations of typical farming activities are also held.

Visiting hours:	Monday–Friday: 08:30–16:00
	Saturday–Sunday: 09:00–16:00
Entrance:	Charged
Tel:	803 6086

Transport Technology Museum

This museum contains exhibits on different matters which are not necessarily connected with transport. These include Meteorology in South Africa, including the work of the Weather Bureau, Research on Antarctica, Merchant Shipping, Civil Aviation, the Department of Transport, Airport Services, the Development of Roads, and Urban Transport.

Location:	Forum Building, cnr Bosman & Struben Streets
Visiting hours:	Mon–Fri 08:00–16:00
	Closed weekends
Entrance:	Free
Tel:	290 2016

Millennium Gallery Courtyard

Bottom:
Millennium Gallery, Groenkloof

Pioneer Museum, Silverton

Outside the city, but not too far away, are also many interesting spots worth a visit.

Tswaing (eco museum)

This is the first eco museum in South Africa. It is a meteorite crater that goes back more than 200 000 years with a saline lake leaving soda and salt deposits during the dry season. Tswaing means 'place of salt'. There is also an information centre. The area surrounding the museum is important for its fauna and floral diversity. More than 300 bird species have already been identified at Tswaing.

Location:	40 km northwest of Pretoria
Visiting hours:	Mon–Sat 09:00–16:00
	Sun 11:00–16:45
Entrance:	Charged
Tel:	(01214) 98730

Sammy Marks Museum

This splendid residence on the farm Swartkoppies outside the city was built by Sammy Marks (1843–1920). Marks was one of the first industrialists in the South African Republic and a mining and farming pioneer who owned a distillery and other factories at Eerste Fabrieken (first factories) not far from his farm, east of the present Mamelodi.

The house was occupied by family members until 1978 and has been preserved in its original form. It contains magnificent furniture ordered by Marks from overseas as well as exquisite cutlery and crockery.

The garden in front of the house was the pride of Sammy's wife Bertha and stood under the supervision of an Austrian gardener. In the 1890s a rose garden was started for which rose trees were imported from Europe. The rose garden was restored during 1987–88 and today the whole formal garden serves as one of the best examples of a mid-Victorian garden belonging to an upper class family in South Africa.

Guided tours are offered through the house on the hour and on the half hour. Enjoy refreshments in the tea garden or book an elegant Victorian picnic, play a game of croquet or tour through the rose garden. Dinner is offered in the wine cellar (book in advance) or you can meet the Scottish ghost if you wish!

Sammy Marks Museum

Location:	23 km east of Church Square along the Old Bronkhorstspruit Road (route R104), the extension of Church Street
Visiting hours:	Tues–Fri 09:00–17:00
Entrance:	Charged
Tel:	803 6158

Sammy Marks

This Jewish entrepeneur was born in Lithuania in 1843. At the age of 16 he emigrated to Sheffield in England where he started a workshop for the finishing of knives. In 1868 Marks came to South Africa, making a living as an itinerant trader in jewellery in the Western Cape.

After the first reports of the discovery of diamonds in Griqualand-West Marks moved to the diamond fields accompanied by his brother-in-law Isaac Lewis. The two men started to trade in miners' requisites and soon progressed to prospecting and diamond trading. Later they bought several farms north of the Vaal River for supplying the miners at Barclay-West and Kimberley with firewood.

During the gold rush at Barberton in Mpumalanga in 1885 the firm of Lewis & Marks obtained control of the profitable Sheba Gold Mining Company. But it was after the discovery of the Witwatersrand gold-bearing reef that Lewis & Marks really became prominent. The firm soon diversified, supplying coal to the mines from its coal-mine near Vereeniging.

Shortly afterwards Marks & Lewis took over the government concession for the distilling of spirits and started a series of new industries at Eerste Fabrieken on the farm Hatherley east of Pretoria. These included a glass factory, a leather tannery and shoe factory, as well as fruit and meat canning. Other enterprises in which the firm became involved were the planting of fruit orchards and maize farming. Marks acquired a large share in a syndicate which had an exclusive concession for producing explosives for use in the mines. He also took the first steps to establish an iron and steel industry based on scrap iron which led to the founding of the Union Steel Corporation in 1911.

Marks was a friend of President Paul Kruger and an acquaintance of Kruger's arch imperialist enemy, Cecil John Rhodes, prime minister of the Cape Colony from 1890 to 1896. As a mark of respect for Kruger he donated money in 1895 for a statue of the president. In exchange Kruger allowed him to use the government mint for one day in 1899 to mint the now famous gold tickeys (three-penny pieces) as souvenirs for his friends. When the war clouds started to gather in the late nineties he made many attempts to avert a clash between the Boers and the British. After the outbreak of war between the Republics and Britain in 1899 Marks exerted himself to facilitate a peaceful settlement.

After the Anglo-Boer War (1899–1902) he became a loyal supporter of the Het Volk political party led by General Louis Botha. Following the formation of the Union of South Africa in 1910 he was nominated as a member of the Senate, the upper house of parliament, which he remained until his death.

Marks made handsome donations to several causes, inter alia a Jewish school in Pretoria. Sammy Marks Square, the shopping complex bounded by Van der Walt, Vermeulen, Prinsloo and Church Streets, was named after him. The ornamental fountain at the entrance to the Pretoria Zoo was donated by him to the government of the South African Republic and stood in the centre of Church Square before the Kruger Statue was moved there in 1954.

He died in 1920 at the age of 76 and was buried in the Rebecca Street cemetry, Pretoria. ■

Air Force Museum

This museum depicts the history of the South African Air Force. The exhibits include old aircraft, uniforms, medals and paintings.

Location:	Swartkops Air Force Base
Visiting hours:	Mon–Fri 08:00–16:00
	Sat–Sun 10:00–16:00
Entrance:	Free
Tel:	71 1211

Willem Prinsloo Agricultural Museum

The museum has as its theme the development of agriculture in Gauteng Province. The exhibits therefore include horse-drawn vehicles, farming implements and other farming equipment. The original farm homestead, built in 1882, depicts the lifestyle of rural people a century ago. There is also a traditional Ndebele hut with its attractive decorations.

Farming activities of yesteryear can also be viewed: a donkey pulling a water pump; ploughing with oxen; candle making; milking cows by hand; dressing of thongs; bread baking; etc.

An annual mampoer (home-brewed liquor or 'moonshine') festival is held at the museum.

There is a restaurant 'Tant Miertjie se Kombuis' (Aunt Miertjie's Kitchen) which serves traditional farm fare.

Willem Prinsloo Agricultural Museum

Smuts House, Irene

Location:	Along the R104, i.e. the Old Bronkhorstspruit Road (the extension of Church Street through Silverton). The museum is about 35 km from Church Square. The N4 to Bronkhorstspruit is signposted as well.
Visiting hours:	08:00–16:00
Entrance:	Charged
Tel:	(01213) 44171

Smuts House

This museum is housed in the home of the late General Jan C Smuts, one of the most famous South Africans of the 20th century. Smuts was prime minister of South Africa twice and an international statesman of note.

The corrugated iron-and-timber home on the farm Doornkloof was bought by General Smuts after it had served as officers' mess at the headquarters of the British forces in Middelburg, Mpumalanga, during the Anglo-Boer War and was re-erected on the farm. Some additions have been made but the house is substantially the same as it was a century ago. The general's study, where he indulged in his favourite occupations of

botany and philosophy, forms the centre piece of the house. His collection of botanical specimens also forms part of the contents and the herbarium, pantry and kitchen have been restored as historical rooms. A statuette of Smuts showing him on Table Mountain which he loved to climb, is to be seen in front of the house and the grounds contain other interesting relics of the general's career. A dirt road leads from the house to the koppie (hill) where the Smuts's ashes were strewn and where there is a monument to the Smuts family.

The museum and adjacent tea garden in their tranquil surroundings are open seven days a week. The grounds around the museum come alive with the hustle and bustle of the Irene Village Arts and Crafts Market on the second and last Saturday of every month.

Location:	The farm Doornkloof, near Irene. Travel along the R21 towards Johannesburg International Airport and take the Irene/Rietvlei turnoff. Turn right on to Nelmapius Road and follow the signpost after about 5 km.
Visiting hours:	Mon–Fri 09:00–16:30 Sat–Sun 09:30–17:00
Entrance:	Charged
Tel:	667 1176

J C Smuts

Jan Christian Smuts (1870–1950) was consecutively the State Attorney of the South African Republic (Transvaal Republic) (since 1898), Boer general in the Anglo-Boer War of 1899–1902, minister in the cabinet of Louis Botha in the Transvaal colony after the war (1907–1910) as well as in Botha's cabinet after the formation of the Union of South Africa in 1910, commander of the British troops in East Africa during the war of 1914–1918 and member of the Imperial War Cabinet in Britain, one of the initiators of the League of Nations, Prime Minister of South Africa (1919–1924), leader of the opposition in parliament (1924–1933), deputy prime minister (1933–1939), prime minister once more (1939–1948), again leader of the opposition (1948 until his death in 1950), Field Marshall of the British Army in the Second World War, one of the founders of the United Nations Organization and author of the preamble to its charter.

In addition Smuts was a philosopher of note and author of the book *Holism and evolution* (1926), as well as a recognized botanist: he experimented with grasses on the farm and one of the finger grasses (Digitaria) was called after him; he also wrote the introduction to the publication *The grasses and pastures of South Africa* which was published (after his death) in 1955. Smuts was the recipient of 27 honorary degrees and several military decorations, Fellow of the Royal Society, chancellor of Cambridge University and the University of Cape Town, and Freeman of 17 world cities. ■

Left: Memorial for Jan Smuts, west of Union Buildings

The first three statues below are those of state presidents of the South African Republic (Transvaal Republic) and cover virtually the whole history of the Republic (1852–1902). A visit to all three can therefore be described as a 'Presidents' route'.

Although they are not discussed in chronological order, it is recommended that they be visited in the order discussed since Church

Statues and public sculptures

Square, where the Kruger statue stands, is the natural starting point for any exploration of the city and its history.

President Paul Kruger statue

This statue is, apart from the Voortrekker Monument, the historical symbol most closely associated with Pretoria. Paul Kruger was the State President of the South African Republic (Transvaal Republic) from 1883 to 1902. He was a father figure statesman who personified nineteenth-century Afrikaner nationalism in its struggle against British imperialism. Kruger died in 1904 having spent the last four years of his life in voluntary exile after the British had occupied Pretoria in June 1900 during the Anglo-Boer War (1899–1902).

The Kruger statue is the most famous public work of the sculptor Anton van Wouw. Kruger's eyes are cast slightly downward as if looking at a crowd of people at his feet. His strong figure has an air of steadfastness about it. The four Boer sentries portray loyalty and the spirit of despondency after the loss of the Republic's independence. The figure with his left elbow on his knee and his chin resting on his closed hand is regarded as one of Van Wouw's finest sculptures. The four relief panels

The history of the Kruger statue

The well-known Transvaal industrialist Sammy Marks was initially a great admirer President Paul Kruger, and in 1895 he donated a sum of money to the government of the South African Republic to have a statue made of Kruger. The statue was designed by a young Dutchman, Anton van Wouw, who later accepted citizenship of the Republic. Van Wouw was at that time a cartoonist with a newspaper in Pretoria and the Kruger statue was his first important work. He designed a model of the President on a high pedestal surrounded by four Boer sentries. Later Van Wouw became one of the best-known sculptors in South Africa.

Van Wouw made the sculpture in Rome where it was possible to cast the pieces in bronze. Marks meanwhile had a base of red Scottish granite erected for the statue on Church Square. While Van Wouw was doing the work, the Anglo-Boer War broke out in 1899 and President Kruger suggested that the erection of the statue should be postponed.

Meanwhile the pieces of the statue were cast in Rome and shipped to Delagoa Bay (Maputo) in Mozambique where they were placed in a warehouse. When the British forces occupied Pretoria in June 1900, Marks lost interest in the project. The four figures of the Boer sentries were donated to Lord Kitchener, the British military commander, who had seen photographs of them. Kitchener subsequently had them shipped to London. But the pieces of the Kruger figure remained behind in Delagoa Bay.

In 1904 Kruger died in exile. The next year the granite base was removed from Church Square to Prince's Park three blocks west of the Square where the municipal bus depot is today. In Prince's Park the Kruger figure, without the four surrounding figures, was unveiled in 1913. Several unsuccessful attempts were made to get back the four Boer sentries and at last by 1921 they were back in Pretoria through the mediation of General Jan Smuts, then Prime Minister of South Africa.

Eventually the complete group of statues was unveiled on Kruger's 100th birthday (10 October 1925) in front of the railway station at the top of Paul Kruger Street. Many people and cultural organizations were not happy with the site and finally the group was moved and unveiled in the present position on Church Square on 10 October 1954. ■

on the base depict scenes from Kruger's career. The group of statues fits in very well on Church Square with the Raadsaal – the parliament building of the South African Republic, to the south – and the other historic buildings around the Square.

President M W Pretorius and Andries Pretorius

Placed in the City Hall gardens, Paul Kruger Street, opposite the Transvaal Museum. M W Pretorius was the first state president of the South African Republic. He was president twice, from 1857 to 1860 and

President M W Pretorius

President T F Burgers

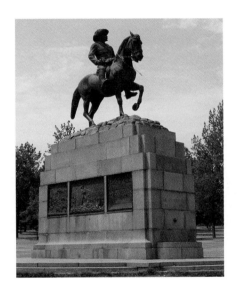

General Louis Botha

General J B M Hertzog

again from 1864 to 1871. In the interim period (1860–1863) he was president of the Orange Free State.

Pretorius was the founder of Pretoria. In 1853 he bought two farms along the Apies River with a view to establishing a seat of government. The town was proclaimed in 1855 and in 1860 it became the seat of government. It was called after his father, Andries Pretorius. Andries Pretorius was the leader of the Voortrekkers in their epic battle against the Zulu army of Dingane at Blood River in 1838 and was subsequently one of the leaders of the Voortrekker state north of the Vaal River.

Andries Pretorius is the figure on horseback with M W (Marthinus Wessel) Pretorius standing. Coert Steynberg was the sculptor.

President T F Burgers

Thomas François Burgers was president of the South African Republic from 1872 until 1877 when the republic was annexed for Britain by Sir Theophilus Shepstone. His statue is in the park named for him, Burgers Park.

Burgers was a progressive thinker who inherited a developing state whose problems he tackled with great zest. He brought about a number of reforms. Two matters, however, caused his presidency to end in disaster – an abortive scheme to build a railway to Delagoa Bay (Maputo) in Mozambique, and the war against the Pedi chief Sekhukhune in the north-eastern part of the Transvaal. The campaign against Sekhukhune was led by Burgers himself but ended inconclusively. Sekhukhune accepted a peace treaty but rejected it shortly afterwards.

When the Transvaal was annexed by Shepstone in April 1877 the 'Pedi problem' was still unsolved. The annexation proclamation was met with only a strong letter of protest by Burgers and he was suspected of collusion with Shepstone. Burgers disappeared quietly from the scene and died in obscurity and poverty in the Cape Colony in 1881.

The Burgers statue is the work of Moses Kottler. The right hand is in an almost pleading gesture. This refers to the fact that Burgers was a progressive thinker who often tried in vain to persuade his subjects to modernize.

It is fitting that the statue should stand in the park which owes its existence to him. At his request land was set aside in 1874 for a botanical garden; this subsequently became Burgers Park.

J G Strijdom

The bronze head of Strijdom under a triangular dome on Strijdom Square is the work of Coert Steynberg. Strijdom was Prime Minister of South Africa from 1954 to 1958.

The horses on a column forming the centre of a fountain is the work of Danie de Jager. The layout of the complex was designed by architects Hans Botha and Roelf Botha.

Kudu

Two kudu, the most graceful of the large South African antelope, adorn the entrance to the ABSA Bank building between Van der Walt and Andries Streets, on the steps to Strijdom Square. The sculptor was Willem de Sanderes Hendrikz.

Other works of sculpture outside the city centre are:

Voortrekker woman with children

The centre piece between the two flights of steps leading to the entrance to the Voortrekker Monument symbolizes the civilization and Christianity that were maintained and developed by the women during the Great Trek. The sculptor is Anton van Wouw.

Corner figures

The four figures on the corners of the Voortrekker Monument depict the Trek leaders Piet Retief, Andries Pretorius and Hendrik Potgieter as well as the Unknown Voortrekker Leader and together they form a symbolic guard of honour. The sculptor was Frikkie Kruger.

Arnold Theiler

Theiler (1867–1936) was the great pioneer of veterinary research in South Africa. His work was internationally recognized and he was the most famous veterinarian of his time. He was born in Switzerland and came to the South African Republic in 1891. He was requested in 1908 to start the research institute at Onderstepoort. Under his leadership the research station became famous. As a result of his research work a number of animal diseases were eradicated in South Africa while remedies were discovered for others. The granite statue of a sitting Theiler holding a magnifying glass is by Coert Steynberg. It was the first full figure statue, i.e. not only a bust, sculpted from granite in South Africa. It is placed at the main entrance to the Veterinary Research Institute, Onderstepoort.

Sir Arnold Theiler

The main building at Onderstepoort with the statue of Arnold Theiler in the foreground

Equestrian statue of Louis Botha

Louis Botha (1862–1919) was the first prime minister of the Union of South Africa from 1910 to 1919. He was also the Commandant-general of the Boer forces for part of the Anglo-Boer War (1899–1902) and prime minister of the Transvaal Colony after the institution of responsible government (1907–1910). At the end of the First World War he represented South Africa at the Peace Treaty of Versailles.

The equestrian statue on the lawn in front of the Union Buildings in Church Street is by Coert Steynberg.

J B M Hertzog

Hertzog (1866–1942) was a High Court judge in the Orange Free State Republic (1895–1899), a general in the Anglo-Boer War (1899–1902), cabinet minister in the Orange River Colony (1907–1910), cabinet minister in the first cabinet after Union (1910–1913), founder of the National Party (1914), and Prime Minister of the Union of South Africa from 1924 to 1939.

The statue is placed in the Union Buildings garden in Government Avenue and the sculptor is Coert Steynberg.

Jan Smuts

This bronze bust of J C Smuts, Prime Minister of South Africa 1919–1924 and 1939–1948, is the work of Danie de Jager. It has a semicircular colonnade behind it and was erected on the western lawn of the Union Buildings.

Striving

This symbolic sculpture at the Provincial Administration Building, cnr Pretorius and Bosman Streets, showing a group in pursuit of higher ideals and education, is the work of Moses Kottler.

Glanstoring

This 'Tower of Splendour', a pyramidal sculpture in glass, iron and bronze by Coert Steynberg has as theme the mineral wealth of Gauteng and the provinces that used to be part of Transvaal. It is in Pretorius Street, part of the works of art adorning the Provincial Administration Building.

Tamed freedom

This Afrikaner bull in bronze being led by a man is by Hennie Potgieter. It stands on a small patch of grass east of the Provincial Administration Building. It symbolizes a nation guided by the needs of its people. Freedom is curbed by the young man (the leader) who brings order and leads the the bull (the nation), actually stronger than himself, in accordance with its needs.

The sower and the reaper

Hennie Potgieter is the sculptor of this sculpture against the wall of the building of the Land and Agricultural Bank of South Africa, cnr Paul Kruger and Visagie Streets.

Applause

State Theatre, cnr Prinsloo and Church Streets. Two stylized hands raised upwards in the classic ballet poise. The sculptor is Danie de Jager.

Family group

This group in front of the Civitas Building, cnr Andries and Struben Streets, which houses sections of the government Department of the Interior dealing with the registration of births and deaths, etc, was executed by Danie de Jager.

Tamed freedom

The sower and the reaper

Abstract form in stainless steel

Civitas Building, cnr Struben and Andries Streets, sculpted by Mike Edwards.

Abstract sculpture in stainless steel

SA Reserve Bank, cnr Prinsloo & Church Streets. The sculptor is Johan van Heerden.

Seated figure

This piece in front of the Sanlam Centre, cnr Pretorius & Andries Streets, is by Eduardo Villa.

Vulcan and Prometheus

These figures by Hennie Potgieter at the Iscor headquarters at Thaba Tshwane depict the Greek mythological figures Vulcan and Prometheus in bronze. Iscor is the Iron and Steel Corporation of South Africa, the largest producer of iron and steel on the continent of Africa.

Vryheid

The creator of this classical woman's figure on top of the dome, Old Raadsaal, representing freedom, is unknown. Like the building it dates back to 1891.

Iscor headquarters at the entrance to Thaba Tshwane where the statue of Vulcan and Prometheus stands

Overleaf:
Sammy Marks Fountain,
Pretoria Zoo

Bartholomew Dias statue   *Mercury, Union Buildings*

Idasa Wall, Visagie Street

Sammy Marks Fountain

The fountain at the zoo entrance, Boom Street, was donated by the nineteenth century industrialist and benefactor, Sammy Marks. It originally stood on Church Square but was moved to its present position to make way for the Kruger statue. It was executed by W Macfarlane & Co and is dated 1905.

Atlas figures

The sculptor is A Broadbent and the figures on top of the domes on the Union Buildings' side wings bear the same date as the completion of the Union Buildings, 1913.

Mercury

This figure in the amphitheatre in front of the Union Buildings is by A Broadbent and dated 1913.

Monument donated by West-German government

This relief work in the garden of the Pretoria Art Museum is of a woman with a child in her arms, a young boy at her side and a sheep-dog at her feet. It was presented to the people of South Africa in appreciation of the thousands of food and other parcels sent in the post-war years to a war-ravaged Germany. Emil Schweikerdt, founder of the art dealers Schweikerdt Art Centre & Gallery, Fehrsen Street, Brooklyn, established the support organization. The monument was presented to South Africa in about 1955 but was erected and unveiled only in 1964. The artist is unknown.

Monument in honour of Bartholomew Dias

Arcadia Park, in front of Pretoria Art Museum, cnr Wessels and Schoeman Streets, Arcadia. This monument in the shape of a Portuguese bark at sea on a podium honours Bartholomew Dias who discovered the sea route from Europe to India in 1488. It was donated by the Portuguese community in Pretoria and was unveiled early in 1989.

Eland

At the University Road entrance to the campus of the University of Pretoria two eland figures in relief appear on the two inside columns. This was done when the entrance was named Elandspoort after the farm of that name on which the university is situated. Elandspoort was one of the two farms on which the town of Pretoria was laid out.

Villa sculptures

Apart from the museum of steel sculptures by Eduardo Villa at the University of Pretoria there are also a few of these impressive abstract works at different points on the campus.

Villa was born in Italy and came to South Africa as a prisoner of war during the Second World War. He elected to stay in South Africa and subsequently became one of the country's foremost sculptors.

The Idasa wall

This work of art offers an unusual experience, not to be missed. It is situated on the corner of Visagie and Prinsloo Streets in the old part of Pretoria but out of the CBD. The house that first occupied the stand belonged to a member of the wealthy Verdoorn family who had built a Victorian mansion on it. In the 1950s and 60s it was a boarding house and then the house was demolished. Unisa later used the site for temporary accommodation while its new campus on the hill above Fountains Circle was being built. It now houses the Independent Democratic Association of South Africa (Idasa).

Idasa commissioned artist Neels Coetzee to design an attractive wall and parking area. The requirement was that the wall should represent the roots of the South African nation and express any particular achievements by South Africans.

The roots are represented by the Zimbabwe-ruins-type wall, gleaned from ruins discovered in South Africa's Northern Province, and the wattle poles that played an important part in housing. The country is depicted by huge granite stones arranged like a koppie (hill) with veld grass around them. The concrete knucklebones were developed by a South African engineer and are used world wide to stop erosion by seawater.

Pretoria Art Museum

Pretoria Art Museum

The Pretoria Art Museum is built in a park bordered by Wessels, Schoeman, Johann and Park Streets (entrance in Wessels St). It has been in existence since 1964 and has built up a collection of more than 3000 works of mainly South African art, including paintings, sculpture, graphics, tapestries, photographic art and ceramics. The museum also

Art galleries and collections

houses a small collection of valuable 17th century Dutch paintings, part of the Michaelis collection which was bequeathed to the three capitals of South Africa, Cape Town (legislative), Bloemfontein (judicial) and Pretoria (administrative), by the late Lady Michaelis. Before the museum was built, the city council acquired various works of art, mostly by South African artists, which were housed in municipal offices and in the passages of the city hall. The collection is possibly the most representative of South African art, which developed parallel to European art because the best-known South African artists studied or lived in Europe as well. Some prominent artists from various parts of Europe settled permanently in South Africa and made an important contribution to local art. Likewise, some South African artists settled in England or Europe, but they generally still spent some time in South Africa and this interchange was valuable and enriching to SA art. The museum is well worth a visit.

Visiting hours: Tuesday to Saturday 10:00–17:00
Wednesday 10:00–20:00
Sunday 10:00–18:00
Closed on Monday
Guided tours: May be booked in advance for 10 or more at 344 1807/8
Admission: Charged

Association of Arts Pretoria

This gallery exhibits and sells the works of young, talented artists as well as well-known, more established artists on a rotating basis. It offers one-man as well as group exhibitions lasting around three weeks, and it has a permanent exhibition of works of art for sale.

Location: 173 Mackie Street, New Muckleneuk
Admission: Free
Enquiries: Tel: 346 3100/346 3110

University of Pretoria

University of Pretoria art collection

The university owns a permanent collection comprising works of mainly South African artists.

Location: University of Pretoria, Lynnwood Road, Hatfield
Enquiries: Tel: 420 3036

*Association of Arts Pretoria,
Mackie Street (off Queen Wilhelmina Ave), New Muckleneuk*

Open Window Art Academy, Rigel Ave South, Erasmusrand

Puppet collection

The collection contains more than 1000 puppets for educational and entertainment purposes.

Location:	Education & Legal Studies Building, cnr Faculty & Tindall Roads (close to Lynnwood Road)
Visiting hours:	By appointment only
Admission:	Charged
Enquiries:	Tel: 420 3031

Van Gybland-Oosterhof Collection

This collection was donated to the university and is regarded as the largest collection of objects on the House of Orange, the Dutch Royal House, outside the Netherlands.

Location:	Ou Lettere (Old Arts) Building, Main Campus (entrance cnr Lynnwood Road & Roper Street)
Visiting hours:	By appointment only
Admission:	Free
Enquiries:	Tel: 420 3031

Van Tilburgh Collection

This collection consists mainly of antique Dutch furniture and works of art as well as centuries-old Chinese ceramics.

Location:	Ou Lettere Building, main campus (entrance cnr Lynnwood Road and Roper Street)
Visiting hours:	By appointment only
Enquiries:	Tel: 420 3100

Eduardo Villa Museum

This museum contains a large number of striking steel sculptures donated to the University by the Italian-born South African sculptor Eduardo Villa. It is housed in an historic library building which serves the purpose extremely well. Some of Villa's works in steel can also be seen outside on the campus.

Location:	Old Merensky Library Building, Main Campus (entrance cnr Lynnwood Road & Roper Street)
Visiting hours:	Monday to Friday: 9:00–16:00
Admission:	Free
Enquiries:	Tel: 420 3031

Van Wouw House Museum

This house (designed by Norman Eaton) was originally the property of the well-known South African Dutch-born sculptor Anton van Wouw. Van Wouw was inter alia responsible for the Kruger statue on Church Square and the Voortrekker woman and children at the Voortrekker Monument. The collection in the house museum consists of 84 small sculptures as well as paintings.

Location:	299 Clark Street, Brooklyn
Visiting hours:	Tuesday–Friday: 10:00–16:00
	Saturday: 10:00–12:00
Enquiries:	Tel: 46 7422

Unisa Art Gallery

The gallery of Unisa (University of South Africa) is an academic gallery open to the public. Temporary exhibitions are presented from time to time.

Location:	Theo van Wyk Building, B Block
	Preller Road, Muckleneuk
Visiting hours:	Monday to Friday: 10:00–15:30
	Saturday: 14:30–16:30
	Closed on public holidays
Admission:	Free
	Guided tours on request
Enquiries:	Tel: 429 6255

Engelenburg House

This is the collection of the late Dr F V Engelenburg, consisting of paintings, sculptures, silver and bronze ware, furniture, porcelain, carpets and ceramics.

Location:	Ziervogel Street, Arcadia (Meintjeskop)
Visiting hours:	Monday to Friday: 8:00–16:00
	Public holidays and weekends by appointment only
Admission:	Free
Enquiries:	Tel: 323 5082 (o/h); 328 5085 (a/h)

Commercial galleries

Aléta Michaeletos
Tel: 47 6777
  The Loop 20A, Lynnwood

Buchels Art & Framing
Tel: 46 2893
  Rautenbach Avenue 211, Waterkloof

Hoffer Gallery
Tel: 322 3670
   395 Schoeman Street

Galerie Estelle Rossouw
Tel: 348 9203
   St Georges Court, Rodericks Road, Lynnwood

Martin Koch Gallery
Tel: 43 2777
   1089 Pretorius Street, Hatfield

Millennium Gallery
Tel: 46 8217
Cell: 083 263 5842
   Cnr Engelenburg Street & George Storrar Drive, Groenkloof

Monica Wood Gallery & Studio
Tel: 46 1303
Cell: 082 893 8170
   480 Charles Street, Menlo Park

Montmartre Gallery
   Charles Street, Menlo Park

Open Window Academy
Tel: 347 1740
   410 Rigel Ave South, Erasmusrand

Schweickerdt Art Centre & Gallery
Tel: 46 5414
   Vatika Centre, Fehrsen Street, Brooklyn

Millennium Gallery, Groenkloof

Stained-glass window by Leo Théron, abstract design for a private home

Supreme Framers
Tel: 345 1849
Barnard Street, Elardus Park

Tugwell Gallery
Tel: 46 0211
Brooklyn Mall, Lange Street, Brooklyn

Zona Boshoff Gallery
Tel: 346 1719
Brooklyn Mall, Lange Street, Brooklyn

Artists' studios

An artist who is willing to receive small groups of visitors strictly by appointment at his studio, is **Leo Théron**. He creates windows from 2 cm thick glass set in concrete, and watercolour paintings. His studio in Brooklyn is easily accessible. Tel: 46 4330.

Alice Elahi is one of Pretoria's senior artists, well-regarded as landscape painter, mainly in oils and watercolours. She will receive small groups of visitors strictly by appointment and subject to circumstances. Tel: 46 3959.

There is an abundance of shopping centres in the Greater Pretoria area. The central business district as well as the suburbs abound with shops and shopping complexes. Most of these centres contain a supermarket or hypermarket and a range of other shops as well as restaurants. Some also have cinemas. Only the larger centres are included in the list below.

Shopping

Consult the map of the city where many of the major centres are indicated.

Shopping centres

Central and Sunnyside/Arcadia

Arcadia Centre
cnr Beatrix & Vermeulen Streets

De Bruyn Park
cnr Vermeulen & Andries Streets

Fedsure Forum
cnr Van der Walt & Pretorius Streets

Kingsley Centre
cnr Beatrix & Church Streets. This centre contains a tenpin bowling alley.

Nedbank Plaza
cnr Beatrix & Church Streets

Sammy Marks Square
the block bounded by Vermeulen, Prinsloo, Pretorius & Van der Walt Streets

Sancardia Centre
cnr Church & Beatrix Streets

Sanlam Centre
cnr Pretorius & Andries Streets

Sunnypark
cnr Jeppe (which becomes Beatrix to the north and Mears to the south) & Esselen Streets

Tram Shed
cnr Van der Walt & Schoeman Streets

Candles made by Klaus Wasserthal

Eastern suburbs

Atterbury Value Mart
cnr Atterbury Rd & Manitoba Drive, diagonally across from Pick 'n Pay complex, Faerie Glen

Brooklyn Mall
cnr Fehrsen & Lange Streets, New Muckleneuk

Brooklyn Square
cnr Middel & Veale Streets, New Muckleneuk

Groenkloof Plaza
George Storrar Drive, Groenkloof

Hatfield Plaza
cnr Hilda & Burnett Streets, Hatfield

Hatfield Square
opposite Hatfield Plaza

Die Jaart
Duncan Street, Hatfield. This shopping centre with its unusual design creating a number of interesting corners and passages is worth a visit, not only for the architecture, but also because of a number of out-of-the-ordinary shops and eating places.

Lynnridge Mall
just off Lynnwood Rd near its corner with Rubida Street

Menlyn Park
cnr Atterbury Rd & Lois Street, Menlyn

Menlyn Retail Park
cnr Lois Street & Menlyn Drive, Menlyn

Pick 'n Pay complex
cnr Atterbury Rd & Manitoba Drive, Faerie Glen

Waterglen Park Centre
Menlyn Drive, Waterkloof Glen

Southern suburbs

Castle Walk
Lois Avenue, Erasmuskloof

Centurion Park
Lakeside, Centurion
The shopping complex is situated next to a large man-made lake which makes for a relaxed atmosphere with a pleasant route for strollers along the lake. Boat trips can be taken on the lake and a water organ provides attractive entertainment at night.

Elardus Park Shopping Centre
Delmas road

Monument Park Shopping Centre
Skilpad Road, Monument Park

Northern suburbs

Gezina City
Frederika Street, Gezina

Jakaranda Centre
Frates Road, Rietfontein

Kolonnade Centre
Zambesi Drive. This centre contains the only ice skating rink in Pretoria.

Madelief Centre
Daan de Wet Nel Drive, Dorandia

Mayville Centre
Van Rensburg Street, Mayville

Wonder Park
along the R513 west of Pretoria North

Die Jaart, Duncan Street

Barclay Square, Sunnyside

Brooklyn Mall

Speciality shops

There are many specialist shops in and around the city. These include art dealers which usually provide a picture framing service, antique dealers, boutiques, curio shops specializing in African curios, camping stores, etc. These cannot all be listed here and tourists should consult the *Yellow Pages* telephone directory where these dealers are listed alphabetically under different categories. Since stores dealing in camping equipment are of special interest to tourists they are listed below.

The *Oeverzicht Art Village* is worth a special mention. Situated on the corner of Gerhard Moerdijk and Kotze Streets in Sunnyside this complex, housed mostly in restored and renovated houses dating from the early part of the century, contains a number of art and craft shops as well as restaurants providing a variety of fare.

Another speciality shop worth mentioning is *Klaus Wasserthal* at 88 Celliers Street, Sunnyside, south of Esselen Street. This shop specializes in candles and holders, pottery, carpets and printed fabrics – including the famous Rorke's Drift work from Kwazulu-Natal with its distinctly African flavour – baskets, toys and gifts.

Hatfield Square, Burnett Street

Camping stores

Camping stores are of particular significance to some tourists and therefore a list of these stores is given here.

The Backpacker, Duncan St, near Brooklyn Mall

The Backpacker
Duncan Street, Brooklyn

The Big Five CC
Hatfield Plaza, Burnett Street, Hatfield, & Kolonnade Centre, Zambesi Drive
Outdoor gear and clothes

Cape Union Mart
Brooklyn Mall, cnr Lange & Fehrsen Streets, New Muckleneuk

ME Stores
Sanlam Plaza West, Schoeman Street
Camping equipment

Trappers Trading
Sanlam Centre, cnr Andries & Pretorius Streets, city centre, & Menlyn Centre, cnr Atterbury Rd & Lois Drive, Menlyn
Outdoor gear & clothing

Centurion City on the lake

Flea and craft markets

A large number of flea markets where a variety of stalls offer paintings, art and crafts, clothing, shoes and other leather goods, household articles and a whole variety of inventive and original creations by persons working from home, operate at regular times in different parts of the city. Some of these markets are open daily and others fortnightly or monthly.

Burnett Street, Hatfield
Side-walk stalls
Daily 08:00–17:00

Centurion Boulevard
Tel: 654 2560
Lenchen Ave, Centurion
Sunday: 08:30–17:00

Fedsure Forum
Tel: 322 2803
Cnr Van der Walt & Pretorius Streets, central
Daily 08:00–17:0

Gezina City/Galleries
Tel: 335 3039
Frederika Street, Gezina
Sat 08:00–13:00

Gift Acres
Tel: 807 0010

Lynnwood Road, east of Gen Louis Botha Drive
Sat & Sun 10:00–16:00

Hatfield Flea Market
Tel: 342 3769

Hatfield Shopping Centre, Burnett St, Hatfield
Sun & public holidays 09:30–17:30

Kingsley Centre
Tel: 341 7530

Cnr Beatrix & Church Streets, central
Daily 08:00–Late evening

Magnolia Dell
Tel: 98 1557

Junction of Walker Street & Queen Wilhelmina Drive, Muckleneuk.
First Saturday of each month. Sometimes a moonlight market is held
on a Friday evening.

Marabastad stalls

Special mention should be made of the shopping area in Marabastad, an
area north-west of the city centre, whose history as an Indian and black
trading and residential area goes back a century and a half. Apart from
interesting old-style Indian-owned shops in the main street, Boom
Street, and African-owned shops in the side streets where one can buy
such things as natural African remedies, there is an area just north of
Boom Street where stalls operate every day during normal business

Centurion City shopping and office complex

Burnett Street, Hatfield, where this dealer operates daily

For sale at craft market, Magnolia Dell

Magnolia Dell art market, first Saturday of the month

Meet you at the Farmers' Market, early Saturday morning

Goats go too!

Esselen Street, Sunnyside, on Saturday and Sunday

hours. Although not a flea market in the conventional sense these stalls sell the sort of wares one often encounters at flea markets: clothes, shoes and other leather goods, bric-a-brac, etc. A walk through Boom Street and the stalls will give the visitor a decidedly third-world shopping experience.

Papatso
On the way to the Carousel Casino and entertainment centre on the N1 north (on the way to Pietersburg) is this original centre for local arts and crafts.

Smuts House/Irene Village Market
Tel: 667 1659

Nellmapius Rd, Irene
Second & last Sat of each month: 09:00–14:00

State Theatre/Strijdom Square
Tel: 322 1665

Cnr Church & Van der Walt Streets, city centre
Mon–Fri 08:00–17:00
Sat 08:00–13:00

Sunnypark Flea Market
Tel: 342 7556

Cnr Jeppe & Esselen Streets, Sunnyside
Sat 08:00–14:00
Sun 11:00–17:00

Technopark Boeremark (Farmers' Market)
Tel: 86 8031

Opposite CSIR, Meiring Naudé Drive
Early Saturday morning, starting at 06:00
This market is managed by the Transvaal Agricultural Union and offers a variety of farm produce as well as other goods.

Ubuntu Market
Tel: 802 0333

N4 East, some 20 km east of Pretoria. Take the Boschkop/Donkerhoek Off-ramp, turn right and travel 2 km along the gravel road.
Every second Saturday of the month 09:00–15:00

Wonder Park
Tel: 654 2560

Old Brits road (R513), Akasia
Sat 08:00–14:00

Wonderboom Flea Market
Tel: 444 0691

Zambezi Drive, Wonderboom
Weekends

Zoo Craft Market
On the pavement next to the main entrance to the zoo in Boom Street a variety of African handcrafts such as beadwork, wood-carving, etc is sold every day from early to late. This is not a flea market in the normal sense of the word but it has admirable gifts and souvenirs of a typical African nature for the tourist and is therefore worth visiting.

Klaus Wasserthal
candle and gift shop, Sunnyside

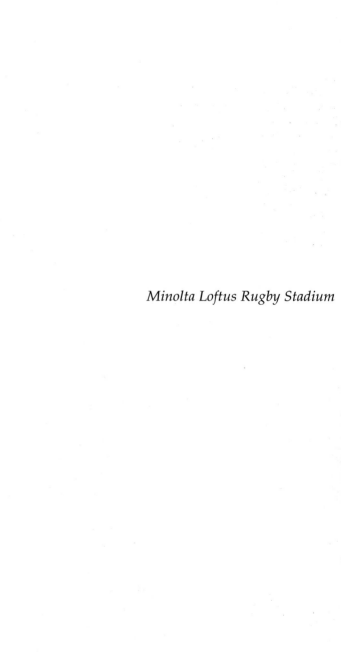

Minolta Loftus Rugby Stadium

13

Pretoria is home to a large number of sport stadiums. However, the three discussed here have international status or have housed international meetings or contests.

Minolta Loftus

This rugby stadium is one of five international test match venues in South

Sport stadiums

Indoor sport centre, University of Pretoria, South Street extension

Pilditch Athletics Stadium with the West End swimming bath left of it

Africa where many a dramatic rugby test match has been played before capacity crowds. The stadium was originally called after a well known Pretoria lawyer, Robert Loftus Owen Versfeld, the founder of organized sport in Pretoria. The stadium has a capacity of over 60 000 and is definitely worth a visit for rugby enthusiasts.

Pilditch

This modern athletics stadium was called after Gerald Pilditch, a sporting pioneer of Pretoria. The stadium with its tartan track and other modern facilities is one of the premier athletics venues in South Africa. It is located next to the Pretoria International Showgrounds where a commercial show is held annually at the end of August–beginning of September. Some livestock is also shown, but its origin was industrial, not agricultural.

Centurion Park

Centurion Park is an international cricket venue situated in the fast-growing Centurion municipality south of Pretoria. The stadium is the home of Northern Transvaal cricket and a number of five-day and one-day internationals have been played there.

There are many places of worship of different denominations in Pretoria. The majority of these are church buildings of the three Afrikaans churches, but there are also a large number of churches of other denominations as well as non-Christian places such as mosques. The Meriammen Temple in Marabastad has already been discussed under 'Historical buildings'.

14

Places of worship

Only some of these places can obviously be discussed here. Those dealt with are fairly representative and worth visiting from an historical or aesthetic viewpoint.

Queen Street Mosque

This historical mosque is completely hemmed in by modern office blocks and so well hidden that many passers-by in the nearest street would hardly be aware of its presence in the heart of the city. Between Andries and Van der Walt Streets is Queen Street, connecting Church and Vermeulen Streets. Halfway down Queen Street is an arcade which seems to end at a gate. Behind the gate is a 'forecourt' where a notice requests one to remove one's shoes before stepping into the mosque. Some twenty metres to the right is the mosque itself. The foundation stone of the brilliant white mosque was laid in 1928, but the history of the site goes back to 1896. In that year the Moslem community bought the site, but for many years a wood-and-iron building served as a place of prayer. The mosque was designed and built in 1927 by a group of Moslems from the Cape.

Queen Street Mosque

The prayer hall of the mosque is striking in its simplicity. As is customary, there is no furniture, apart from the wooden wall cabinets with their glass fronts behind which the Quran is kept. On the floor is a carpet of amber and gold.

Amidst all the towering blocks the mosque forms a haven of tranquility and serenity where Moslem men come regularly to pray.

St Alban's Anglican Cathedral

This cathedral at 327 Schoeman Street is also of historical significance. The first building on the site was erected in 1872 by the Royal Engineers. The first part of the present building was designed by the well-known Sir Herbert Baker and built in 1905. The rest was completed by the British architect E W N Mallows.

This is a typical Anglican cathedral built in the classical style, with stained glass windows and the usual Gothic cross ground plan. The modern glass-and-concrete windows are the work of Leo Théron.

Greek Orthodox Church, Lynnwood Road

Greek Orthodox Church

Situated on the corner of Lynnwood Road and Roper Street, opposite the main entrance of the University of Pretoria. The building is not old but at present some works of art are being added to the inside of the church.

Old Synagogue, Paul Kruger Street

Synagogue, Paul Kruger Street

Not in use as a synagogue for many years, it nevertheless has an interesting façade and has been declared a national monument. Situated between Vermeulen and Proes Streets.

Sacred Heart Roman Catholic Cathedral

This cathedral was designed in 1932/33 by the Irish-born architect B J Glinch and is a good example of the New Gothic architecture. The twin towers with the large stained-glass window between them gives the northern face of the building a particularly attractive and inviting front. The atmosphere inside the cathedral is enhanced by twelve stained-glass side windows, which help to make the building a devoted space amidst the hustle and bustle of the city outside.

Loreto Roman Catholic Church

This modern church building stands in contrast to the traditional Sacred Heart Cathedral discussed above. It is in the modern idiom, with white plastered walls, but designed in such a way that the sacred atmosphere is unmistakable, even from the outside. The interior, with biblical scenes in stained glass set in concrete along the two long side walls, executed by the well-known Pretoria artist Leo Théron, is something very special which is worth a visit.

The church is in Woodlands Drive, Queenswood, next to the Loreto School.

Catholic Church, Celliers Street, Sunnyside, which also houses windows by Leo Théron

Dutch Reformed Church Universiteitsoord

Unlike many Protestant churches, which may be rather stark and often with little aesthetic appeal, this church, which serves the student congregation of the University of Pretoria, is a gem of architectural design. Despite its simplicity the interior is dominated by two features: the cone-shaped steeple, which swoops up above the pulpit to allow in light through narrow and high stained-glass windows on either side, and the extremely attractive use of face-brick. The latter feature is made all the more striking by the interesting textures created by the liberal use of rough half bricks. The architect was Jan van Wijk, who also designed the Afrikaans Language Monument on the mountainside at Paarl. The building was completed in 1967 but its timeless beauty is sure to survive as long as it stands. Unlike most Afrikaans churches this building is open to the public and can be viewed during normal office hours. The church is situated east of the University of Pretoria and two blocks away from Lynnwood Road, on the corner of Duxbury and Herold Streets in Hillcrest.

The three Afrikaans 'sister' churches

The original Afrikaans church that developed in South Africa split up to become three separate denominations (after the Voortrekkers settled in Transvaal). They are still Calvinistic protestant, and the English translation of their names remains Dutch Reformed. In Afrikaans there are subtle differences in the titles. Soon after Pretoria was founded, each of the three denominations built a church, but even before the town was formally founded, it was the site of a Reformed Church congregation. A primitive church building was erected on the market square (now Church Square). The building caught fire and was burnt down. Some years after the town was planned, each religious group bought its own piece of land. The Reformed Church finally bought ground on the south-west corner of Du Toit and Vermeulen Streets. The church building erected there at the turn of the century still serves the Pretoria congregation.

President Kruger belonged to what was colloquially called the 'Dopper' Church, and its church building, equally impressive, was erected right opposite the President's house, where he often took the morning service himself. It still serves the Pretoria congregation. The largest of the three church groups built its church on the corner of Vermeulen and Koch Streets. Koch Street was renamed Bosman Street in honour of Dr H S Bosman who for many years served there as minister of the NG Church. It is still the church building for the Pretoria congregation. General Jan Smuts was buried from this church and the religious service during the inauguration of South Africa's first State President, C R Swart, was held there in 1961. Each of the three church buildings has beautiful wood panelling, a magnificent pipe organ and a pulpit worth seeing. ■

Footnote:

For many years members of the 'sister' churches have been discussing unification. However, there always seems to be a point or two on which it is impossible to agree – perhaps the same minute reasons that split them up in the first place?

Should you be interested in viewing a church building, there is often a secretary or sexton in an office somewhere at the back, usually in the morning. Worth a try!

Opposite: NG Church Universiteitsoord

'Hervormde' Church, Du Toit Street

Kruger's (Dopper) Church, Church Street West

Bosman Street Church, cnr Vermeulen Street

156

*Unisa campus from the air with
the Union Buildings in the
background left*

Educational centres

Pretoria is perhaps the South African city with the largest number of schools, colleges and tertiary institutions in the country. Greater Pretoria is home to three universities, a regional campus of a fourth, two technicons, two technical colleges, a teachers' training college (next to Unisa) and a very large number of state as well as private schools.

Educational, research and conference centres

Part of Vista University, Pretoria

Afrikaans Boys High School,
Lynnwood Road

University of South Africa (Unisa)

The history of this university is intertwined with that of tertiary education in South Africa. University education in South Africa started in 1858. In that year a board of examiners was created due to the need for local education for attorneys and other professional men. In 1873 it became the University of the Cape of Good Hope which was, however, purely an examining body. The actual teaching was done by two colleges, the South African College in Cape Town and the Victoria College in Stellenbosch. In 1916 the examining institution became known as the University of South Africa. Shortly afterwards the above-named colleges became autonomous as the University of Cape Town and the University of Stellenbosch. The remaining tertiary institutions were then affiliated under the University of South Africa.

After a number of the younger institutions had become autonomous between 1922 and 1946 the University of South Africa continued to function but switched to distance or correspondence education in the latter year. It has grown to be the biggest university in South Africa with more than 120 000 students drawn from all parts of the globe.

The university used to be housed in buildings in the city but in 1971 it was moved to the new campus on Muckleneuk Ridge. Additions have been made to the buildings so that a sprawling complex on the ridge meets the eye as one approaches the city from Johannesburg International Airport via the R21 or from Johannesburg via the Fountains traffic circle.

From its vantage point on top of the ridge the university campus affords good views of the southern part of the city. The university has an impressive library building containing a book collection of some 1,5 million volumes apart from 300 000 other items and 7000 periodical titles. Unisa has a permanent art collection as well as a collection of cycads – protected plants which are the almost extinct remainder of a group of plants that once formed the dominant vegetation type some 300 million years ago and of which an individual specimen may become hundreds or even thousands of years old.

Tel: 429 3111
Muckleneuk Hill

Graduation day

Break between classes, University of Pretoria

University of Pretoria

The University of Pretoria, with more than 28 000 students, is the largest Afrikaans medium university in the country. It is also the only South African university with a veterinary faculty and it has a fine research record in both the natural and human sciences. The campus contains several art collections and historical buildings.

The first step towards a university in Pretoria was taken in 1908 when a branch of the Transvaal University College of Johannesburg was established in the city. The Johannesburg institution had come into existence two years earlier in 1906. In 1910 the Johannesburg branch was transformed to the South African School of Mines and Technology which was to become the University of the Witwatersrand in 1922. The Pretoria branch meanwhile developed independently concentrating on the human sciences. Colloquially it was known as the TUC (TUK in Afrikaans) and its students as Tukkies, a name still used today.

In 1930 the Transvaal University College attained autonomy and two years later, in 1932, it chose to become an Afrikaans language institution – only the second tertiary institution for Afrikaans speakers who constituted the majority of the white population. Today it offers tuition in English as well as Afrikaans as the need has increased.

There are several historical buildings on the campus of the University of Pretoria. These include the Ou Lettere Gebou (Old Arts Building) and the Old Merensky Library as well as the reconstructed Kya Rosa homestead, all of which have been discussed in the section *Historical buildings* under 'Architecture'.

University of Pretoria campus

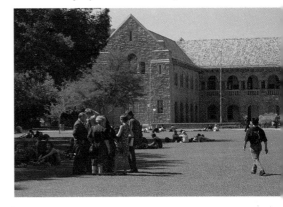

There are two art collections on the campus, the van Tilburgh collection and the van Gybland Oosterhoff collection, and the van Wouw collection in the Van Wouw House in Brooklyn. All three are dealt with under 'Art collections'.

A few blocks east of the university is a sport complex which boasts probably the best equipped indoor sport centre in the country. The whole sport complex is extremely picturesque being situated along a stream, the Hartebeestspruit, in which two lakes were built – one near the indoor sport centre which is used for canoeing and rowing practice, and another near the tennis courts. In the latter is an island which serves as a breeding colony for cattle egrets and other birds. It is one of only two or three cattle egret breeding colonies on the highveld plateau. The area surrounding the lake is a haven of tranquility where it is scarcely noticeable that busy motor freeways pass close by.

Tel: 420 3111
Main entrance: Lynnwood Rd, Hillcrest

Technikon Pretoria

Technicons are experiencing a flourishing period in South African education. For many years a dichotomy used to exist with schools at one end of the scale and universities at the other. Over the past few decades the accent on the tertiary level has shifted away from the traditionally academically oriented universities to technicons which are more vocationally oriented. The Technikon Pretoria with its attractive new campus is a case in point.

Vista Mamelodi campus

The technikon has six faculties: Art, Economic Sciences, Engineering, Environmental Sciences, Information Sciences and Natural Sciences. The courses within these faculties range from chemistry, architecture and civil engineering to computer science, film/video technology, food technology, information technology, marketing, opera, power engineering, textile design and travel and tourism.

The modern campus design complements this beehive of educational activity. The attractive lay-out on the hilly terrain is enhanced by the architecture. Many of the buildings have stained glass windows set in concrete designed by the well-known Pretoria artist practising this art form, Leo Théron.

Tel: 318 5911
Lady Selborne (off D F Malan Drive)

Medical University of Southern Africa (Medunsa)

The Medical University of Southern Africa came into being in 1975 as the first truly comprehensive health science centre in Africa. The first students were admitted in 1978 and in 1981 the first graduation ceremony took place where inter alia 34 MBChB degrees – the basic qualification for general medical practitioners in South Africa – were awarded.

The institution underwent continual expansion and today the complex includes an Animal Hospital and a Dental Hospital in addition to the large Ga-Rankuwa hospital which serves as academic hospital for the medical faculty. Because of the dire need for science teachers in the black community a Faculty of Basic Sciences was started and the first students were admitted in 1989. An optimum enrolment of some 4000 for the whole university by the year 2000 is envisaged.

Medunsa was started as a university exclusively for blacks, but today – like all other universities in South Africa – it is open to all races and only academic considerations serve as criteria for admission.

Tel: 529 4111
Situated north-west of Rosslyn, at GaRankuwa

Research centres

Council for Scientific and Industrial Research (CSIR)

The CSIR was established in 1945 to conduct research in the natural sciences, especially with regard to the applicability of research findings in industry. Today it has units for building technology, communication/

information networking technology, food science/technology, manufacturing/aeronautical systems technology, materials science/technology, roads/transport technology, satellite applications, technology for development, and water/environment/forestry technology. The CSIR cooperates with the South African Bureau of Standards.

The CSIR is situated on an attractive 200 acre hilly terrain to the east of the city known as Scientia. There is a large modern conference centre. Some of the units have displays for the visitor.

Tel: 841 2911
Meiring Naudé Road, next to the N1

Human Sciences Research Council (HSRC)

The HSRC is the human science counterpart of the CSIR. It undertakes research in the human sciences with special reference to the development needs of the country. The research includes opinion surveys, constitutional studies, market research, crime and other sociological studies, educational and psychological studies.

The building housing the HSRC at 134 Pretorius Street is interesting in design, the main feature being the curved walls which have eliminated long clinical looking passages in an attempt to make it more user friendly. The building has won a design award for concrete buildings.

The HSRC has a bookshop with easy access from the street where the organization's publications are for sale, as well as a permanent art collection in the same venue.

Tel: 202 9111
134 Pretorius Street, central city

South African Bureau of Standards (SABS)

The SABS was established in 1945 to contribute, by the promotion of quality and standardization, towards the strengthening of the economy of South Africa and towards enhancing the quality of life of its people. The bureau has done this by rendering a comprehensive standardization, certification and testing service of a high quality to industry, commerce and the consumer.

Apart from the head office in Pretoria the SABS has regional offices in five cities as well as Namibia, a national electrical test facility between Pretoria and Johannesburg, a coal laboratory at Richards Bay and a veterinary laboratory in East London. For a few years, from 1956 to 1961, the SABS was amalgamated with the CSIR, and today the two organizations still cooperate in some matters.

The SABS played a pivotal role in planning the decimalization of the South African currency which eventually took place in February 1961. The same applies to the metrication of weights and measures for which an Act was passed in 1974 and the introduction of television in South Africa in 1976. In 1983 the Fuel Research Institute was also incorporated with the SABS as the National Institute for Coal Research, with the SABS taking over the routine analysis of coal exported from Richards Bay, the main coal exporting port.

The SABS also operates a marking scheme for products for which national mark specifications exist. The SABS certification mark serves as a testimonial that the product complies with the specification, and that the supplier maintains an efficient and appropriate quality control system. The organization also provides training for personnel of companies involved in the implementation, evaluation and maintenance of quality control systems. The SABS has made contributions in many other fields: preparing specifications for apparatus for monitoring the breath alcohol levels of motorists; the compilation of a listing scheme for manufacturers of assessed capability; providing facilities for the testing of motor vehicles with regard to the compulsory safety specifications; drawing up a uniform set of building regulations for the country; formulating regulations for the safe transportation of dangerous goods by air; etc.

A design institute is attached to the SABS whose mission is to foster the economic and technological development of South Africa through the promotion of design and to act as a centre for design promotion in southern Africa. It focuses on industry, education and information. Design achievers awards are made annually.

Tel: 428 7911 (SABS); 428 6332 (Design Institute)
George Storrar Drive, Groenkloof

Veterinary Research Institute, Onderstepoort

The Veterinary Research Institute was founded by Sir Arnold Theiler and owes its origin to the rinderpest which broke out in 1896. Initially the institute was situated at Daspoort west of Pretoria but later it was moved to Onderstepoort north of the city. Apart from the Veterinary Research Institute which falls under the state department of Agriculture, Onderstepoort also houses, across the road from the institute, the Faculty of Veterinary Science of the University of Pretoria of which Theiler was the first dean (see box on Theiler).

The institute continues to render excellent service to the agricultural sector in South Africa as well as other African countries and the rest of the world, and many animal diseases have been effectively neutralized or brought under control as a result of the knowledge gained at

Onderstepoort. Ever so often when an animal disease outbreak of some kind occurs, either in South Africa or elsewhere, it is only the knowledge and expertise of this institute that stands between the farmer and total devastation.

There is an Arnold Theiler Museum at the Institute which depicts his enormous life work.

Arnold Theiler, scientist extraordinaire

Arnold Theiler was born in Switzerland in 1867. He studied in the natural sciences and obtained a diploma in Veterinary Science in 1889. After practising privately as a veterinarian for about a year he heard that the government of the South African Republic was looking for a young veterinarian and decided to come to South Africa. In September 1891 he started a private practice in Pretoria. He immediately started to gain as much knowledge as possible of the unknown animal diseases in a strange continent.

In March 1896 rinderpest broke out in present-day Zambia and spread southwards from the Zambesi River. In May of that year Theiler was appointed state veterinarian of the South African Republic assigned to find a vaccine for the disease. The rinderpest quarantine station at Daspoort west of Pretoria was transformed into a vaccine institute where two researchers from France did research with Theiler in 1897. They could not do more than confirm his findings. He had achieved a measure of success with the simultaneous injection of virulent blood and an immune serum from recovered animals. However, in an attempt to fully substantiate his results scientifically he hesitated to publish his findings. Meanwhile the later famous Robert Koch, who was appointed by the government of the Cape Colony and applied the same methods, published his findings and so received the credit. Nevertheless some 4 500 000 animals died before the epidemic had run its course.

In 1902 Theiler was appointed State Veterinary Bacteriologist. During the period 1902–1907 no fewer than 100 of his articles were published.

In 1908 the laboratory at Daspoort moved to the present site at Onderstepoort. In 1910 Theiler was appointed to the post of Director of Veterinary Research of the Department of Agriculture at Onderstepoort. Because of the heavy load of administrative work which interfered with his research work, he resigned in 1917 and the following year became Director of Botulism Research at Armoedsvlakte near Vryburg in the Northern Cape.

In 1919 Theiler once again accepted the post of Director of Veterinary Research and Teaching with the task of starting a faculty of veterinary science at the Transvaal University College, the forerunner of the University of Pretoria. The faculty came into being in 1920 with Theiler as dean and one of the first six professors. From 1925 he was professor in the Department of Tropical Medicine of the University College and in March 1927 he went on pension upon reaching the retirement age. Theiler returned to Switzerland but travelled extensively and still occupied himself with veterinary matters, attending international conferences, etc. He died in London in 1936.

At a time when veterinary science in the formal sense was still unknown Theiler, in the face of ignorance and prejudice, brought into existence an institute which was to become the greatest and most important veterinary institute in the world. Through his unrelenting research work and his many findings, expressed in 250 publications, Theiler placed South Africa on the scientific map of the world and he can be regarded as the most famous veterinarian of his time.

The honours bestowed on him include six honorary doctorates and membership, honorary membership or associate membership of many scientific societies and bodies of academics in a number of countries.

The granite statue of Theiler in front of the institute building is by Coert Steynberg. It was unveiled in 1939 and his ashes rest underneath the statue. ■

Conference centres

Only conference centres within the municipal boundaries of greater Pretoria and Centurion have been listed here.

ABSA Conference Centre
Tel: 548 0170/9
Fax: 548 1204

Besembiesie Road, Montana Park
Conference rooms: 11; maximum delegate capacity: 100

African Window
Tel: 324 6082
Fax: 328 5173

Visagie Street, between Bosman & Schubart Streets
Conference rooms: 1; maximum delegate capacity: 90

Akasia Town Hall
Tel: 549 3857
Fax: 549 3655

Dale Avenue, Akasia
Conference rooms: 1; maximum delegate capacity: 500

Arcadia Hotel
Tel: 326 9311
Fax: 326 1067

515 Proes Street, Arcadia
Conference rooms: 2; maximum delegate capacity: 35

Best Western Pretoria
Tel: 341 3473
Fax: 44 2258

230 Hamilton Street, Pretoria central
Conference rooms: 1; maximum delegate capacity: 20

Boulevard Protea Hotel
Tel: 326 4806
Fax: 326 1366

186 Struben Street
Maximum delegate capacity: 200

Castle Walk Restaurant
Tel: 546 9146

Madelief Centre, Daan de Wet Nel Drive, Dorandia
Maximum delegate capacity: 15

Centurion Lake Hotel
Tel: 663 1825
Fax: 663 2555

1001 Lenchen Road, Centurion
Conference rooms: 6; maximum delegate capacity: 160

City Library
Tel: 308 8337
Fax: 308 8873

Sammy Marks Square, Pretoria Central
Conference rooms: 3; maximum delegate capacity: 220

CSIR Conference Centre
Tel: 841 3809/841 3822
Fax: 841 3827/841 2051

Meiring Naudé Road, Brummeria
Conference rooms: 2; maximum delegate capacity: 450

Diep in die Berg
Tel: 807 0111/3
Fax: 807 0112

Cnr Disselboom & Hans Strijdom Ave, Wapadrand
Conference rooms: 5; maximum delegate capacity: 120

Edelweiss Function and Conference Centre
Tel: 808 1016
Fax: 808 0625

Plot 79, Kameeldrift
Conference rooms: 5; maximum delegate capacity: 300

Espada Ranch
Tel: 811 0024/811 0518
Fax: 811 0503

Tiegerpoort, from Lynnwood Rd extension

Farm Inn Hotel
Tel: 809 0266
Fax: 809 0146

Lynnwood Rd, next to Silver Lakes Golf Estate
Maximum delegate capacity: 120

GMBA (Pta) Conference
Tel: 342 3970/1
Fax: 342 3932

300 Hill Street, Arcadia
Conference rooms: 1; maximum delegate capacity: 10

Hamilton Conference Centre
Tel: 324 2892
Fax: 323 3544

140 Hamilton Street, Arcadia
Maximum delegate capacity: 72

Holiday Inn Garden Court
Tel: 322 7500
Fax: 322 4972

Cnr Van der Walt & Minnaar Streets
Conference rooms: 3; maximum delegate capacity: 70

Holiday Inn Crown Plaza
Tel: 341 1571
Fax: 44 7534

Cnr Church & Beatrix Streets, Arcadia
Conference rooms: 6; maximum delegate capacity: 350

Holiday Inn Express
Tel: 320 1060
Fax: 320 1208

632 Van der Walt Street
Conference rooms: 1; maximum delegate capacity: 15

Human Sciences Research Council Conference Centre
Tel: 302 2426
Fax: 302 2479

134 Pretorius Street
Conference rooms: 6; maximum delegate capacity: 310

Institute of Catholic Education: Santa Sophia
Tel: 346 1438

129 Main Street, Waterkloof
Conference rooms: 2; maximum delegate capacity: 130

Karos Manhattan Hotel
Tel: 669 0165
Fax: 320 1252

Cnr Scheiding & Andries Streets
Conference rooms: 5; maximum delegate capacity: 60

Leriba Lodge
Tel: 660 3300
Fax: 660 2433

End Street, Clubview, Centurion
Conference rooms: 5; maximum delegate capacity: 80

Monument Conference Centre
Tel: 21 6230
Fax: 323 0772
Cell: 082 552 3300

Voortrekker Monument, Eeufees Road
Conference rooms: 4; maximum delegate capacity: 2000

Naka Safari Lodge
Tel: 808 5133

Moloto-Murrayhill Rd, Kameeldrift
Maximum delegate capacity: 20

Premos
Tel: 313 0064

11 State Artillery Rd, Pretoria West
Conference rooms: 19; maximum delegate capacity: 120

Pretoria Hof Hotel
Tel: 322 7570
Fax: 322 9461

Cnr Pretorius & Van der Walt Streets
Maximum delegate capacity: 120

Roodevallei Country Lodge
Tel: 808 1700
Fax: 808 1130

Plot 81, Zeekoeigat, Kameeldrift
Maximum delegate capacity: 300

Saint George Hotel
Tel: (011) 316 1254/316 4780
Fax: (011) 316 1254

58 Old Pretoria Road, Rietvlei Dam
Maximum delegate capacity: 1500

Sammy Marks Convention Centre
Tel: 323 7458
Fax: 323 7449

314 Church Street, Sammy Marks Square
Maximum delegate capacity: 2100

Silver Lakes Country Estate
Tel: 807 0219
Fax: 87 2889

Lynnwood Rd extension, Pretoria East
Maximum delegate capacity: 60

Sinodale Conference Centre
Tel: 322 8900
Fax: 322 8928

234 Visagie Street
Maximum delegate capacity: 624

Technikon Pretoria
Tel: 318 5453
Fax: 318 5459

Staatsartillerie Road, Pretoria West
Maximum delegate capacity: 200

Telkom Conference Centre
Tel: 311 4611
Fax: 311 2720

153 Proes Street, Telkom Tower North
Maximum delegate capacity: 120

Wonder Waters Lodge
Tel: 543 0068

Opposite Wonderboom Nature Reserve, Annlin
Conference halls: 4

Pretoria is situated centrally enough to allow day trips to be undertaken to a number of interesting tourist attractions. In some cases more than one of these places can be fitted into a single day trip. Although attractions in and around Johannesburg, such as Gold Reef City, are close enough to Pretoria to be visited in one day, they are associated with Johannesburg rather than Pretoria and are not included here.

Day drives from Pretoria

Information on them can be found in general South African tourist guides or guides dealing with Johannesburg.

The South African Mint and Coin World

The South African Mint, official manufacturer of South African coins, is definitely worth a visit. Since 1988 the mint has operated as a registered private company, the South African Mint Company (Pty) Ltd, whose only shareholder is the South African Reserve Bank. At Coin World, which forms part of the Mint complex, visitors can view a display of South Africa's rich coin heritage. Here they can also strike their own proof quality R5 coin on 'Oom Paul', the oldest working mint press in the world. A 'Coin Walk' factory tour for visitors is conducted through the plant twice daily. At a retail outlet in Coin World visitors can purchase coins which constitute excellent investments. These include proof sets of current coins as well as proof quality gold Kruger rands, including the 1 ounce, $\frac{1}{2}$ ounce, $\frac{1}{4}$ ounce and $\frac{1}{10}$ ounce 22 carat gold coins. The 1 oz coin won the award for 'The most popular coin' at the Singapore Coin Show in February 1998. Other collectors' coins available include the Natura series which has featured the 'Big Five' – the lion, rhinoceros, elephant, buffalo and leopard –

Petroport on the Great North Road (Cecil Rhodes's dream was of a continuous road from the Cape to Cairo)

Premier Mine Museum

and the Protea series with the theme 'Children' for 1998. There are also the R1 and R2 gold coins whose revival have proved very popular and continue with the 'San' and 'Coelacanth' coins, while the Marine Life theme is continued on the R2 silver coin and the silver tickey ($2\frac{1}{2}$ cents), depicting the Jackass penguin. Coin World is open seven days a week from 09:00 to 15:30.

The mint is surrounded by large grounds containing a variety of small game.

Tel: 677 2342/677 2911
Tours: Twice daily Monday to Friday, 09:00 & 15:30.
For persons over the age of 12 only.
Booking is essential.

Premier Diamond Mine

This world famous diamond mine is situated in the small town of Cullinan, some 45 km east of Pretoria. The mine became famous when the world's largest diamond, the Cullinan diamond, over 3000 carats, was found there in 1905. The diamond was named after Sir Thomas Cullinan who discovered a huge diamond pipe there in 1902. The diamond was bought by the Transvaal government and donated in 1907 to the British monarch King Edward VII on his birthday. It was subsequently cut into smaller stones, the largest of which, a drop-shaped stone of more than 500 carats, was laid into the royal sceptre with the second largest being used in the royal crown. The other stones cut from the original also form part of the British royal collection.

Cullinan village (Premier Diamond Mine)

Tourist Bureau, Premier Diamond Mine

*A modern
dairy farm near Pretoria*

Cosmos along the road in March-April

After having been in operation for 95 years the mine is still visited by many tourists. A visit includes a guided tour of the works, including a view from the look-out point into the man-made crater. Visitors can view replicas of the famous stones cut from the Cullinan diamond, as well as a display showing the various stages of diamond cutting.

In the mine grounds can also be seen miners' cottages from the pioneering days of the mine.

Getting there:	Leave Pretoria along Schoeman Street and travel east along the N4 towards Witbank and Mpumalanga. Take the Cullinan/Rayton turn-off and follow the R515 for about 15 km to Cullinan. Follow the signposts to the mine on the side of the town.
Tel:	305 2911
Tours:	Conducted Monday to Friday at 9:30, 10:00 and 13:30 and Saturday and Sunday at 10:00.
Admission:	Charged
Further information:	Premier Diamond Tours P O Box 7 CULLINAN 1000

Overleaf: Hartbeespoort Dam

Hartbeespoort Dam area

This dam (lake) with its surrounding area some 35 km west of Pretoria is a favourite recreational spot for both Pretorians and people from Johannesburg. The dam offers fishing, water sport and yachting facilities. The road from Pretoria to Rustenburg crosses the dam wall and goes through a short tunnel in the mountainside. The dam is formed by a 59 m high concrete wall across a gap in the Magaliesberg range through which the Crocodile River flows. The dam contains sufficient water to irrigate 40 000 acres of land. A scenic drive can be taken around the dam. Interesting kiosks, curio shops, farm stalls, picnic spots and private resorts are passed along the way on either side of the dam. At the flea market on the Rustenburg side some interesting items can be bought at exceptionally reasonable prices, for example semi-precious beads and polished stones.

The picturesque village alongside the dam also contains a private zoo, the Hartbeespoort Dam Snake and Animal Park, situated right next to the dam. The zoo is small but it contains lions, tigers, cheetahs, panthers, pumas and leopards as well as a snake section. The zoo is open from 08:00 to 17:00. Chimpanzee and seal shows take place at 12:00 and 15:00 on weekends and public holidays and snake handling demonstrations are also held. A curio shop is attached to the zoo.

Passenger cruises on the dam lasting 20 minutes can be taken from a mooring at the zoo.

Curios and crafts, Hartbeespoort Dam

Kosmos village

Inland beach, Hartbeespoort Dam

Tan' Malie's curiosity shop (and eats!)

Hartbeespoort Dam

Curio market Hartbeespoort Dam (west side, on the road to Rustenburg and Sun City)

A cableway on the Pretoria side takes visitors to the top of the Magaliesberg range next to which the dam is situated. The bottom station of the cableway is about two km east of the zoo on the road from Pretoria outside the village. From the top of the mountain some 400 m above the dam exquisite views may be enjoyed over the surrounding countryside. Near the top cable station is a platform from where hang gliders take off to follow the air currents. Over weekends visitors may be lucky enough to see them floating gracefully down. The Magaliesberg is the home of the protected black eagle, the top of most of the range being conservation area.

Getting there: Travel west along Church Street West, past the cemetery on the right, and turn right at the first traffic light after the cemetery into D F Malan Drive. After about 200 m turn left onto the N4 at the Brits/Rustenburg signpost. Follow this toll road for some 27 km right up to its end and take the Pelindaba off-ramp. Turn right over the freeway and after two km left at the T-junction signposted Hartbeespoort Dam. Carry on straight along this road for 10 km until you reach the village on the shore of the dam. The zoo and snake park is in the heart of the village on the left. To cross the dam wall, carry on with this road. A traffic light is at the start of the tunnel after which the road crosses the dam wall.

For information on other attractions in the Brits/Hartbeespoort region contact the Brits Publicity Office at tel: (012) 318 9274 or fax at the same number (ask for fax line).

De Wildt Cheetah Research Centre

One of the success stories in game preservation and the plucking of an endangered species from the teeth of extinction is that of the Cheetah Research Centre at De Wildt, some 40 km north-west of Pretoria.

The graceful spotted cat, with its smaller head and more streamlined build than the leopard, is the fastest mammal on earth, capable of speeds up to 112 km (70 miles/hour) over short distances (see box). But this agile carnivore, though admirably equipped to hunt for food, became the hunted because of its striking coat. The number of cheetahs therefore became dangerously depleted during the 20th century.

In 1971 the Cheetah Research Centre was established to breed these magnificent animals in semi-captivity. Because of the shy nature of cheetahs the project was initially greeted with scepticism. But after more than 25 years it has proved an astounding success with more than 400 cubs having been born at De Wildt. The aim is always to reintroduce them into the wild.

Apart from cheetah the centre has also successfully bred other endangered species such as the wild dog, brown hyaena, Cape vulture, suni (the second smallest antelope), blue duiker (another small antelope), and the riverine rabbit, the latest success being the Egyptian vulture.

A special place of honour at De Wildt is occupied by the king cheetahs. They are distinguished from the ordinary cheetahs by their markings. Their spots are larger and flow into heavy black stripes and blotches. They are a genetic variation and not a separate species.

Getting there: Travel west along Church Street West and, after passing Church Street Cemetery on the right, turn right in D F Malan Drive at the large traffic light intersection. Carry on for 5 km from Church Street along D F Malan Drive and turn onto the R80 at the cloverleaf interchange. Follow this road for 7 km and turn left onto the R513 on the way to Brits. Carry on for 21 km along the R513 until you see the signpost to the Cheetah Research Centre on the left.

Guided tours by arrangement only at the following times: Saturday and Sunday at 09:00 and 14:15; Thursday 10:00. Book well in advance. *No children under six.*

Tel: 504 1921.

Admission: Charged

The cheetah: a unique large cat

Like the leopard, the cheetah has been hunted for its attractive spotted fur, for preying on farmers' livestock, and simply for 'sport'. Unlike the leopard, which stalks its prey, the cheetah is a chaser. This graceful cat can reach a speed of up to 112 km (70 miles/hour) when chasing its prey. However, it can sustain this speed only for about 300 metres. In reaching this high speed it takes strides of up to 7 m, making it the fastest mammal on earth. By comparison the second fastest African animal is the springbok which is capable of 96 km (60 miles/hour), while the elephant can charge at 40 km.

The average cheetah stands about 85 cm (2 ft 9.5 inches) high and at about 54 kg (121 lb) for an average male and 43 kg (97 lb) for an average female, it is considerably lighter than the leopard. A leopard has shorter legs and is a lot more powerful than a cheetah. The spots on the two species also differ. The leopard tends to have spots on the legs, flanks, hindquarters and head and rosettes over the rest of the body. The rosettes are the most obvious feature which differentiates leopards from cheetah. The cheetah has solid spots only. The underparts of the body are whitish and the tail is spotted for one third of its length, after which there are three black rings, while the tip of the tail is off-white. A leopard's build is much more solid and stocky than a cheetah's.

Characteristic of the cheetah is the 'tear mark', a narrow black band running down from the inner corner of each eye to the corners of the mouth. This adds a somewhat sorrowful touch to the cheetah's face, almost as if the marks have been caused by a lot of tears shed over its endangered state.

A cheetah does not roar like a lion. It purrs, growls and hisses. Cheetahs are more peace-loving than the other large cats and are therefore sometimes driven from their catch by lions and hyaenas. Because of their peaceful nature they are more easily tamed.

The natural habitat of the cheetah in South Africa is the Northern Cape and the Northern Province and Mpumalanga, but they are widespread in the countries north of South Africa. ■

Stalking cheetah

De Wildt Herbal Centre

Margaret Roberts has gained renown as a herbalist through her books and television appearances. The centre is her herb garden, which contains thousands of indigenous and exotic herbs, some for medicinal use, others for culinary purposes and yet others purely for their fragrance.

The owner has an encyclopedic knowledge of herbs and their uses and in her garden against the slopes of the Magaliesberg her knowledge is imparted to visitors every Wednesday. A visit to the different parts of the garden is a fascinating experience. The visitor leaves with a greatly enhanced knowledge of the healing properties of some herbs and the cooking virtues of others while a walk through the fragrant herbs invigorates the lungs and in fact the whole system.

There is a shop where herbs and herbal products such as soap, cream, lotions, potpouri, pomanders, etc, are on sale. A tea garden serves herbal tea and scented scones, and herb plants can be purchased at the nursery.

Getting there: The Herbal Centre is situated along the R513. Follow the directions for the De Wildt Cheetah Research Centre and travel one km further.

Hours: Open **Wednesday only** 08:30–16:00

Tel: 504 1729

Admission: Charged

Impala, the most common buck found on game ranches and in reserves

Naka Safari Lodge

This fairly new game ranch only 30 km north-east of Pretoria offers various exciting out-door activities. There are daily game drives, hiking trails, horse riding and mountain-bike trails. As the name Naka (meaning horn) implies, the game consists mainly of ungulates (buck) plus small cats and rodents.

Accommodation is available in luxuty chalets and an á la carte restaurant is on the ranch.

Getting there: Take the N1 to Pietersburg, then the turn-off for Zambesi Road/Cullinan. Turn right to Cullinan. Turn left at the 4-way stop about 3 km on (the old Moloto Road). Carry on for about 20 km to the turn-off left to Murrayhill (a dirt road). The Naka turn-off is about 500 m on, to your right.

Admission: Charged. Booking is essential.

Tel: 808 5133

Woodstock Ostrich Farm

Ostrich farming is usually associated with the district of Oudtshoorn in the Little Karoo area of the southern Cape. But a thousand kilometres away in the north, several enterprising farmers have started breeding ostriches. A tour of the Woodstock farm teaches one everything about this strange bird: its particular qualities, breeding habits, the uses of the meat and feathers, etc.

Getting there: Take the R513 to Brits (see the description of the route to De Wildt Cheetah Research Centre). Pass the Cheetah Research Centre and you will find the ostrich farm on the right.

Facilities: Ostrich braai/barbeque

Tel: 504 1084

Dr Robert Broom

Dr Robert Broom at the Sterkfontein excavations. He is pointing to a skull in the rock.

Dr Broom was born in Paisley, Scotland, in 1866. He acquired several degrees between 1887 and 1905, including a medical degree in 1895 and a doctorate in natural sciences in 1905.

After visiting the USA and spending five years in Australia he came to South Africa in 1897. Initially he was professor of geology and zoology at the Victoria College in Stellenbosch, the predecessor of the University of Stellenbosch. He then spent the years 1916 to 1929 at Douglas near Kimberley, practising as a medical doctor. But he regarded himself in the first instance as a paleontologist. He also spent short periods elsewhere in the country.

His interest in paleontology was stimulated by his early contact with Sir Richard Owen, Britain's foremost paleontologist, and he was determined to explore the remarkable fossil wealth of the Cape which Owen had already described. In 1934 Broom was appointed to a special post as paleontologist at the Transvaal Museum in Pretoria. Here he was free to devote his time to the discovery of ape-men. Since Professor Raymond Dart's discovery of the *Australopithecus* scull at Taung in the northern Cape in 1924 there had been great doubt whether that fossil was indeed related to human predecessors. Broom realized that more specimens would have to be found if Dart's theory was to be substantiated. Within twelve years he made the sites around Krugersdorp – Sterkfontein, Kromdraai and Swartkrans – famous by his discovery of the fossils of ape-men. This convinced many scientists of the unique human characteristics of these beings.

In 1950 his book *Finding the missing link* appeared which contained a popular account of his opinion regarding the origin of humans. He was the first scientist to realize that more than one line of ape-men existed and that not all the early australopithecines were in the line of origin of *Homo sapiens*.

His most famous discovery was the skull subsequently dubbed Mrs Ples, short for *Plesianthropus transvaalensis*, but later reclassified as *Australopithecus africanus*.

For a discussion of the significance of this find in 1947, see the box on Mrs Ples under **Museums**.

Broom died in Pretoria in 1951. He was made a fellow of the Royal Society (FRS) in 1920, one of the few South Africans to receive this honour. He was the recipient of numerous honorary degrees, medals, honorary memberships of professional societies and other awards. His bibliography comprises 456 publications between 1885 and 1952. ■

Sterkfontein Caves

Fossils are normally regarded by the public as dusty bony remains, some millions of years old, which are hardly capable of exciting the interest of ordinary people. However, the remains of early man and his predecessors have yielded some fascinating finds in South Africa. Early man can be broadly divided into two groups: the australopithecenes (pre-humans) and the three groups belonging to the genus Homo (humans). These are Homo habilis (handy man, some 1.8 million years ago), Homo erectus (man who walks upright, one million years ago), and Homo sapiens (wise man, the only hominid species alive on earth today). Fossil remains of all three these groups have been discovered in southern Africa.

In 1947 an extremely well-preserved skull of a young woman was discovered at the Sterkfontein caves near Krugersdorp on the West Rand. The species she belonged to was eventually classified as Australopithecus africanus, but originally the scientist who recognized the importance of the discovery, Dr Robert Broom, named the skull of this early man-ape of two million years ago Plesianthropus transvaalensis. Subsequently it became known as Mrs Ples.

The Sterkfontein caves were discovered by a gold prospector in 1896. The single cave initially found, subsequently proved to be the entrance to an interconnected series of caves. There are a number of chambers, the largest being 23 m high and 91 m long, as well as an underground lake at a depth of 40 metres. A statue of Dr Broom examining Mrs Ples stands at the entrance to the caves.

Spectacular dripstone formations are to be seen inside the caves but many of the stalactites and stalagmites were unfortunately damaged and removed during early limestone and bat-guano gathering activities. Fortunately the caves are protected today. They form part of a nature reserve and are the property of the University of the Witwatersrand. Guided tours are conducted every 30 minutes. The caves are being considered for declaration as a World Conservation site.

Getting there: Travel south along the N1 and follow the Krugersdorp freeway (R28 or N14). About 10 km before reaching Krugersdorp (which is about 75 km from Pretoria) turn right on the R563 where the way to the caves is signposted. The turn-off to the caves is about 5 km along this road on the left.

Hours: Tuesday to Sunday: 09:00–16:00. Closed Mondays.

Admission: Charged

Facilities: Museum, restaurant and picnic site

Wonder Cave

South-west of Pretoria, more or less halfway between Pretoria and Johannesburg, in an area that has become world famous for its paleontological sites, is a cave of rare beauty. Although the cavern was discovered a century ago, it was opened to the public only in 1991. The darkness inside has been dispelled by floodlights which show the breathtaking rock formations with their many stalactites and stalagmites to good effect. The cave consists of a single chamber, 50 m wide by 125 m long and 40 m high, which can be reached only through an opening in the roof, but a lift provides comfortable access.

Tours of this 2000 million year old cave are conducted every 90 minutes.

Getting there: Travel south along the N1 and take the R28 to Krugersdorp – the same route as that to Sterkfontein Caves. After some 27 km on the R28 you will pass the signpost to the Lion Park on the left. The turn-off to the Wonder Cave is some 3 km after that on the right along the R512. Travel 7 km on the R512 and turn left at the sign to the Rhino Reserve and the Wonder Cave. The Cave is about 10 km along this road. The Rhino Reserve is on the same road.

Hours: Daily, including public holidays, 08:00–17:00. Guided tours every 90 minutes.

Admission: Charged

Tel: (011) 957 0106

Rhino Nature Reserve

Situated next to the Wonder Cave and in close proximity to the Sterkfontein Caves at Kromdraai, some 35 minutes' drive from Pretoria, is a small private reserve where rhinos roam the grassland free with other game such as buffaloes (like rhinos, one of the Big Five), giraffes, zebras, jackals and antelope. The prehistoric-looking rhino in its natural habitat is worth a visit. Rhinos are estimated to have been on earth some 60 million years and both the so-called white and black rhino are under threat of extinction (see box).

Good gravel roads provide access to most parts of the reserve.

Getting there: See the description of the route to the Wonder Cave

Hours: Daily, including public holidays, 08:00–17:00.

Facilities: Game drives in an open vehicle and walks by arrangement. Braai (barbeque) and picnic area, swimming pool, and overnight accommodation in thatched chalets.

Tel: (011) 957 0109

The rhino: prehistoric 'tank' of the Big Five

Of the Big Five of Africa – the lion, leopard, elephant, buffalo and rhinoceros – the rhinoceros is definitely the most awe-inspiring and formidable looking. The large body, which it can move surprisingly swiftly, the tough pantzer-like skin, the small eyes and that lethal-looking horn all add up to that appearance.

Rhinos have been on earth more than 60 million years. There are five species of rhino, three in Asia and two in Africa. All five are in danger of extinction. The two South African species are the so-called white rhino and the black rhino. These names are misleading, however, since they are neither white nor black. The white rhino is square-lipped and the black rhino hook-lipped. The shape of their lips has everything to do with their diets. The square-lipped rhino is a grazer who feeds on short grass, while the hook-lipped one is a browser who uses the upper lip to grab leaves and work them into its mouth.

Most rhinos are to be found in KwaZulu-Natal. Successful breeding programmes by the Natal Parks Board at Hluhluwe and other game reserves have led to an increase in the number of square-lipped (white) rhinos but the hook-lipped (black) variety is still in great danger. Reintroduction of rhinos to reserves in other parts of South Africa has also taken place in the past few decades.

The greatest danger to the continued existence of rhinos is poaching which is done to obtain the horn. Rhino horn, which actually consists of a compacted hair-like substance, is often used in the Middle East to make handles for ceremonial daggers, while in some countries it is used as an aphrodisiac. Powdered rhino horn is also highly valued in the Far East as an ingredient for certain medicines.

The square-lipped rhino is more placid than the hook-lipped variety but both should be respected. Both varieties are surprisingly light on their feet and mobile and can reach speeds of up to 50 km (30 miles) per hour. ■

Krugersdorp Game Reserve and Ngonyama Lion Lodge

Close to Sterkfontein Cave and the Rhino Nature Reserve is another reserve which offers the visitor a truly African experience. The Krugersdorp Game Reserve and Ngonyama Lion Lodge is situated in a stretch of virgin bush and grassland west of Krugersdorp. The reserve contains a variety of game such as rhino, hippopotamus and giraffe as well as over 200 species of birds. The lions are in a separate enclosure where they can be viewed at close quarters in a natural setting.

There is an airfield next to the reserve, which makes it accessible to visitors from any part of the country. However, it is only about 40 minutes' drive from Pretoria.

The accommodation includes thatched cottages as well as luxury units and a well-equipped caravan park.

Getting there:	Travel to Krugersdorp along the R28 as directed for Sterkfontein Caves. Instead of turning off onto the R563, carry on another 6 km from there and look out for the signpost on your left.
Facilities:	Tarred roads through the reserve. Restaurant, picnic facilities.
Tel:	(011) 665 4342/665 1735 (011) 953 1797/953 1770
Further information:	P O Box 5237 Krugersdorp West 1742
Admission:	Charged

Lion Park

The wish of many an overseas tourist to see the king of the beasts, the lion, in its natural surroundings can be realized within about 40 minutes' drive from Pretoria. The Lion Park contains a separate enclosure with about 60 lions in a typical African savannah setting. These magnificent animals can be viewed at close quarters from the safety of one's vehicle.

A 10 km game drive takes the visitor through the rest of the park which contains a variety of game such as zebras, buck, ostriches and black wildebeest, and through the large lion enclosure.

At the end of the drive there is a restaurant, a swimming pool, a curio shop and a colourful reconstructed Ndebele village.

Getting there: Drive towards Johannesburg along the N1. Pass the Midrand/Allandale Road turn-off and take the N1 (Bloemfontein/Kimberley) route where it splits from the M1 (Johannesburg) and N3 (Durban) routes. Travel along the N1 for about seven km and take the William Nicol Road off-ramp. Turn right along William Nicol Road to Fourways. Turn left at Fourways onto Witkoppen Road, drive 400 m and turn right at the first traffic light into Cedar Road. Travel for about 8 km until a stop street is reached. Turn left and travel about 2 km to the Lion Park on the left.

Hours: Open daily, including public holidays, 08:00–16:30

Admission: Charged

Zebras, always a delightful sight, are very adaptable and can be seen in zoos as well as in game parks

Seeing lions remains the supreme experience, therefore it may be worth your while to visit a local lion park if you cannot make it to Kruger Park

Giraffe have beautiful eyes

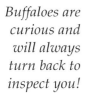

Buffaloes are curious and will always turn back to inspect you!

The Lippizaner Centre

The magnificently graceful, disciplined and precision-drilled Lippizaner horses which perform once a week at Kyalami are unique outside Europe. They are of the same stock as the Lippizaners which still perform in the famous Spanish Riding School in Vienna in Austria.

The forbears of the South African horses belonged to a Hungarian nobleman who fled his native land during the turmoil after the Second World War. Twelve horses from the stud of the nobleman, Count Jankovich Besan, were sent to Bavaria and then to England. From there he brought them to South Africa in 1948. The present Lippizaners are descendants of those twelve.

Initially the team of performing horses stood under the directorship of a former Polish cavalry officer. They have been performing in South Africa since 1965.

The stallions perform a number of different precision patterns as well as leaps which only these intelligent animals can be trained to execute. These movements have their origin in the cavalry exercises used during the Middle Ages to intimidate and disperse foot soldiers.

Getting there: Take the N1 to Johannesburg. Pass the first off-ramp to Midrand and about 30 km south of Pretoria, take the second one marked Midrand/Allandale Road. Turn right and continue along Allandale Road until you reach the entrance to Kyalami race track. Turn right. The Lippizaner Centre signpost is about 500 m along this road on the left. Follow the signs from there.

Performances: Every Sunday at 11:00. No performance from mid-October to mid-November. Booking can be done at Computicket or tickets bought at the door.

Admission: Charged

Crocodile River Arts and Crafts Ramble

At Broederstroom, some 45 minutes' drive west of Pretoria, is an art and crafts route where the visitor can travel from studio to studio viewing the work of the different artists and craftsmen and see some of them at work as well. Many of the studios have galleries attached. Some sixteen artists and craftsmen form part of the route and a large variety of art and craft forms are represented. These include painting, sculpture, ceramics, pottery, jewellery, stained glass, wrought iron work, knitwear, etc.

There are a number of farm stalls and tea gardens along the route where the visitor can acquire home-made fare or have tea and scones and other delights. Hotels cater for more substantial meals.

Getting there: Travel to Hartbeespoort Dam by taking Proes Street (one-way) westward. Where Proes Street runs into a T-junction

with D F Malan Drive, turn right and after 100 m left into
Vom Hagen Street, which becomes the N4 (west). Carry
on straight along this Magalies Toll Road for about 27 km
to the end of the toll road and take the off-ramp signposted Hartbeespoort Dam/Pelindaba. Turn left towards
Pelindaba and follow this road for 6 km to where the R512
joins it on the left south of the Hartbeespoort Dam.
Broederstroom is just 4 km away. Look out for signposts
to studios along the R512 as well as before turning left
onto it.

Hours: Saturday and Sunday on the first weekend of every
month from 09:00 to 17:00

Admission: Free

Lesedi African Cultural Village

Near Broederstroom, some 45 minutes' drive from Pretoria, lies a cultural village with traditional Zulu, Xhosa, Pedi and Basotho homesteads
in the foothills of the Magaliesberg range. This village offers the visitor
a rare, decidedly African cultural experience. Each homestead is inhabited by a rural African family which maintains an authentic ethnic
lifestyle. This gives the visitor the opportunity to experience the culture of the Zulu, Xhosa, Pedi and Basotho people at close quarters.
There are also overnight facilities in the form of neat additional huts. In
the evening visitors can experience an African-style feast in the central
boma or meeting place. The meal is followed by a display of traditional
dancing. Day visitors can also join these nightly experiences before
they leave or they can enjoy a Monati Lunch.

   Lesedi also makes it possible for couples to get 'married' in the traditional Zulu way. However, these marriages are not recognized by the
state or the courts of law.

Getting there: Broederstroom is situated directly south of the Hartbeespoort Dam. Follow the directions for the Crocodile River
Arts and Crafts Ramble. Take the R512 and travel about 5
km until you see the signpost to the Lesedi Cultural
Village on the right.

Information: Cell: 082 600 5000

Loopspruit Wine Estate

Winemaking in South Africa is usually associated with the Western
Cape with its Mediterranean climate and historic wine farms and wine
routes. But over the past decade or two viticulture has taken off in the
north as well. The Loopspruit Wine Estate, spread over some 20 ha and
the only award-winning wine estate north of the Vaal River, affords visitors to the capital the opportunity to see the wine-making process at

close quarters. A tour of the cellar takes one through the different stages of the process.

Getting there:	Take the N4 highway to Witbank. After about 45 km, just before getting to Bronkhorstspruit, take the Ekandustria off-ramp and continue past Ekandustria on the road to Kwa Mahlanga for about 32 km. Turn right at the Nooitgedacht sign. Loopspruit is on your left.
Hours:	08:00–16:00
Admission:	Charged
Tel:	(01212) 24303

Ndebele Tribal Village

The Ndebele are known for their colourful dresses and beadwork as well as their beautifully decorated homes. Traditional Ndebele women wear not only the exquisite dresses but also layer upon layer of brass or other metal rings around their necks and lower legs.

A tribal village north-east of Pretoria displays this wonderful artwork to good effect.

Getting there:	Take the N4 highway to Witbank. After about 45 km take the Bronkhorstspruit/Ekandustria off-ramp. Turn left onto the R568 and carry straight on for about 32 km. Turn right at the Nooitgedacht sign. The village is on your right.
Hours:	Tour times: 08:00–17:00. The tour presentation lasts 45 minutes or more. Demonstration advice: Mon: 13:00–16:00; Tue, Wed and Thu: 08:00–16:00; Fri: 08:00–12:30
Tel:	(01212) 20894
Admission:	Charged

Warmbaths Spa

A little more than an hour's drive north of Pretoria along the N1 is the town of Warmbaths, which owes its existence to its hot mineral springs. Around these springs a modern resort has grown.

The hot mineral water is thought to have special healing qualities. The water of different hot springs in South Africa are rich in different minerals which are believed to be healing agents. The spring at Warmbaths is one of those whose alkaline water contains mainly sodium carbonate and sodium bicarbonate. These minerals are thought to combine with the temperature of the water emerging from the earth at 49 °C to work wonders for ailments such as rheumatism. The complex at Warmbaths includes a health centre incorporating an indoor pool with strong underwater jets to provide therapeutic treatment for sufferers.

Ndebeli mural art

But Warmbaths also provides for the holidaymaker. There are a number of large outdoor hot and cold pools set in pleasant bushveld surroundings.

The complex is open to day visitors.

Accommodation for visitors who want to stay longer is in the form of chalets in natural surroundings as well as a hotel. There is also a well-appointed camping and caravan site.

Getting there: Take the N1 north from Pretoria to Pietersburg for about 90 km. Before entering the Kranskop Toll Road take the R516 turn-off left to Warmbaths. The town is 8 km from the N1.

Details: The Aventura Warmbaths Resort is open daily 07:00–17:00 throughout the year.

Further information:

Aventura Warmbaths

P O Box 75

WARMBATHS

0480

Tel: (014) 736 2200

Bushveld game reserves near Warmbaths

For the day visitor who would like to take in a game reserve in the true Bushveld region there are a number to choose from. Only four of these are mentioned here which are within fairly easy reach of Pretoria on a day trip. For more info on the Warmbaths vicinity contact the local Tourist Information Centre at tel: (014) 736 3694.

Sondela Nature Reserve is situated close to the town of Warmbaths. Instead of turning left towards the town from the N1, turn right and travel four km towards Settlers where the entrance to the reserve is situated. This smallish reserve of 5000 ha abounds with wildlife and birds. Tel: (014) 736 4304/5/6.

Mabalingwe Nature Reserve is 28 km west of Warmbaths on the R516 road to Rooiberg and Thabazimbi. The reserve has over a hundred thatched chalets. Accommodation is usually available and day visitors are also welcome. Telephone to book. On a game drive 48 species of game and 170 bird species can be observed. There are elephants, hippos and rhino but no lions. Trackers are available for walking trails through the indigenous bushveld. Safaris on horseback under supervision are offered as well. Amenities include airstrip, hot and cold swimming pools, tennis courts and barbecue. Tel: (014) 736 2334/5.

The turn-off to *Mabula Game Lodge* is 5 km further on the same road as Mabalingwe (33 km from Warmbaths). This bush retreat boasts the Big Five as well as hippo's. The visitor can drive around himself or undertake

Overleaf:
African elephant,
giant of the bush

a horseback trail ride. Booking is essential. Mabula also has an airstrip (tel: (014) 734 0012).

Borakalalo Game Reserve is further west than Mabula Game Lodge and slightly more remote, but the Tswana name means 'the place where people relax' and indeed, it feels like the heart of Africa and does allow the visitor to experience the peace of the bush. The reserve is located around a dam and contains elephants, giraffes, zebras, white rhino, leopards and several antelope species. Directions are the same as for Mabula Game Lodge. Travel past the Mabula turn-off up to Leeupoort which is some 65 km from Warmbaths. Turn off to Leeupoort and just outside the mining town turn left again at the fork and travel another 35 km to Borakalalo. The approximately 35 km from Leeupoort is a dirt road. The reserve can also be reached along a tarred road via the town of Brits (tel: (011) 465 5423/4).

For the route through Brits and for information on other attractions in the Brits/Hartbeespoort region, contact the Brits Publicity Office at tel 318 9274 or fax the same number (ask for a fax line).

Sun City and the Lost City

The Sun City and Lost City complex in the Pilanesberg north-west of Rustenburg is one of the best-known tourist attractions in South Africa. It is about two and a half hours by car from Pretoria. Part of the attraction of this tourist playground lies in the fact that it is situated far from urban centres slap in the middle of the Bushveld. It attracts some two million visitors per year.

The complex is the brainchild of the founder of Sun International Hotels, Sol Kerzner. Today it consists of eight different components. These are the original Sun City Hotel, the Cascades hotel, the Cabanas hotel, the entertainment centre, the Valley of Waves, the tropical jungle, the Palace of the Lost City, the Gary Player Country Club and the Lost City Golf Course.

The Sun City Hotel

This luxury hotel was the original component of the complex and it overlooks the man-made lake and Gary Player Golf Course. It contains a large casino, an equally large pool deck, several restaurants, cinemas and a theatre which has often been used for overseas theatrical productions and extravaganzas.

The Cascades

This is the second of four hotels in the complex. As the name indicates the theme is cascading waters and the garden of the hotel contains no fewer than twelve waterfalls. The lush jungle around it is home to scores of exotic birds.

The Cabanas

This hotel, situated near the man-made lake in the complex to which it has direct access, caters mainly for families. The emphasis here is on outdoor entertainment and the facilities include a mini golf course and an adventure playground.

The Entertainment Centre

This huge centre is packed with slot machines of various kinds, video games, a bingo saloon, and a number of cinemas, restaurants and boutiques. It also houses the Superbowl which was opened by a Frank Sinatra performance. A bridge from this centre brings you to the ruins of the lost city through impressive sculpture and past the Eternal Flame to the Valley of Waves.

The Valley of Waves

In keeping with the fantasy theme of the whole complex, this attraction provides a tropical bathing spot in the heart of the bushveld. Here the visitor can relax on an artificial beach of white sand with palm trees and thatched umbrella shades around him. Giant waves emanate from a cliff of stone in front of his eyes to roll out on the beach sand. Several water slides add to the attraction of this fantasy feature.

The tropical jungle

Next to the valley of waves is another wonder world in the form of a tropical jungle. It contains half a million exotic and indigenous trees and other plants, and features no less than 5000 species of forest trees, including the impressive baobab transported from the Northern Province to be transplanted here.

The Palace of the Lost City

This luxury hotel caps everything in the complex and certainly counts among the world's top hotels. Here the imagination has certainly had free rein. Everything has been done in the superlative degree, creating an air of wonder and fantasy. Visitors are usually overwhelmed by the scale of it all and the great attention paid to detail. Impressive statues of wild animals guard the entrance and in one of the courtyards is a life-size statue of a famous Kruger National Park elephant.

The foyer, Palace of the Lost City

Gary Player Country Club and Lost City Golf Course

There are two golf courses in the complex. The famous Gary Player Country Club Course, which borders on the man-made lake, is the venue for the annual Sun City Million Dollar Golf Challenge. By contrast, the course at the Lost City offers a desert experience and live crocodiles at the 13th hole as well as a driving range.

Sun City Timeshare

These self-catering, fully equipped timeshare units are affiliated with RCI and are exchangeable for points or other units. If available, they can also be rented in the ordinary way. A free bus service does the rounds to the other features and the complex has its own swimming pools and braai facilities.

Crocodile farm

This interesting feature is situated at the entrance to the complex.

Getting there: Take the N4 West towards Hartbeespoort Dam. Cross the dam wall or take the road around the dam by following the signposts. After the dam carry straight on, passing the curio market and stalls, followed by orange orchards. Look out for the signposts to Sun City on your right. The entrance to the complex is about 70 km from the Hartbeespoort Dam.

Details: Open 24 hours every day. Admission charged. Several operators run regular bus and plane trips to Sun City.

Further information:

Sun International Central Reservations
P O Box 784487
Sandton 2146

Tel: (011) 780 7800

Ludwig's Roses

On the N1 north, about 21 km from Pretoria, is Ludwig's Roses, an extensive rose nursery where new roses are regularly bred. It is open to the public seven days a week and a tea garden provides refreshments.

Casinos

There are several casinos within easy reach of Pretoria.

The easiest to reach are the Carousel, about 65 km from Pretoria on the N1 north to Pietersburg, and Caesars, about 50 km away on the East Rand road, just 5 minutes past Johannesburg International Airport to the left.

Entertainment

Cinemas

Full information is on the show page every day in the local newspapers. Tickets for movies and most theatre productions can be bought at Computicket where information is available as well. Credit cards accepted.

Computicket branches are at the **State Theatre**, cnr Church and Prinsloo Streets; **Sanlam Centre**, cnr Andries and Pretorius Streets; **Sunnypark** (in Clicks); **Hatfield Plaza**, Burnett Street; **Brooklyn Mall**, Fehrsen Street; **Centurion Shopping Centre**, Centurion Lake; **The Tram Shed**, Van der Walt Street; **Glenfair Shopping Centre**, Lynnwood Road; **Menlyn Centre**, cnr Atterbury Road & Lois Avenue; **Lynnridge Mall**, Lynnwood Road; **Jakaranda Centre**, Frates Road, Rietfontein; **Pretoria North**, cnr Rachel de Beer and Ben Viljoen Streets; and **Kolonnade Centre**, Zambesi Drive, Montana.

Cinemas are to be found at the following shopping centres:

Carousel Casino, N1 north

Brooklyn Mall
Tel: 346 3435
    Cnr Lange & Fehrsen Streets,
New Muckleneuk

Centurion Centre
Tel: 663 2034
    Lenchen Street, Centurion

Sterland Cinema complex,
Pretorius Street, Arcadia

Hatfield Plaza
Tel: 342 2932
> Burnett Street, Hatfield

Kolonnade Centre
Tel: 548 0382
> Zambezi Drive, Montana

Menlyn Centre
Tel: 348 8611
> Cnr Atterbury Road & Lois
> Ave, Menlyn

Sammy Marks Square
Tel: 326 6614
> Cnr Van der Walt &
> Vermeulen Streets, central

Sterland Centre
Tel: 341 7568
> Cnr Beatrix & Pretorius
> Streets, Arcadia

Sunnypark
Tel: 341 9226
> Cnr Esselen & Jeppe Streets,
> Sunnyside

The Tram Shed
Tel: 320 4300
> Cnr Van der Walt &
> Schoeman Streets, central

Drive-in cinemas

The local newspapers carry a daily page with full information of shows and times.

Wonderboom 1&2
Tel: 567 1108
> Zambezi Drive, Sinoville

Zwartkops
Tel: 374 4902
> R55, Zwartkops

Theatres

State Theatre
Tel: 322 1665
> Church Street, between
> Prinsloo & Van der Walt
> Streets

There are five different theatres in this building and plays, opera, musicals and other productions are presented throughout the year. Information on what is on can be obtained from the above number or in the local press.

Breytenbach Theatre
Tel: 44 4834

137 Gerhard Moerdijk Street,
Sunnyside

Café Riche Basement Theatre
Tel: 328 3173

Café Riche Building, Church
Square West

Little Theatre
Tel: 322 7676

Skinner Street, central

Teaterhuisie
Tel: 341 9205

Oeverzicht Art Village
Cnr Gerhard Moerdijk & Kotze
Streets, Sunnyside

Ice rink

Kolonnade Ice Arena
Tel: 548 2450

Kolonnade Shopping Centre
Zambezi Drive, Montana

Vilamoura Restaurant interior

Atteridgeville and Saulsville Taverners Association
Tel: 373 8635

Mareka Street, Atteridgeville
Contact person: Elias Nkonyane

Gauteng Jazz Foundation
Tel: 373 0446

Contact person: Jaja Seema

Hot Air Balloon Company
Tel: 205 1021

Fly over mountain and lake scenery only 20 minutes from Pretoria.

Indoor go-karting
Tel: 323 5064

Lower basement, Sancardia Shopping Centre
Cnr Church & Beatrix Streets, Arcadia

Kingsley Tenpin Bowling
Tel: 44 5314

Kingsley Centre
Cnr Beatrix & Church Streets, Arcadia

Menlyn 19th Hole & Go-karts
Tel: 47 4110

Cnr Gen Louis Botha Drive & Serene Street, Menlyn

19th Hole Putt-Putt Centurion
Tel: 663 4021

Lenchen Street, Centurion

19th Hole Putt-Putt, Sunnyside
Tel: 341 3013

Cnr Jeppe & Park Streets, Sunnyside

Pretoria East Arena
Tel: 991 4778

Atterbury Value Mart
Atterbury Road, Pretoria East
Activities: Action Cricket & Action Netball

Pretoria Indoor Grand Prix
Tel: 327 1116

Pretoria Showgrounds, Hall G

Zone 4 Laser Games
Tel: 323 1848

Arcadia Shopping Centre
Beatrix Street, Arcadia

Ducking about – you may find unexpected fellows sharing the park!

Taking to the water to get away from it all – Hartbeespoort Dam

Golfing around at Brooklyn Mall

Shot! Pretoria offers a full range of golf courses, driving ranges and mini-golf or putt-putt.

Restaurants

The following is an up to date list of restaurants at the time of writing. 'Central' in the locality indicates that it is situated in central Pretoria.

Alex's
Tel: 322 1106

Steakhouse
Sanlam Centre, Pretorius
Street, central

Algarve
Tel: 322 3669

Portuguese & a la carte
SAAU Building, Schoeman
Street, central

American Dream
Tel: 322 1846

Pub lunches
Sanlam Centre, Pretorius
Street, central

Barrel Inn
Tel: 327 1856

A la carte & pub lunches
53 Mitchell Street, Pretoria West

Beefeater
Tel: 542 2366

A la carte/Pub lunches
Waterbok Street. Akasia

Bel-A-Pizza
Tel: 804 3988

Pizza/Pasta
Shop 34, Buckle Street, Silverton

Bella Vida
Tel: 997 2483

Portuguese
Moreleta Centre, Rubenstein
Drive, Moreleta Park

Billy's Village
Tel: 44 8018

Steakhouse
The Village, 34 Esselen
Street, Sunnyside

Blue Crane
Tel: 46 7615

A la carte/Coffee shop
Cnr Melk & Boshoff Streets,
New Muckleneuk

Böhmerwald
Tel: 326 7658

A la carte/German/Provincial
85 Paul Kruger Street, central

Boston BBQ
Tel: 543 0037

Buffet dishes
Lavender/Braam Pretorius
Streets, Pretoria North

Boston BBQ
Tel: 807 2250

Buffet dishes
Gift Acres, Lynnwood Road,
Lynnwood Ridge

Boston BBQ
Tel: 46 1238

Buffet dishes
78 George Storrar Drive,
Groenkloof

Brass Inn, The
Tel: 327 1302

A la carte
458 Mitchell Street, Pretoria
West

Brasserie de Paris, La
Tel: 342 5057

French
525 Duncan Street, Hatfield

Bronco Canyon Spur
Tel: 98 4423

Steakhouse & pub lunches
Sunbird Park Centre, Sunbird
Street, Garsfontein

Brooklyn Square

Cnr Veale & Middel Sts
New Muckleneuk
15 restaurants for all tastes

Buddies
Tel: 329 3025

Steakhouse
353 Voortrekkers Street,
Capital Park

Bugsy
Tel: 332 2274

Steakhouse
C de Villiers Centre, Cadonia
Ave, Waverley

Café Amics
Tel: 342 0326

A la carte/Bar/Coffee shop
Hatfield Square, Burnett
Street, Hatfield

Café Barcelona
Tel: 345 3602

A la carte/Bar/Coffee shop
Elardus Park Shopping
Centre, Elardus Park

Café Lisboa
Tel: 46 9087

Portuguese/Seafood
Monument Park Centre,
Skilpad Rd, Monument Park

Café 41
Tel: 46 5216

A la carte/Coffee shop
Groenkloof Plaza, George
Storrar Drive, Groenkloof

Camel Tavern, The
Tel: 342 6655

A la carte
Hatfield Rendezvous,
367 Hilda Street, Hatfield

Camelot
Tel: 663 1166

Steakhouse/Seafood/Carvery
Anglo American Building,
Gerhard Street, Centurion

Can Ton
Tel: 47 6426/47 7921

Chinese/Cantonese
Glenfair Centre, Daventry
Road, Lynnwood Manor

Cantina Tequila
Tel: 46 5276

Mexican
Brooklyn Plaza, Middel Street,
New Muckleneuk

Capital Chinese
Tel: 342 8022

Chinese
No 2, Block 4, Hatfield Square,
Burnett Street, Hatfield

Caraffa
Tel: 346 3181

Italian Trattoria
46 Selati Street, Alphen Park

Carvings & Cravings
Tel: 341 7047

A la carte
Kingsley Centre, Cnr Pretorius
& Beatrix Streets, central

Casa José
Tel: 46 8068

Steakhouse
Waterkloof Centre, Waterkloof

Castle Walk
Tel: 45 3370

Steak/Seafood/Potjiekos
Lois Ave, Erasmuskloof

Castle Walk
Tel: 546 9146

Steak/Seafood/Potjiekos
Madelief Shopping Centre,
Daan de Wet Nel Ave,
Pretoria North

Chagall's
Tel: 342 1200

A la carte/French
924 Park Street, Arcadia

Birdwatching at the Blue Crane

Chatterley's
Tel: 44 7920/341 0805

A la carte/Seafood/Steaks
473 Church Street, Arcadia

Cheers
Tel: 804 1212

A la carte
Nedbank Centre, Pretoria
Road, Silverton

Coffee Bean, The
Tel: 47 1436

German/Bar lunches/Bar &
Coffee shop
Lynnridge Mall, Lynnwood
Road, Lynnwood Ridge

Crawdaddy's
Tel: 341 6205

Seafood/Steak/Chicken
57 Esselen Street, Sunnyside

Crazy Nut
Tel: 46 2874

Vegetarian/Buffet
Brooklyn Square, Middel
Street, New Muckleneuk

Crazy Prawn
Tel: 997 0600

Seafood/A la carte
Moreleta Centre, 680
Rubenstein Drive, Moreleta
Park

Crown and Beggar
Tel: 326 8136

German/Bar lunches
Shop 15, Standard Bank
Building, Van der Walt Street,
central

Cynthia's
Tel: 46 3220/46 3229

A la carte
Maroelana Centre, Maroelana
St, Maroelana

Day 'n Nite Grill
Tel: 341 3039

A la carte
202 Esselen Street,
Sunnyside

Diep in die Berg
Tel: 807 0111

A la carte
Hans Strijdom Drive, off
Lynnwood Extension

Downtown
Tel: 348 6910

A la carte
69 Lynnburn Road, Val de
Grace

Dragon Garden
Tel: 998 6233

Chinese/Take-aways
Shop 3, Niesewand Street,
Constantia Park

Fingers
Tel: 44 2923

A la carte
1st Floor, Sunnypark Centre,
Esselen Street, Sunnyside

Gerard Moerdijk
Tel: 344 4856

Traditional South African
752 Park Street, Arcadia

Gino's Grill
Tel: 57 6078

A la carte/Carvery
Wonder Waters, Old
Warmbaths Road,
Wonderboom

Gino's Pizzeria
Tel: 807 0638

Pizza/Pasta/A la carte
10 Wapadrand Centre,
Lynnwood Road, Wapadrand

Gerard Moerdijk Restaurant

Giovanni's
Tel: 344 4070

Italian/A la carte
529 Jorissen Street,
Sunnyside

Giovanni's
Tel: 44 8323

Italian/A la carte
151 Esselen Street,
Sunnyside

Giovanni's
Tel: 346 3344

Italian/A la carte
118 Brooklyn Mall, New
Muckleneuk

Giovanni's
Tel: 342 0286

Italian/A la carte
Rendezvous Centre, Hilda
Street, Hatfield

Globe Trotter
Tel: 323 2957

A la carte
228 Pretorius Street, central

Gloria
Tel: 21 5075

A la carte
233 Pretorius Street, central

Godfather, The
Tel: 663 1859

A la carte/Steaks/Pub lunches
Biella Centre, Lenchen Street,
Centurion

Golden City
Tel: 346 3880/465 650

Chinese
32 Pinaster Street,
Hazelwood

Golden Eagle Spur
Tel: 343 7100

Steakhouse
501 Jorissen Street,
Sunnyside

Grants
Tel: 326 4806

A la carte
Boulevard Protea Hotel,
186 Struben Street, central

Greek Easy, The
Tel: 342 5199

Greek
370 Hilda Street, Hatfield

Greentrees Water
Tel: 326 7407

A la carte
Nedbank Centre, Church
Street, Arcadia

Green Trees
Tel: 341 7181

Steakhouse/Roadhouse
76 Harmony Street,
Muckleneuk

Hillside Tavern
Tel: 47 5119

Restaurant & Pub
Rynlal building, 320 The
Hillside, Lynnwood

Homestead
Tel: 341 1790

A la carte
Cnr Shoeman/Hamilton/Park
Streets, Arcadia

Hong Kong
Tel: 46 9221/2

Chinese
Shop 29-30, Brooklyn Mall,
Brooklyn

Il Bacio
Tel: 341 0689

Pizza/Pasta
286 Esselen Street, Sunnyside

Il Bacio
Tel: 342 2921/342 1679

Pizza/Pasta
1st Floor, Nedbank Forum,
Burnett Street, Hatfield

Indian Ocean Company
Tel: 803 6006

Portuguese/Seafood/Deli
374 Rossouw St, Murrayfield,
off N4 witbank

Jacaranda
Tel: 341 1571

Buffet Carvery/Set menu
Holiday Inn, Crn Beatrix &
Church Streets

J D Blonde's
Tel: 346 5067

A la carte
Middel Street, New
Muckleneuk

Keg & Hound
Tel: 43 6460

Traditional English
pub/Restaurant
107 Arcadia Street, Hatfield

Keg & Feather
Tel: 998 5475

Traditional English
pub/Restaurant
Waterglen Centre, Menlyn
Drive (off Louis Botha Drive),
Waterkloof Glen

Keg & Musket
Tel: 663 1081

Traditional English
pub/Restaurant
Southlake Centre, Centurion

La Cantina
Tel: 322 4211

Italian/Pizza/Pasta
393 Pretorius Street, central

Lady Annabel's
Tel: 341 7090

A la carte
Sunnypark, Esselen Street

Lady Chatterley's
Tel: 083 263 3017

Seafood/A la carte
1211 Prospect Street, Hatfield

La Fragola
Tel: 44 4134

Italian
36 Jeppe Street, Sunnyside

La Gondola
Tel: 348 3359

Italian/Pizza/Pasta
Shop 61, Lynnwood Galleries,
Rosemary/Diana Streets,
Lynnwood

Lai Jing
Tel: 348 7021

Chinese
Shop 6,7,8, Newlands Plaza,
Dely Road, Newlands

La Madeleine
Tel: 44 6076

French/Belgian
258 Esselen Street, Sunnyside

La Maison
Tel: 43 4341

French
235 Hilda Street, Hatfield

La Pampa
Tel: 348 4200

A la carte
St Georges Court, 426
Rodericks Road, Lynnwood

La Pentola
Tel: 329 4028

Italian/A la carte
97 Soutpansberg Road,
Riviera

La Perla
Tel: 322 2759

Swiss/Continental
Didacta Building, 211 Skinner
Street, central

La Pizza
Tel: 326 2105

Italian
165 Schoeman Street, central

La Stalla
Tel: 809 0460

Italian/A la carte
Lynnwood Road Extension,
Tweefontein

Le Chalet
Tel: 76 1832

A la carte/Seafood/Steaks
522 Voortrekkers Road,
Gezina

Le Temps des Fondues
Tel: 341 3004

French/Swiss/Fondue
91 Gerard Moerdijk Street,
Sunnyside

Lin Wah
Tel: 45 5515

Chinese
Erasmusrand Centre, Rigel
Ave, Erasmusrand

Luinis Pizzeria
Tel: 342 1050

Italian/Pizza/Pasta
283a Lynnwood Road, Menlo Park

Magic Samovar
Tel: 341 9500

Russian/Czech
115 Gerard Moerdijk Street, Sunnyside

Maharani Cuisine
Tel: 347 1377

Indian curries/Seafood
Castle Walk Shopping Centre, Erasmuskloof

Meet and Eat
Tel: 43 3822

Steakhouse
413 Hilda Street, Hatfield

Meet and Eat
Tel: 55 4615

Steakhouse
570 Gerrit Maritz Street, Pretoria North

Menews
Tel: 326 4353

Seafood/Bar lunches
Sancardia Centre, 524 Church Street, Arcadia

Mickey's
Tel: 342 7140

Steakhouse
497 Hilda Street, Hatfield

Mieke's
Tel: 341 2526

A la carte/Dutch
92 Meintjes Street, Sunnyside

Mike's Kitchen
Tel: 87 3291

A la carte/Family fare
Barnard Street, Elardus Park

Mike's Kitchen
Tel: 663 1940

A la carte/Family fare
Cnr Lenchen Ave/Embankment Road, Centurion

Ming Woo
Tel: 663 1888

Chinese
Lake Terrace, Centurion Centre

Ming Yuan
Tel: 807 2357

Chinese/Mong BBQ
12 Farm Road, Willow Glen

Misha's
Tel: 73 5833

A la carte
Kilner Park Galleries, Kilner Park

Mongolian BBQ
Tel: 44 3423

A la carte/Buffet
Provisus Building, 523 Church Street, Arcadia

Monument
Tel: 323 0772

A la carte/Buffet
Voortrekker Monument, Schanskop

Mozzarella's
Tel: 342 8266

Italian/Pizza/Pasta
Hatfield Square, Burnett Street, Hatfield

Oeka Toeka
Tel: 341 0084

Boerekos (traditional Afrikaans food)
119 Gerard Moerdijk Street, Sunnyside

O'Gallito
Tel: 342 6610

Portuguese/Seafood
367 Hilda Street, Hatfield

Ohio Spur
Tel: 342 0556

Steakhouse
Hatfield Square, Burnett Street, Hatfield

O'Hagan's Irish Pub & Grill
Tel: 63 2345/663 3089

Grills
Von Willich Ave, Centurion

O'Hagan's Irish Pub & Grill
Tel: 47 1425

Grills
Newlands Plaza, Lois Road,
Newlands

O'Hagan's Irish Pub & Grill
Tel: 328 7040/328 7042

Grills
87 Soutpansberg Road, Villieria

O'Hagan's Irish Pub & Grill
Tel: 807 2783

Grills
Lynnwood Road extension,
next to Wilgers Hospital

Oscar's
Tel: 341 2812

American/Mexican burgers
501 Beatrix Street, Arcadia

Pacha's
Tel: 46 5063/46 4336

A la carte
22 Dely Road, Hazelwood

Palmyra
Tel: 325 3466

Arabic
113 Beatrix Street, Arcadia

Panarotti's
Tel: 548 0500

Pizza/Pasta
Kolonnade Shopping Centre,
Montana

Panarotti's
Tel: 348 7001/348 8093

Pizza/Pasta
376 Garsfontein Road, Menlyn

Panaroti's
Tel: 663 6153/663 6107

Pizza/Pasta
Southlake Centre, Centurion

Pancho Villa
Tel: 46 5140

A la carte/Mexican
103 Club Avenue, Waterkloof
Heights

Pavarotti's
Tel: 323 4221

A la carte
Sammy Marks Square,
Church Street, central

Pheasant's Nest
Tel: 811 0494

A la carte
Menlyn Road, Tierpoort

Pinocchio
Tel: 43 6651

A la carte
260 Paul Kruger Street, central

Pipachiri
Tel: 341 7001

Pizza/Pasta
Kingsley Centre, Beatrix
Street, Arcadia

Pipachiri
Tel: 341 1176

Pizza/Pasta/Chicken/Ribs
Esselen Street, Sunnyside

Porterhouse
Tel: 98 5522

Steakhouse
Waterglen Park, Menlyn
Drive, Menlo Park

Porterhouse
Tel: 663 3955

Steakhouse
De Nunpen Building,
Centurion Centre, Centurion

Presley's
Tel. 807 0690

A la carte
18 Struland St, off Lynnwood
Rd, Lynnwood Ridge

Pride of India
Tel: 346 3684

Indian/A la carte
Groenkloof Plaza, George
Storrar Drive

Prime Cut, The
Tel: 341 7148

Steakhouse
Kingsley Centre, Cnr Beatrix
& Church Streets, Arcadia

Red Eagle Spur
Tel: 44 8262

Steakhouse
Sterland Centre, Beatrix
Street, Arcadia

Rio Grande Spur
Tel: 320 0900

Steakhouse
Holiday Inn Garden Court, Van der Walt Street, central

Ritrovo
Tel: 46 5173

Italian/A la carte
Waterkloof Heights Centre, 103 Club Ave, Waterkloof Heights

Roberto's
Tel: 320 4020

Italian/A la carte
The Tramshed, Schoeman Street, central

Roberto's
Tel: 46 7258/9

Italian/A la carte
Brooklyn Centre, Fehrsen Street, New Muckleneuk

Rockefeller 555
Tel: 322 7635

Buffet
Karos Manhattan Hotel, 247 Scheiding Street, central

Rugantini's
Tel: 803 4053

Italian/A la carte
Murrayfield Centre, Rubida/Rossouw Streets, Murrayfield

Sacramento Spur
Tel: 549 2274

Steakhouse
Wonderpark Centre, Brits Road, Karen Park

Saddles
Tel: 325 4422

Steakhouse
Sancardia Centre, cnr Church/Beatrix Streets, central

Safika
Tel: 46 9269

African & Vegetarian
27 Maroelana Centre, Maroelana Street, Maroelana

Salzburg
Tel: 323 1384

Austrian/A la carte
240 Vermeulen Street, central

Santa Barbara Spur
Tel: 543 1349

Steakhouse
Sinoville Centre, Sinoville

Santa Rosa Spur
Tel: 663 4117

Family fare
1279 M Crawford Ave, Centurion Centre

Santorini
Tel: 346 3672

Greek/A la carte
Fehrsen Street, Brooklyn

Sebastian's
Tel: 663 1973

A la carte
West Street, Lyttelton Manor

Silver Chief
Tel: 47 2290/348 9386

Steakhouse
376 Garsfontein Drive, Newlands

Silver Ridge Spur
Tel: 47 7949

Steakhouse/Kiddies Corner
Lynnridge Mall, Lynnwood Road, Lynnwood Ridge

South East
Tel: 809 0090/809 0449

Japanese/Teppanyaki
Lynnwood Road extension, The Willows

Status
Tel: 58 3953

A la carte
12 Rosslyn Plaza, De Waal Street, Rosslyn

Steak 'N Ale
Tel: 62 2721

Steakhouse
66 Botha Ave, Lyttelton Manor

Stefano's
Tel: 44 9792

Italian
Pencardia, Pretorius Street, Arcadia

Steers
Tel: 342 2904

Steakhouse
313 Lynnwood Road, Menlo Park

Talk of the Town
Tel: 328 7190

Light meals
180 Visagie Street, central

Taormina
Tel: 998 9204

Italian/A la carte
Garsfontein Park Centre, 645
Jacqueline Drive, Garsfontein

Taras Bulba
Tel: 44 3765

Steakhouse/Seafood
209 Hamilton Street, Arcadia

Taverna Dionysos
Tel: 346 4762

Greek
Maroelana Centre, Maroelana
Street, Maroelana

Terassa
Tel: 342 0326

Cajun &
Mediterranean/Tappas Bar
Iparioli Office Park, Duncan
Street, Hatfield

Thirties
Tel: 44 6792

A la carte
17 Sunnypark, Esselen Street,
Sunnyside

Thyme & Again
Tel: 348 4816

A la carte
Glenfair Sanlam Centre,
Lynnwood Road, Lynnwood

Tien Chu
Tel: 807 0508

Chinese
York House, The Highway
Road, The Willows

Tijuca Churrascaria
Tel: 346 3610

Brazilian buffet & barbeque
Monument Park Shopping
Centre, 87 Skilpad Road,
Monument Park

Toothpix
Tel: 379 5930

Seafood
494 Moot Street, Hermanstad

Toureiro
Tel: 327 4763

Seafood/Steaks
314 Church Street West,
Pretoria West

Toureiro
Tel: 46 6540

Seafood/Steaks
Waterkloof Centre,
Waterkloof Road, Waterkloof

Trastevere
Tel: 322 3026

Italian/Pasta/Pizza
407 Church Street, Arcadia

Trattoria Nardi
Tel: 341 8283

Italian/Pizza/Pasta
Barclay Square Centre, Cnr
Leyds/Rissik Streets,
Sunnyside

Trofa
Tel: 327 6331

Portuguese
339 Church Street, Pretoria
West

Venezia
Tel: 46 7747

Italian/Pizza/Pasta
Maroelana Centre, Maroelana

Vilamoura
Tel: 346 1650

Portuguese/Seafood
273 Middel Street, New
Muckleneuk

Villa do Mar
Tel: 46 5140

Seafood/Portuguese
103 Club Ave, Waterkloof
Heights

Villa San Giovanni
Tel: 548 2980

Continental
Kolonnade Centre, Zambesi
Drive, Montana

Village Green, The
Tel: 348 7536

A la carte
Menlyn Park Centre, Menlyn

Vivaldi
Tel: 46 8828

A La Carte
New Muckleneuk Centre,
Bronkhorst Street, New
Muckleneuk

Wakita Spur
Tel: 548 2506

Steakhouse
Shop No 30, Kolonnade
Centre, Zambesi Drive,
Montana

Wangthai
Tel: 346 6230

Thai Restaurant
281 Middel Street, New
Muckleneuk

Wild Boar, The
Tel: 44 1483

Steakhouse
1st Floor, Ancor Building, 85
Jeppe Street, Sunnyside

Yuet Wah
Tel: 323 2377

Chinese
137 Beatrix Street, Arcadia

Zappa's
Tel: 803 6122

Steak/Seafood/Chinese/Italian
378 Rossouw Street,
Murrayfield

Zillertal
Tel: 322 4080

A la carte
Louis Pasteur Building,
Prinsloo Street, central

Pubs and taverns

Barristers Tavern
Tel: 324 1207
Van Erkom Arcade, 217 Pretorius Street, central

Barristers Tavern
Tel: 21 6379
Cnr Paul Kruger & Vermeulen Streets, Pretoria central

Bootleggers
Tel: 47 2025
Glenwood Centre, Glenwood Road, Lynnwood Glen

Camel Tavern, The
Tel: 342 6655
367 Hilda Street, Hatfield

Castle Walk Tavern
Tel: 45 3370
Cnr Lois & Nossob Ave, Erasmusrand

Castle Walk Tavern
Tel: 546 9146
Madelief Centre, Daan de Wet Nel Street, Pretoria North

Hillside Tavern
Tel: 47 5119
320 The Hillside, Lynnwood

McGinty's
Tel: 342 0490
Hatfield Square, Hatfield

McGinty's
Tel: 341 2085
230 Beatrix Street, Arcadia

McGinty's
Tel: 991 3261
Shell Faerie Centre, Selikats Causeway, Faerie Glen

O'Hagan's Irish Pub & Grill
Tel: 342 9103
Duncan Walk, Duncan Street, Hatfield

O'Hagan's Irish Pub & Grill
Tel: 63 2345
Von Willich Ave, Centurion

O'Hagan's Irish Pub & Grill
Tel: 47 1425
Newlands Plaza, Lois Road, Newlands

O'Hagan's Irish Pub & Grill
Tel: 328 7040/328 7042
87 Soutpansberg Road, Villieria

O'Hagan's Irish Pub & Grill
Tel: 807 2783
Lynnwood Road extension, next to Wilgers Hospital

Sports Frog
Tel: 342 3959
1048 Burnett Street, Hatfield

Coffee shops

Amadeus
Tel: 323 6903
Koedoe Arcade, Pretoria central

Burgundy's Lounge
Tel: 348 1688
Menlyn Park Centre, Upper level

Café Florian
Tel: 346 3314
Brooklyn Mall, Fehrsen Street

Café le Tram
Tel: 320 4017
Tram Shed, Van der Walt St, Pretoria central

Café Montmartre
Tel: 21 6111
Burlington Arcade, Church Street, Pretoria central

Cafe Paradiso
Tel: 44 3622
Sunnypark Centre, Esselen St, Sunnyside

Café Riche
Tel: 328 3173
2 Church Square West, Pretoria central

Café Rossini
Tel: 46 5912
Brooklyn Mall, New Muckleneuk

Coffee at Burgundy's
Tel: 341 2276
Barclay Square, Rissik Street, Sunnyside

Coffee at Burgundy's
Tel: 342 5870
1119 MBI House, Burnett Street, Hatfield

Coffee at Burgundy's
Tel: 348 9111
Menlyn Park Centre, Menlyn

Coffee at Burgundy's
Tel: 548 2131
Kolonnade Centre, Zambesi Drive, Montana

Coffee at Burgundy's
Tel: 663 1937
Centurion Centre, Centurion

Grapevine, The
Tel: 44 6910
204 Sunnyside Galleries, Esselen St, Sunnyside

Greenfields
Tel: 362 6095
Cnr Hilda & Burnett Streets, Hatfield

Greenfields
Tel: 348 4999
Glen Gables, Cnr Lynnwood Rd & Gen Louis Botha Drive, Lynnwood

Greenfields
Tel: 320 7071
State Theatre foyer, Church Street, central

House of Coffees
Tel: 21 7268
Thibault Building, Pretorius Street, Pretoria central

Java
Tel: 362 3226
285 Lynnwood Road, Lynnwood

Koffiehoekie
Tel: 330 2340
Upper level, Jacaranda Centre, Rietfontein

Latin Coffee Bar & Grill
Tel: 320 8178
429 Church Street, Arcadia

Matjiesfontein
Tel: 807 131
183 Ou Klipmuur Ave, Willow Glen

Pebbles
Tel: 322 0289
24 Polley's Arcade, 231 Pretorius St, Pretoria central

Pepper Tree
Tel: 44 5281
Hotel 224, Leyds Street, Arcadia

Ritz Coffee Bar
Tel: 320 4196
Shop 3B, The Tramshed, Van der Walt St, Pretoria central

Rio Tech
Tel: 21 5244
396 Church Street, Pretoria central

Tiffiny's
Tel: 346 2480
Brooklyn Mall, Fehrsen Street

Tea Gardens

Café Rose
Tel: 342 2064
Venning Park, Eastwood Street, Hatfield

Café Wien
Tel: 320 0229
Burgerspark, Jacob Maré Street, Pretoria central

Country Lane
Tel: 345 2096
Waterkloof Agricultural Holdings, Waterkloof

Déjà vu
Tel: 329 3539
78 Annie Botha Ave, Riviera

Die Stoep
Tel: 335 6609
404 Nicholson Street, Mayville

Edelweiss
Tel: 808 1016
Moloto Road, Roodeplaat Dam

Jan Smuts House
Tel: 667 1176
Doringkloof, Irene

Ludwig's Rose Farm
Tel: 544 0144
Off N1 Motor Way, Wallmansthal exit

Prince of Wales
Tel: 322 2805
Melrose House, Scheiding Street, Pretoria central

Plumbago
Tel: 348 7773
Gen Louis Botha Drive, Lynnwood

Sammy Marks
Tel: 803 6158
Sammy Marks Museum, Old Bronkhorstspruit Rd

Shelanti
Tel: 663 3450
263 Jean Ave, Centurion

Sinkhuis, Die
Tel: 329 0762
59 Lys Street, Riviera

Zebediela
Tel: 991 4535
1029 Zebediela Street, Faerie Glen

Tea garden in Venning Park, Schoeman Street, among the roses

Hotels (5 star)

The Sheraton
Tel: 429 9999
Fax: 429 9300

Cnr Wessels and Church Streets
Arcadia (opposite Union Buildings)

Accommodation

Hotels (4 star)

Centurion Lake Hotel
Tel: 663 1825
Fax: 663 2760

1001 Lenchen Avenue,
Centurion

Holiday Inn Crown Plaza
Tel: 341 1571/341 1764
Fax: 44 7534
Toll-free: 0800 11 77 11

Beatrix Street

Hotels (3 star)

Arcadia Hotel
Tel: 326 9311
Fax: 326 1067

515 Proes Street

Diep in die Berg
Tel: 807 0111/3
Fax: 807 0112

Cnr Disselboom & Hans
Strÿdom Ave, Wapadrand

Farm Inn, The
Tel: 809 0266
Fax: 809 0146

Oasis Farm, Lynnwood Road
extension

Hotel Best Western Pretoria
Tel: 341 3473
Fax: 44 2258

Central reservation office: 341 3473
Fax: 341 4449
Toll-free: 080011 2889

World-wide reservations
Toll-free: 080012 0886

230 Hamilton Street

Karos Manhattan Hotel
Tel: 322 7635
Fax: 320 0721

Cnr Scheiding & Andries
Streets

Carousel Hotel,
Great North Road (N1)

Leriba Lodge
Tel: 660 3300
Fax: 660 2433

End Street,
Centurion

Other hotels & lodges

Boulevard Protea Hotel
Tel: 326 4806
326 5231
Fax: 326 1366

186 Struben Street

Capital Protea Hotel
Tel: 322 7795
Fax: 322 7797

390 Van der Walt Street

Court Classique
Tel: 344 4420
Fax: 344 4419

Cnr Becket & Schoeman
Streets, Arcadia

Courtyard, The
Tel: 342 4940
Fax: 342 4941

950 Park Street, Arcadia (Cnr
Hill Street)

Hatfield Manor Hotel
Tel: 342 3019
Fax: 342 1412

Cnr Burnett & Festival
Streets, Hatfield

Holiday Inn Express
Tel: 320 1060
Fax: 320 1208

632 Van der Walt Street,
Berea

Holiday Inn Garden Court
Tel: 342 1444
Fax: 342 3492

Cnr Pretorius & End Streets,
Hatfield

Hotel Formula 1
Tel: 323 8331
Fax: 323 8325

81 Pretorius Street (between
Bosman and Potgieter Streets)

Hotel Host International
Tel: 341 7455
Fax: 341 7455

573 Church Street East

Hotel 224
Tel: 44 5281
Fax: 44 3063

Cnr Schoeman & Leyds
Streets

Town Lodge, Atterbury Rd, near
Menlyn Shopping Mall

La Maison
Tel: 43 4341
Fax: 342 1531

235 Hilda Street, Hatfield

Park Lodge Hotel
Tel: 320 8230
Fax: 320 8230

Cnr Andries & Jacob Maré Streets

Pretoria Hof Hotel
Tel: 322 7570
Fax: 322 9461

291 Pretorius Street (Cnr Pretorius & Van der Walt Streets)

Roode Vallei Country Lodge
Tel: 808 1700
Fax: 808 1130

Plot 81, Kameeldrift (some 20 km north-east of the city centre)

Town Lodge
Tel: 348 2684

Atterbury Road (next to N1) Menlo Park

Victoria Hotel
Tel: 323 6052
Fax: 323 6052

200 Scheiding Street (opposite railway station)

Villa Via Luxury Hotel
Tel: 342 9130
Fax: 342 9131

Cnr Pretorius & Orient Streets, Arcadia

Furnished apartments

Clara Berea Lodge
Tel: 320 5665
Fax: 322 5601

Cnr Andries & Clara Streets, Berea

Clutton's Executive Apartments
Tel: 343 3238
Fax: 343 3238

266 Wessels Street, Arcadia

Don Apartments
Tel: 341 0098
Fax: 341 5552

599 Pretorius Street, Arcadia

The Don Arcadia 2
Tel: 343 3811
Fax: 343 0722

672 Schoeman Street, Arcadia

The Don Arcadia 3
Tel: 344 4100
Fax: 343 809

634 Park Street

Executive Cottages
Tel: 348 8698
Fax: 997 2222

14 Losch Place, Moreleta Park (Eastern suburbs)

Orange Court Lodge
Tel: 326 6346
Fax: 326 2492

540 Vermeulen Street, Pretoria central

Sentinel Executive Apartments
Tel: 343 3440
Fax: 343 7291

734 Arcadia Street, Arcadia

Trafalgar Court
Tel: 344 4100
Fax: 343 2809

634 Park Street, Arcadia

Unicadia
Tel: 347 7702

734 Park Street, Arcadia

Ute's Holiday Apartment
Tel: 997 2334
Fax: 997 2334 – ask for fax

Sunnyside

Boarding houses

AJO Centre
Tel: 326 4189
    235 Visagie Street

Ararat Youth Centre
Tel: 44 4355
    27 Troye Street

Capital Inn
Tel: 44 4261
    579 Church Street

Constantia Residence
Tel: 44 9247
    566 Schoeman Street

Fairmont
Tel: 344 0742
    622 Pretorius Street

Len Dan Accommodation
Tel: 344 2733
    708 Church Street

Nix Hotel
Tel: 341 5903
    72 Rissik Street

Panorama Inn
Tel: 344 3010
    706 Arcadia Street

Riantes Residence
Tel: 44 2715
    587 Church Street

Solario
Tel: 322 4119
    327 Visagie Street

The Foundation
Tel: 323 7181
    129 Vermeulen Street

Backpackers hostels and organizations

Pretoria Backpackers
Tel: 343 9754
Fax: 71 4383
    34 Bourke Street, Sunnyside

Sunnyside Backpackers
Tel: 343 7499
    430 Reitz Street, Sunnyside

Word of Mouth Backpackers
Tel: 341 9661
Fax: 341 1232145
    Berea Street, cnr Mears Street, Muckleneuk

Guest houses & bed & breakfast establishments

Central reservations offices

Bed and Breakfast Association of Pretoria
Tel: 083 212 1989
Fax: 083 8212 1989

Farm Holidays Association
Tel: 333 8021

Guest House Association of Pretoria
Tel: 43 3711/98 4515/344 4850

Hospitality and Touring
Tel: 361 3597
E-mail: handt@global.co.za

Jacana Country Homes
Tel: 346 3550/1/2
Fax: 346 2499

Pretoria Guest House Reservations
Tel: 46 5327
Fax: 46 9276
Cell: 082 566 3958

Rikita Guest Houses
Tel: 46 8779
Cell: 082 494 7812

Central Pretoria and eastern and southern suburbs

Amici Bed & Breakfast (C)
Tel: 344 5094
Cell: 083 449 8640

179 Beckett Street, Arcadia

Anderson Guest House (E)
Tel & Fax: 362 2710

*Brooklyn Guest Houses
Central Reservations Tel:* 362
1728/362 4993
13 Anderson Street, Brooklyn

Anne's Guest House (EE)
Tel: 807 2089/807 2027
Fax: 807 3693
Cell: 083 250 4663/083 272 5120
E-mail: annerich@satis.co.za

(Satour accredited and B&B
Association of Pretoria)
374 Erlon Street, The Willows

Annette's Bed & Breakfast (SEE)
Tel & Fax: 998 5772

522 Jonathan Street,
Waterkloof Glen

Aquarius Guest House (EE)
Tel: 803 2403
Fax: Ask for fax
Cell: 082 893 9342

Cnr Rosalind & 119 Rubida
Street, Murrayfield

Avalon (E)
Tel: 362 3151
Fax: 362 3151

(Satour Accredited, B&B
Association of Pretoria
281 Brooks Street, Brooklyn

Battiss Guest House (EE)
Tel & Fax: 46 7318

Fook Island, 92 20th Street,
Menlo Park

Bay Berry House (S)
Tel: 46 6627
Fax: 46 3076
Cell: 082 562 5820

86 Frans Oerder Street,
Groenkloof

Bay Tree Guest House, The (S)
Tel: 44 2462
Fax: 44 5596

(Satour accredited, Guest
House Association of SA)
225 St Patrick's Road,
Muckleneuk

B' Guest House (C)
Tel: 344 0524
Fax: 344 4023

751 Park Street, Arcadia

Bed & Breakfast in Brooklyn (EE)
Tel & Fax: 46 3172
Cell: 082 451 7433

373 Pienaar Street, Brooklyn

Berg Villa (C)
Tel: 342 8451
Fax: 342 8452
Cell: 083 268 9087

790 Government Avenue,
Arcadia

Birdwood Guest House (C)
Tel: 43 4905
Fax: 342 3997

(Satour accredited and B&B
Association of SA)
976 Arcadia Street, Arcadia

Blair Castle Guest House (EE)
Tel: 807 2875

Meadow Avenue, Willow
Glen

Blue Angel (EE)
Tel: 346 5800
Cell: 082 553 1276

941 Duncan St, Brooklyn

Bond Street Guest House (C)
Tel: 344 2767
Fax: 344 5082
Cell: 083 260 8323

18 Bond Street, Clydesdale
(Sunnyside area)

Bosau Guest House (EE)
Tel: 804 1728/804 9121
Fax: 804 1093
Cell: 083 227 8276

88 Van der Merwe Ave,
Silverton Ridge

Brandon House (SSE)
Tel & Fax: 45 1833

345 Aquilla Road, Waterkloof
Ridge

Brooklyn Guest House (C)
Tel: 362 1728
Fax: 362 1727

*Central Reservations Brooklyn
Guest Houses Tel: 362 1728/
362 4993*
128 Murray Street, Brooklyn

Brooklyn Lodge (EE)
Tel: 46 3936/7/8
Fax: 46 2988

Cnr Bronkhorst & Tram
Streets, New Muckleneuk

Brooks Cottage (C)
Tel: 362 3150
Fax: 323 0052
Cell: 082 448 3902

283 Brooks Street, Brooklyn

Bryntirion House (C)
Tel: 343 7092
Fax: 343 7076
Cell: 082 5544543

195 Pine Street, Arcadia

Cabriere Guest House (SSE)
Tel: 347 6284
Cell: 083 459 4073

377 Rigel Ave, Erasmusrand

Carmen Guest House (SSE)
Tel & Fax: 347 9051
Cell: 082 574 3864

258 Waenhuiskrans Street,
Erasmusrand

Chancellor's Court (C)
Tel: 344 1404
Fax: 344 0465

797 Park Street, Clydesdale
(Sunnyside area)

Chapters Guest House (EE)
Tel & Fax: 46 9059

31 Murray Street, Brooklyn

Christ Alone Bed & Breakfast
(EE)
Tel: 43 2420

58 Doreen Street, Colbyn

Clydesdale Cottage (C)
Tel: 344 2988
Cell: 082 550 5938

417 Kirkness Street, Clydesdale

Colbyn Guest Lodge (EE)
Tel & Fax: 43 6426
Cell: 083 284 6379

107 Amos Street, Colbyn

Cornerstone Bed & Breakfast
(SSE)
Tel: 348 8716
Cell: 082 576 7040

209 Kassia Ave, Newlands

Country Estate Exotica (EE)
Tel: 807 1700/2
Fax: 807 1701

Plot 76 Lynnwood Road, The
Willows

De Zoete Inval Guest House
(EE)
Tel: 998 8081
Fax: Ask for fax

1017 St Bernard Drive,
Garsfontein

De Zoete Verblijf (C)
Tel: 341 9239
Fax: 341 9239
Cell: 082 955 0372/082 964 3737

114 Gerhard Moerdijk Street,
Sunnyside

Die Werf (EE)
Tel: 991 1809
Fax: 991 0674

Plot 66, Olympus Drive,
Olympus

Diep in die Berg (EE)
Tel & Fax: 807 0111/3
Cnr Hans Strydom &
Disselboom Ave, Wapadrand

Domein B&B (SSE)
Tel: 45 2997
Fax: 347 1277
Cell: 082 447 5684

Satour accredited, B&B
Association of SA)
Waterkloof

Doorknob Bed & Breakfast (EE)
Tel: 993 5360
Cell: 083 227 4148
Fax: 326 4954

24 La Mancha Gen Louis
Botha Drive, Waterkloof Glen

El Nise Guest House (EE)
Tel: 46 5694
Cell: 082 956 4445
Fax: 346 1644

21 Ninth Street, Menlo Park

Embassy Gasthaus/Kia Ora (C)
Tel: 322 4803
Fax: 322 4816
E-mail: kia-ora@pixie.co.za

257 Jacob Maré Street,
Pretoria central

Emilienne B&B (EE)
Tel: 991 0559
Fax: 991 3851

777 Tiperary Way, Faerie Glen

Estelle's Guest House (NEE)
Tel: 329 0345 (a/h) or
322 7632 x 12 (w)
Fax: 322 7939

807 Antoinette Street, Villieria

Executive Choice for Guests (EE)
Tel: 804 6129
Cell: 083 310 2626

    30 Aloe Avenue, Lydiana

Frauenstein Guest House (C)
Tel & Fax: 343 8477

    453 Berea Street,
    Muckleneuk

Gannabos Guest House (EE)
Tel: 803 2764

    83 Amandel Ave, Val de Grace

Garden Cottage (SSE)
Tel & Fax: 46 2667

    218 Argo Place, Waterkloof
    Ridge

Genadeprag Guest House
(SSE)
Tel: 345 2633
Fax: 428 0712

    25 Tromp Crescent, Elardus
    Park Ext. 1

God's Window (EE)
Tel & Fax: 807 0902
Cell: 082 490 4144

    996 Wagon Wheel Ave,
    Wapadrand

**Green Gables Bed &
Breakfast** (EE)
Tel: 807 2449
Cell: 083 273 5667

    (Satour accredited and B&B
    Association of Pretoria)
    558 Witogie Street, The
    Willows

Green Gates (SSE)
Tel & Fax: 46 2761
Cell: 083 290 3185

    262 Indus Street, Waterkloof
    Ridge

Greenwoods Guest House (EE)
Tel: 348 7929
Fax: 47 1749
Cell: 083 305 9777

    425 Walter Bunton Street,
    Garsfontein

Guest House Seidel (EE)
Tel: 348 6282
Fax: 348 7791

    337 The Rand, Lynnwood

Guineafowl Lodge (EE)
Tel & Fax: 47 5946
Cell: 082 415 1117

    139 Pennys Way, Glenwood
    Village

Hamkari Guest House (EE)
Tel: 991 3195
Fax: 991 1014
E-mail: explorer@iafrica.com

    6 Val's Crescent, Faerie Glen

Hammy's Country Studio (SSE)
Tel & Fax: 480 0650

    Plot No 16, Rietfontein,
    Wingate Park

Harri's Place (EE)
Tel: 997 1617/997 2422
Fax: 997 1617

    5 Claudius Place, Moreleta
    Park

Hatfield B&B (C)
Tel: 362 5387
    1265 Arcadia Street

Haus Bamberg (EE)
Tel: 46 3652
Fax: 346 2060
Cell: 083 3023 210

    (Satour accredited, Guest
    House Association of SA)
    367 Albert Street, Waterkloof

Hospersa Guest House (NN)
Tel: 332 1952

    Cnr Walter & Trumpher
    Streets, Waverley

Howard's Place (EE)
Tel & Fax: 333 2607

    1301 Whisteltree Drive,
    Queenswood

Huis en Haard (EE)
Tel: 342 1618
Fax: 342 5925

    10 Glyn Street, Colbyn

Ingrid's Guest House (EE)
Tel: 807 4167
Fax: 807 1601

    541 Witogie Street, The
    Willows

Inkwazi Bed & Breakfast (EE)
Tel: 997 1376
Fax: 997 1376
Cell: 082 894 4727

    (Satour accredited, B&B
    Association of Pretoria)
    Moreleta Park

Intermezzo Guest House (C)
Tel: 344 2826
Fax: 341 5825

    35 Bond Street, Clydesdale

Isabel's Bed & Breakfast (EE)
Tel: 46 8993
Cell: 083 431 9795

    13 Nuwe Hoop Street, Alphen
    Park

Jadehaus (EE)
Tel & Fax: 807 4507

    533 Rossouw Street, The
    Willows

Jakaranda Lodge (NN)
Tel: 330 2424
Fax: Ask for fax

    Cnr 19th Ave & Swemmer
    Street, Rietfontein

Jane-Anne's Junction (EE)
Tel & Fax: 803 3535
Cell: 083 306 9718

    175 Rubida Street, Murrayfield

**Kaye Rive Health & Stress
Lodge** (C)
Tel: 329 4218
Fax: 329 4235

    259 Soutpansberg Road,
    Rietondale

Kelkiewyn (SSE)
Tel & Fax: 347 7644
Cell: 082 574 7031

    321 Rooiribbok Street,
    Waterkloof Ridge Ext. 11

Kia Ora Embassy Gasthaus (C)
Tel: 322 4803
Fax: 322 4816

    257 Jacob Mare Street,
    Sunnyside

Kleineweide Guesthouse (SSE)
Tel: 345 1666
Fax: 345 3451
Cell: 082 572 0878

    53 Jochem Street, Waterkloof
    Agricultural Holdings

Kloof House (SS)
Tel: 46 4600
Fax: 46 4348

366 Aries Street, Waterkloof Ridge

Kloof House Annex (C)
Tel: 46 4600
Fax: 46 4385

346 Olivier Street, Brooklyn

Kosmos Guest House (C)
Tel: 341 0890/49
Fax: 341 2052

Cnr Rissik & Joubert Street, Sunnyside

Kotana Guest House (EE)
Tel: 997 1464
Fax: 997 1464

699 Toermalyn, Moreleta Park

Krit Guest House (NN)
Tel: 332 2886
Fax: 332 2746

1376 Dickenson Ave, Waverley

La Maison (C)
Tel: 43 4341
Fax: 342 1531

(*** Satour grading and Guest House Association of SA)
235 Hilda Street, Hatfield

La Rochelle (SSE)
Tel & Fax: 46 6815

28 Plough Ave, Waterkloof Ridge

Lily's Lodge (C)
Tel & Fax: 362 0322

163 Lunnon Road, Hillcrest

Little Gem Guest Cottage (EE)
Tel: 361 6769
Cell: 082 920 6602

384C Kings Highway, Lynnwood

"Little Wisley" (SS)
Tel & Fax: 347 1729

607 Goudsnip Street, Monument Park

Loerie Lodge (B&B) (EE)
Tel & Fax: 46 5928

49 Pinaster Ave, Maroelana

Louis John Haven (EE)
Tel: 997 0565

6 Louis John Hills, Louis John Street, Moreleta Park

Lynnwood Manor Bed & Breakfast (EE)
Tel & Fax: 361 1780
Cell: 083 375 4148

19 Hilden Road, Lynnwood Manor

Maldon Guest House (EE)
Tel: 348 4959
Fax: 348 4634

49 Maldon Road, Lynnwood Glen

Malvern Guest House (C)
Tel: 341 7212
Fax: Ask for fax

575 Shoeman Street, Arcadia

Marvol Manor House (SSE)
Tel: 346 1774
Fax: 346 1776

358 Aries Street, Waterkloof Ridge

McWilson's Lodge (EE)
Tel: 803 2139

Meyers Park

Meintjeskop Guest House (C)
Tel: 43 3711/342 0738
Fax: 43 4037
Cell: 082 554 0125

145 Eastwood Street, Arcadia

Mellow Place Country House (EE)
Tel: 46 2887
Cell: 082 578 1683
Fax: 46 5102

1 Thomas Edison Street, Menlo Park

Menlolane Guesthouse & Coffee Shop (EE)
Tel: 46 3518
Fax: 46 4189
Cell: 082 570 6895

28 13th Street, Menlo Park

Merino Bed & Breakfast (SSE)
Tel & Fax: 46 3002
Cell: 082 963 7676

250 Milner Street, Waterkloof

Milner 246 (SE)
Tel & Fax: 46 7180
Cell: 082 566 1496
E-mail: Leo@hixnet.co.za

246 Milner Street, Waterkloof

Mutsago Guest House (E)
Tel: 43 7193
Fax: 43 7635

327 Festival Street, Hatfield

Oorkant Loftus (C)
Tel & Fax: 344 2289/343 2044

439 Kirkness Street, Sunnyside

Ormonde House (C)
Tel & Fax: 343 8453
Cell: 082 490 3654

34 Ormonde Street, Muckleneuk

Oxnead Guest House (EE)
Tel: 993 4515
Fax: 998 9168
Cell: 083 268 6865

802 Johanita Street, Moreleta Park

Pandora Guest House (C)
Tel: 46 2104
Fax: 46 3076

103 Frans Oerder Street, Groenkloof

Papa Joe Slovak and International Guest House (WW)
Tel: 327 0344
Fax: 327 0343

470 Frederick Street, Pretoria West

Paula's Place (EE)
Tel & Fax: 46 5934

333 Charles Street, Brooklyn

Pebble 'n Palms (EE)
Tel: 43 3739
Fax: 43 3739
Cell: 082 577 7575

124 Alcock Street, Colbyn

Premier Guest House (SSE)
Tel & Fax: 46 4894

217 Premier Ave, Waterkloof

Pretoria Accommodation (NN)
Tel: 332 1384 (after 18:00)

1238 Breyer Avenue,
Waverley

Pretoria Guest House (E)
Tel: 335 3188

705 Kensington Avenue, cnr
Fred Nicholson, Parktown

Pretoria-East Guesthouse (EE)
Tel: 998 5915

556 Airedale Street,
Garsfontein

**Queens Gardens Bed &
Breakfast** (EE)
Tel: 333 2281
Cell: 082 415 0720

Queenswood Heights

**Rietvlei View Bed &
Breakfast** (SSE)
Tel: 345 1040
Fax: 345 1042
Cell: 082 412 8848

Plot 11A, View Street,
Waterkloof Agricultural
Holdings

Roastmasters (EE)
Tel: 807 4401
Fax: 807 4370

130 Meadow Ave, Willow
Glen

Ronde Geluk Guest House
(C)
Tel: 341 9221
Fax: 341 9222

570 Pretorius Street, Arcadia

Rose Cottage (C)
Tel: 46 6903

34 College Ave, Bailey's
Muckleneuk

**Rose Cottage Bed &
Breakfast** (C)
Tel: 341 9239
Cell: 082 964 3737/082 955 0372
Fax: 341 9239

House 32, Oeverzicht Art
Village, Gerhard Moerdijk
Street, Sunnyside

Rose Guest House, The (EE)
Tel & Fax: 362 0031
Cell: 082 652 5244

12 & 36 Murray Street,
Brooklyn

Rosetoli (EE)
Tel & Fax: 43 3917

20 Frances Street, Colbyn

Rosslie's Guest House (EE)
Tel: 361 2330
Fax: 348 3047

133 Camelia Ave, Lynnwood
Ridge

Rozenhof (GH) (EE)
Tel: 46 8075
Fax: 46 8085

525 Alexander Street,
Brooklyn

Selous Manor (EE)
Tel: 46 8728
Fax: 46 1980

178 Olivier Street, Brooklyn

Sentosa Guest House (C)
Tel: 344 0205
Fax: 344 0225

170 Smith Street,
Muckleneuk

Shere View Guest Lodge (EE)
Tel: 809 0096/809 0003
Cell: 082 892 7354/083 310 2625
Fax: 809 0177

Plot 15, Shere, Lynnwood
Road extension

Sherwood Forest (C)
Tel & Fax: 344 4850/344 1398
Cell: 082 900 1669

131 Hugh Street, Sunnyside

Silverton Guest House (EE)
Tel: 804 1597
Cell: 082 572 7048
Fax: 804 1597

460 President Street,
Silverton

St Aden's Bed & Breakfast (C)
Tel & Fax: 344 0594
Cell: 083 250 7101
E-mail: martin@ilink.nis.za

360 Berea Street,
Muckleneuk

St Aden's Manor House (C)
Tel & Fax: 344 3562/344 4318
E-mail: martin@ilink.nis.za

605 Jorissen Street,
Sunnyside

Sunset View Bed & Breakfast
(NE)
Tel: 329 1808
Cell: 082 772 2489

219 Union Street, Riviera

Swaeltjie Guest House (EE)
Tel: 811 0496
Cell: 082 410 3189
Fax: 811 0388

Plot 240, Swaeltjie Holdings,
Lynnwood Ridge

Ted's Place (EE)
Tel & Fax: 807 2803

Cnr Wagon Wheel &
Slingeroord Roads, Wapadrand

"That's It" Guest House (C)
Tel: 344 3404
Fax: 343 5270

5 Brecher Street, Clydesdale

Tiptol Guest House (SSE)
Tel & Fax: 346 1934
Cell: 082 414 0325

345 Clark Street, Waterkloof

Two Oaks (Accredited) (EE)
Tel & Fax: 361 3597

407 Om die Berg Street,
Lynnwood

Villa Elonda (EE)
Tel & Fax: 991 1477
Cell: 082 568 6075

509 Mississippi Street, Faerie
Glen

Villa Monica (C)
Tel: 46 5106/342 7099 – ask for fax
Cell: 082 600 0543

308 Hill Street, Arcadia

Villa Sterne (SSE)
Tel: 346 2255

212 Johan Rissik Drive,
Waterkloof Ridge

Villa Willowdene (EE)
Tel: 807 0457

591 Willowdene Street, The
Willows X15

Waterhouse, The (EE)
Tel: 991 2823
Fax: 991 1808

    439 Stonewall Street, Faerie Glen

Whistletree Guest House (EE)
Tel: 333 9915
Fax: 333 9917

    1267 Whistletree Drive, Queenswood

Willows Guest House, The (EE)
Tel: 807 5038
Fax: 807 5344
E-mail: willows@webware.co.za

    29 Beuke Oord, The Willows

Centurion (south of Pretoria)

Bloemhoek Bed & Breakfast
Tel & Fax: 654 6302
Cell: 082 555 6566

    73 Oxford Street, Clubview

Centurion Guest House
Tel & Fax: 664 4685

    277 Van Riebeeck Ave, Lyttelton

Centurion Rendezvous
Tel & Fax: 347 2018
Cell: 082 458 6886

    99 Karin Ave, Doringkloof

Classic Africa
Tel: 666 8565/666 9506
Fax: 666 8565
Cell: 083 325 0675/082 457 7888

    Plot 108, Erasmus Ave, Raslouw, Wierda Park

Doringkloof Guest House (B&B)
Tel & Fax: 667 3382

    207 Ronel Street, Doringkloof

Edgehill
Tel: 667 3561
Fax: 667 2814
Cell: 082 570 3853

    113 Umtata Ave, Doringkloof

Edwards Bed & Breakfast
Tel & Fax: 661 8459

    44 Kestrel Ave, Rooihuiskraal

Green, The
Tel: 660 1769
Fax: 660 1142
Cell: 082 578 4861

    156 Stymie Ave, Clubview-West

Helinda Guest House (B&B)
Tel: 664 0574
Fax: 664 3218
Cell: 082 920 0748

    172 Monument Ave, Lyttelton Manor

Icarus Inn
Tel: 654 6479

    20 Cedar Ave, Clubview

Irene Guest House
Tel: 667 2712
Fax: 667 1858

    43 Arnold Street, Irene

Leriba Lodge (Hotel)
Tel: 660 3300
Fax: 660 3324

    End Street, Clubview

Natanja Guest House
Tel & Fax: 664 6601
Cell: 082 570 3602

    150 Alethea Street, Lyttelton

Pines, The
Tel: 664 4442
Fax: 664 1949
Cell: 083 445 1316

    206 Basden Ave, Lyttelton Agricultural Holdings

2 Calls Accommodation
Tel: 667 1520

North of Pretoria

Hedgehog Guest Cottage
Tel: 549 2925
Cell: 082 892 3028
Fax: 549 1355

    316 Kremetart Ave, Amandasig (NNW)

Little Ibilanhlolo Bushveld Lodge
Tel & Fax: 808 1033

    Kameelfontein (NNE)

Sunbird Guest House
Tel: 546 2233

    366 Danie Theron Street, Pretoria North (NN))

Banking

Banking hours

Most banks are open from 09:00 to 15:30 on weekdays and from 09:00 (or 08:30) to 11:00 on Saturdays.

Foreign exchange

All commercial banks have a foreign exchange department which is open during the above hours. A 24-hour foreign exchange service is available at Johannesburg International Airport. The main branches of the major banks, listed below, all have foreign exchange facilities.

For further details on any particular bank, contact the **Pretoria Tourist Information Bureau** at 313 7694/313 7980 or consult the Pretoria telephone directory.

Major banks

Only head offices/main branches are listed here. Every bank has a number of branches throughout the city where normal banking services are available. Please consult the Pretoria telephone directory.

ABSA Bank
Tel: 320 6700

Volkskas Bank Building
Van der Walt Street

Bank of Athens
Tel: 21 8985

Tomkor Centre
131 Du Toit Street

First National Bank
Tel: 325 2300

Eastern side of Church
Square

Mercantile Lisbon
Tel: 322 6416

Bank of Lisbon Building
394 Paul Kruger Street

Natal Building Society
Tel: 325 2800

259 Pretorius Street

Nedbank
Tel: 21 2541

Nedbank Building
Cnr Andries & Church Streets

Perm Bank
Tel: 326 0981

Sancardia Centre
Church Street, Arcadia

Standard Bank of SA
Tel: 351 3000

Standard Bank Building
Church Street

Credit card facilities

Most credit cards are accepted, as are traveller's cheques, provided they are in an acceptable currency.

Transport and tour operators

Pretoria airport shuttle
Tel: 323 0904
Cell: 082 566 7242

An hourly shuttle operates between Pretoria and Johannesburg International Airport, departing from the Tourist Rendezvous Centre, cnr Prinsloo and Vermeulen Streets.

Coach hire/buses from Pretoria

Baz Bus (The Round South Africa Budget Bus)
Tel: 323 1222/323 7493/439 2323
Fax: 439 2343/323 7488

- No time limit, hop-on hop-off, on-board information, Youth hostels door to door, fun way to meet other travellers, start from anywhere on the route
- Johannesburg/Pretoria – Cape Town – Durban – Johannesburg/Pretoria

Ebersohn Bus Service
Tel: (01464) 2005
Cell: 083 730 7231

- Coaches for hire: 70–75 passengers per coach
- Tours also organized for school/educational groups

Elwierda Coaches
Tel: 664 5880

- Scheduled bus service between Pretoria (State Theatre, Prinsloo Street) and Johannesburg (Carlton Centre, cnr Fox & End Streets)
- Depart: Pretoria/Johannesburg: 06:25 from State Theatre; Mon–Fri 06: 40 from Clubview/Lyttelton off-ramp

- Depart: Johannesburg/Pretoria 16:15 from Carlton Centre back to Pretoria, Mon–Fri

Explorer Coach Lines
Tel: 563 0200

- Coach hire: Luxury (48 seater), semi-luxury (60 seater), board-room coach (28 seater) with boardroom facilities, super luxury (42 seater)

Greyhound Citiliner
Tel: 323 1154 or
Computicket: 328 4040

- Depart from Pretoria Railway Station (east side right next to the station)
- Pretoria to: Cape Town, Durban, Port Elizabeth, Nelspruit, Kimberley, Bulawayo, Mossel Bay/Knysna, Harare

Impala Bus Service
Tel: (011) 974 6561 or
Computicket (credit card payment): 326 4684

- Trips to Sun City from Pretoria on weekends: Saturdays and Sundays, contact Computicket personally (see list of branches under Entertainment)
- Daily trips to Sun City from Johannesburg International Airport
- Coaches for hire

Intercape Mainliner
Tel: 654 4114 or
Computicket personally

- Depart from Pretoria Railway Station (east of station building)
- Pretoria to: Cape Town, Port Elizabeth, East London, Plettenberg Bay, George, Upington, Windhoek

Municipal buses
Tel: 308 0839/308 0840
Municipal City Bus Times:
308 0229
308 0229: Municipal bus hire

- Timetables and fares available from selected chemists, and from the Bus Information Office on Church Square

North Link Transport
Tel: 323 0379

- Coaches from Pretoria to: Pietersburg, Phalaborwa, Louis Trichardt
- Depart from: Pretoria Railway Station

Robbert Bus Service/Coach Hire
Tel: 376 2373
Cell: 083 442 1406

- Coaches for hire

Springbok Atlas Coach Charters
Tel: (011) 396 1053

- Fleet of over 110 vehicles
- Luxury and economy vehicles ranging from 8 to 60 seaters

Sun City Trips/Super Tours
Tel: 341 9239
Cell: 082 964 3737/082 955 0372

- Depart: Tue to Fri: 09:00 from Sammy Marks Square, Cnr Prinsloo & Vermeulen Streets; 17:00 from Sun City, Welcome Centre
- Reservations essential

Translux
Tel: 315 2333

- Departure/Arrival: Pretoria Railway Station
- Pretoria to: Cape Town, Durban, Umtata, Port Elizabeth, Queenstown, East London, Knysna, George, Graaff-Reinet, Cradock, Harare, Lusaka, Bulawayo/Victoria Falls, Beitbridge, Bloemfontein

Transtate Express
Tel: 315 8069/315 8032

- Long distance coaches
- Coach hire

Zimbabwe Travel
Tel: 567 4264

- Luxury coach tours
- Pretoria – Beit Bridge (Bulawayo & Victoria Falls). Trips twice weekly
- Depart from BP service station, cnr Charles Street & Atterbury Road

Car hire

Avis
Tel: 325 1490
Toll free: 0800 02 1111
  70 Schoeman Street, Pretoria central; cnr Atterbury & Charles Sts, next to N1

Budget
Tel: 341 4650
Toll free: 0800 01 6622
  465 Church Street, Pretoria central

Economy Car Hire
Toll free: 0800 011 257
  Centurion

Europcar Inter-rent
Tel: 341 6161
Toll free: 0800 01 1344
  540 Pretorius Street, Arcadia

Imperial
Tel: 323 3259
Toll free: 0800 13 1000
  Cnr Pretorius & Potgieter Streets, Pretoria central

International Car Hire
Tel: 342 3543/4
  1169 Church Street, Hatfield

Pender Car Rental
Tel: 46 8016
Cell: 082 453 8650 a/h
  222 Albert Street, Waterkloof

Tempest
Tel: 324 5007
Toll free: 0800 03 1666
  Boulevard Protea Hotel, Struben Street, Pretoria central

Taxis

City Bug
Tel: 663 6316

City Taxis
Tel: 21 5742/3/4

Dial a Dove
Tel: 333 4424
  333 3103

Five Star
Tel: 320 7513/4

Flash Taxis
Tel: 323 6376
  323 6378

Rixi Taxis
Tel: 325 8072/3/4

Transcab
Tel: 324 5051

Trains

Blue Train (main line)
Tel: 663 6316

Commuter trains – information
Tel: 315 2007

Main line railway:
Departures/arrivals:
Tel: 315 2757

Reservations:
Tel: 315 2401

Lost property/luggage:
Tel: 315 2264

Rovos Rail (Steam train)
Tel: 323 6052
Fax: 323 0843

Magalies Valley Steamer
Tel: 773 9068
Fax: 774 2121

Treat yourself to a steam-train trip

Fly away! Private charter flights can be arranged from Wonderboom Airport, north of the city.

Fly anywhere from Wonderboom Airport

Airports

Johannesburg International Airport

Arrival/departure enquiries:
(011) 975 9963

Airfreight enquiries:
(011) 978 4699

Other enquiries:
(011) 356 1111

Locality: R21 past Kempton Park, east of Johannesburg, south of Pretoria

Grand Central Airport

Tel: (011) 805 3166

Locality: Midrand, south of Pretoria

Lanseria

Tel: (011) 659 2750

Locality: South-western outskirts of Johannesburg

Rand Airport

Tel: (011) 827 8884

Locality: South-eastern outskirts of Johannesburg, near Germiston

Swartkop Airforce Base

Tel: 351 2111

Locality: South-west of Pretoria

Waterkloof Airforce Base

Tel: 672 4911

Locality: South of Pretoria

Wonderboom Airport

Tel: 567 1188

Locality: North of Pretoria

Tour operators

Abba Tours and Safaris

Tel: 323 1332

- Pretoria and game parks

Adventure Travel Africa

Tel: 341 1232

- Day trips, Kruger National Park, Drakensberg, etc

Africa-in Tours & Safaris

Tel: 803 5392

- Botswana, Kruger National Park, Victoria Falls, Chobe

African Vistas Travel & Tours

Tel: 325 7353

- Pretoria, Johannesburg, Soweto, Sun City, Mamelodi, Ndebele, Lion/Rhino Park, & surrounding areas

Barefoot in Africa Adventures

Tel: 664 3246

Tailormade tours, Package tours, Fly-in Safaris, Golf course tours, Transfers

Bill Harrop's Balloon Safaris

Tel: (011) 705 3201

- 'Original' Balloon Safaris and selected Ballooning lodges

Candando Tours

Tel: 348 2871

City Tours Pretoria

Tel: 347 1000

- Pretoria and surrounding areas

C M Louw Tours

Tel: 342 5919
Cell: 083 251 3874

- Pretoria and surroundings

Dinky Safaris

Tel: 46 2345
Cell: 082 579 7823

- Lowveld tours

Drum Beat Safaris

Tel: 46 5959

- Local Pretoria, Local Johannesburg, Soweto, Mamelodi & Atteridgeville, Kruger National Park, Wild Life safaris, Photographic safaris, General tourism and countrywide

Executive Travel Services
Tel: 664 3462
Cell: 082 555 0026

Expeditionary Force
Tel: 667 2833

- Specialized historical tours

Exquisite tours
Tel: 543 0825

- Pretoria, Mpumalanga

Filler Tours
Cell: 082 956 0003/082 552 0915

- Specialize in day outings in and around Pretoria, Diamond and gem cutting works and traditional dinners, etc.

Footsoo Tours
Tel: 323 1332

- Day drives to game parks, trophy hunting, game photography

Freeway Tours
Tel: (011) 366 1747/828 2882

- For an affordable experience, transfers/tours to Sun City, drive through Soweto, Johannesburg, Pretoria, etc.

Get Set Tours
Tel: (0142) 97 2788

Green Rhino African Travel
Tel: 346 4599

Golfing Safaris
Tel: 802 0605

- Specializing in golf tours and packages

Guttera Tours
Tel: 333 2428

- Day tours in and around Pretoria, countrywide as well as Botswana, Namibia and overseas

Holidays for Africa
Tel: 803 4358

- Day tours in and around Pretoria, West coast, Garden Route and Klein Karoo, Mpumalanga and Kruger Park, Swaziland/Zululand and Durban

Inline Travel & Tours
Tel: 323 0450/323 0725

- Pretoria, surroundings and international tours

Inyanga Tours
Tel: 804 1593

- Personalized service: countrywide, especially game farms, flying safaris

Jacana Country Homes and Trails
Tel: 346 3550

- Country homes and cottages, bush camps, farm vacations, hiking, mountain bike and horse riding trails, country and adventure tours

Jimmy's Face to Face Tours
Tel: (011) 331 6109

- Soweto tours from Johannesburg

Kwanvelo
Tel: 348 6972

- Wildlife, day tours, white-water rafting

Loerie African Bush Adventures
Tel: (01211) 59 1324

- Pretoria and other speciality tours

Mag Chri Tours and Safaris
Tel: 664 1873

- SA, Mamelodi, Bo-Karoo, Kruger Park, Mpumalanga, Cape Town & Garden Route, Swaziland, Zimbabwe, Drakensberg, Umfolozi, tours in and around Pretoria

Marabou Safaris and Tours
Tel: (011) 968 1134

Norman and Olive Orsmond
Tel: 46 3172

- Pretoria, Mpumalanga. Satour registered tourist guide

Pretoria Tour
Tel: 330 1400

- Pretoria, Premier Diamond Mine

Prisma Travel
Tel: 341 0923

- Kruger National Park & Mpumalanga, Day tours, Swaziland & Zululand, Cape Town & Garden Route, Zimbabwe

Rainbow Travel
Tel: 346 3245

- Coach operator to Namibia, Zimbabwe and Namaqualand

Registour
Tel: 662 0047/98 1961

- Pretoria, Johannesburg, Mpumalanga

Safari Link
Tel: 348 7453

- Wildlife safaris and adventure, Pretoria and elsewhere

Sakabula Safaris and Tours
Tel: 998 8795

- Pretoria and surrounding areas; countrywide

South African Splendour Safaris and Tours
Tel: 333 2428/808 0990

Silver Cloud Tours and Safaris
Tel: 322 9596

- Shuttle service to and from Johannesburg International Airport, Shebeen and Jazz Club visits, cultural tours to Lesedi and the KwaNdebele Cultural villages, the Kruger National Park, Mpumalanga, Johannesburg and Gold Reef City

Small Five Tours and Safaris
Tel: 342 1639
Cell: 083 442 1480

- Gauteng, North West, Mpumalanga and Kwazulu-Natal, Johannesburg, Pretoria, Soweto, Lesedi, Sun City, Pilanesberg, Lion Park, Heia Safari and Kruger National Park

Sunrica Tours
Tel: 567 5992

- Tours in and around Pretoria

Super Tours
Tel: 341 9239
Cell: 082 964 3737

- Daily Sun City trips, Pilanesberg National Park, Pretoria, Mpumalanga, Kruger National Park

Tebu Travel and Tours
Tel: (011) 973 5329
Cell: 083 753 7637

Terry Wepener
Tel: 998 7823

- Pretoria, Satour registered tourist guide

Thabela Africa Town and Country Tours
Tel: 549 1008

- German guide, tours of Pretoria, Pilanesberg, Lesedi and Cheetah farm

The Baker's Dozen
Tel: 344 3197

- Specialized historical tours of the Union Building; 3 hour tour: groups and children welcome

Tokologo Tours
Tel: 330 0464

- Local, Kruger National Park, Northern Natal, Gauteng, Cullinan, Soweto, Sun City, De Wildt, etc.

Tourist in South Africa
Tel: 366 1747/828 2882
Cell: 083 268 4091

- Kruger National Park, Mabula Lodge, photographic safaris, animal breeding projects, crocodile farms, scenic routes, waterfalls, caves, Boer War graves, Jock of the Bushveld route, historic sites, Soweto, mine tours, Gold Reef City, trout fishing and curio shopping

Turafrica Travel Enterprises
Tel: 341 6089
Cell: 082 555 0026

- Cultural tours to and from South Africa, concentrating on music in its full spectrum. Clients consist of choirs, bands, orchestras, folk dancers, etc. Organize transport, accommodation and performances

Ubuntu Tours
Tel: 993 3163
Cell: 082 855 4602

- Cultural events and informal talk, Ubuntu Kraal in Soweto, Ubuntu wine tasting in Melville. Ideal for tourists, intercultural discourses, corporate education and other interested groups.

Ultimate Tours and Safaris
Tel: 567 2968
Cell: 082 901 1014

- Pretoria, surrounding areas and countrywide

Ulysses Tours and Safaris
Cell: 082 566 5506/082 5727 629

- Pretoria, Cullinan Diamond Mine, De Wildt Cheetah Research Centre, Johannesburg/Gold Reef City/ Soweto, Pilanesberg National Park, Sun City/Lost City, River Rafting, Hartebeespoort and Lesedi traditional village, Hot air ballooning, Loopspruit wine estate, Warmbaths mineral spa, Kruger National Park, Mpumalanga and many other services.

Whizzing Wheels Transfer Service
Tel: 326 5147
Cell: 082 967 2936

- Transfers: Pretoria/Sandton/ Centurion, etc

Wisani Tours
Tel: 373 0797

Wydah Tours
Tel: (011) 781 2093

- Overland tours, Gauteng and surroundings, Cape Town and surroundings, transfers to Sun City, Mpumalanga, etc, local ballooning and guest house accommodation

21

Foreign representation

Algeria (Embassy)
Tel: 342 5074
Fax: 342 6479
    950 Arcadia Street, Hatfield

Angola (Embassy)
Tel: 342 0049
Fax: 342 0049
    1030 Schoeman Street, Hatfield

Argentina (Embassy)
Tel: 43 3524
Fax: 43 3521
    200 Standard Plaza, 440 Hilda Street, Hatfield

Australia (High Commission)
Tel: 342 3740
Fax: 342 4222
    292 Orient Street, Arcadia

Austria (Embassy)
Tel: 46 2483
Fax: 46 1151
    1109 Duncan Street, Brooklyn

Bangladesh (High Commission)
Tel: 343 2105
Fax: 343 5222
    410 Farenden Street, Sunnyside

Belgium(Embassy)
Tel: 44 3201
Fax: 44 3216
    625 Leyds Street, Muckleneuk

Botswana (High Commssion)
Tel: 342 4760
Fax: 342 1845
    24 Amos Street, Colbyn

Brazil (Embassy)
Tel: 341 1741
Fax: 341 7547
    201 Leyds Street, Arcadia

Bulgaria (Embassy)
Tel: 342 3720
Fax: 342 3720
    1071 Church Street, Hatfield

American Embassy
877 Pretorius Street, Arcadia

Canada (High Commission)
Tel: 422 3000
Fax: 422 3053

    1103 Arcadia Street, Hatfield

Chile (Embassy)
Tel: 342 1511
Fax: 342 1658

    5th Floor, Campus Centre,
    1102 Burnett Street, Hatfield

China, People's Republic of
(Embassy)
Tel: 342 4194
Fax: 342 4244

    972 Pretorius Street, Arcadia

Colombia (Embassy)
Tel: 342 0211
Fax: 342 0216

    300 First National
    Building/Plaza, 1105 Park
    Street, Hatfield

Congo, Republic of (Embassy)
Tel: 342 5507
Fax: 46 4315

    960 Arcadia Street, Arcadia

Croatia, Republic of (Embassy)
Tel: 342 1206
Fax: 342 1819

    1160 Church Street, Colbyn

Cuba, Republic of (Embassy)
Tel: 346 2215
Fax: 346 2216

    45 Mackenzie Street, Brooklyn

Czech Republic (Embassy)
Tel: 342 3477
Fax: 43 2033

    936 Pretorius Street, Arcadia

Denmark (Embassy)
Tel: 322 0595
Fax: 322 0596

    8th Floor, Sanlam Centre, Cnr
    Andries & Pretorius Streets

Egypt (Embassy)
Tel: 343 1590
Fax: 343 1082

    270 Bourke Street,
    Muckleneuk

Eritrea (Embassy)
Tel: 333 1302
Fax: 333 2330

    1281 Cobham Road,
    Queenswood

Ethiopia (Embassy)
Tel: 342 6321
Fax: 342 8035

    2nd Floor, Southern Life
    Plaza, 1059 Schoeman Street,
    Hatfield

European Union (Delegation)
Tel: 46 4319
Fax: 46 9923

    2nd Green Park Estates, 27
    George Storrar Drive,
    Groenkloof

Finland (Embassy)
Tel 343 0275
Fax: 343 3095

    628 Leyds Street,
Muckleneuk

France (Embassy)
Tel: 43 5564
Fax: 43 3481

    807 George Ave, Arcadia

Gabon (Embassy)
Tel: 342 4376
Fax: 342 4375

    1st Floor, Southern Life Plaza,
Schoeman Street, Hatfield

Germany (Embassy)
Tel: 427 8900
Fax: 343 9401

    180 Blackwood Street,
Arcadia

Ghana (High Commission)
Tel: 342 5847
Fax: 342 5863

    1038 Arcadia Street, Hatfield

Greece (Embassy)
Tel: 43 7351
Fax: 43 4313

    995 Pretorius Street, Arcadia

Hungary (Embassy)
Tel: 43 3020
Fax: 43 3029

    959 Arcadia Street, Arcadia

India (High Commission)
Tel: 342 5392
Fax: 342 5310

    852 Schoeman Street, Cnr
Eastwood St, Arcadia

Indonesia (Embassy)
Tel: 342 3356
Fax: 342 3369

    949 Schoeman Street,
Arcadia

Iran, Islamic Republic of
(Embassy)
Tel: 342 5880
Fax: 342 1878

    1002 Schoeman Street,
Hatfield

Ireland (Embassy)
Tel: 342 5062
Fax: 342 4752

    Tulbagh Park, 1234 church
Street, Colbyn

Israel (Embassy)
Tel: 342 2684
Fax: 342 2365

    339 Hilda Street, Hatfield

Italy (Embassy)
Tel: 43 5541
Fax: 43 5547

    796 George Avenue, Arcadia

Ivory Coast (Côte d'Ivoire)
(Embassy)
Tel: 342 6913
Fax: 342 6713

    795 Government Avenue,
Arcadia

Japan (Embassy)
Tel: 342 2100
Fax: 43 3922

    Sanlam Building, 353 Festival
Street, Hatfield

Jordan (Embassy)
Tel: 342 8026
Fax: 342 7847

    209 Festival Street, Hatfield

Kenya (High Commission)
Tel: 342 5066
Fax: 342 5069

    302 Brooks Street, Menlo
Park

Korea, Republic of (Embassy)
Tel: 46 2508
Fax: 46 1158

    Block 3, Greenpark Estate, 27
George Storrar Drive,
Groenkloof

Kuwait, The State of (Embassy)
Tel: 342 0877
Fax: 342 0876

    890 Arcadia Street, Arcadia

Lesotho
Tel: 322 6090
Fax: 322 0373

    6th Floor, Momentum Centre,
343 Pretorius Street

Libya
Tel: 342 3903
Fax: 342 3904

    900 Church Street, Arcadia

Lichtenstein – Represented by Swiss Embassy

Luxembourg – Represented by Netherlands Consulate

Malawi (High Commission)
Tel: 342 0146
Fax: 342 0147

    770 Government Avenue, Arcadia

Mali (Embassy)
Tel: 342 7464
Fax: 342 0670

    Suite 106, Infotech Building, 1090 Arcadia Street, Hatfield

Malaysia (High Commission)
Tel: 342 5990
Fax: 43 7773

    950 Pretorius Street, Arcadia

Mauritius (High Commission)
Tel: 342 1283
Fax: 342 1286

    1163 Pretorius Street, Hatfield

Mexico (Embassy)
Tel: 342 5190
Fax: 342 5234

    Southern Life Plaza, Cnr Festival & Schoeman Streets, Hatfield

Morocco (Embassy)
Tel: 343 0230
Fax: 343 0613

    799 Schoeman Street, Arcadia

Mozambique (Embassy)
Tel: 343 7840
Fax: 343 6714

    199 Beckett Street, Arcadia

Namibia (High Commission)
Tel: 342 3520
Fax: 342 3565

    702 Church Street, Arcadia

Netherlands (Embassy)
Tel: 344 3910
Fax: 343 9950

    825 Arcadia Street, Arcadia

New Zealand (High Commission)
Tel: 342 8656
Fax: 342 8640

    1110 Arcadia Street, Hatfield

Nigeria, Federal Republic of (High Commission)
Tel: 343 2021
Fax: 343 1668

    138 Beckett Street, Arcadia

Norway (Embassy)
Tel: 323 4790
Fax: 323 4789

    7th Floor, Sancardia, 524 Church Street, Arcadia

Pakistan (High Commission)
Tel: 46 1080
Fax: 46 7824

    97 Charles Street, Brooklyn

Palestine, State of (Embassy)
Tel: 343 0668
Fax: 343 3458

    580 Kruin Street, Muckleneuk

Paraguay (Embassy)
Tel: 347 1047
Fax: 347 0403

    189 Strelitzia Road, Waterkloof Heights

Peru (Embassy)
Tel: 342 2390
Fax: 342 4944

    Suite 202, Infotech Building, 1090 Arcadia Street, Hatfield

Phillipines (Embassy)
Tel: 342 6920
Fax: 342 6666

    Southern Life Plaza, Cnr Schoeman & Festival Street, Hatfield

Poland (Embassy)
Tel: 43 2631
Fax: 43 2608

    14 Amos Street, Colbyn

Portugal (Embassy)
Tel: 341 2340
Fax: 341 3975

599 Leyds Street,
Muckleneuk

Romania (Embassy)
Tel: 46 6941
Fax: 46 6947

117 Charles Street, Brooklyn

Russian Federation (Embassy)
Tel: 362 1339
342 4630
Fax: 362 0116

Barclay Plaza, Park Street,
Hatfield
Also 316 Brooks Street,
Menlo Park

Rwanda
Tel: 46 0709
Fax: 46 0708

35 Marais Street, Brooklyn

Saudi Arabia
Tel: 343 1426

183 Blackwood Street,
Arcadia

Senegal (Embassy)
Tel: 342 6230
Fax: 342 6260

Infotech Building, 1049
Arcadia Street, Hatfield

Singapore (High Commission)
Tel: 343 4371
Fax: 343 3083

173 Beckett Street, Arcadia

Slovak Republic (Embassy)
Tel: 342 2051
Fax: 342 3688

930 Arcadia Street, Arcadia

Spain (Embassy)
Tel: 344 3875
Fax: 343 4891

169 Pine Street, Arcadia

Sudan, Republic of (Embassy)
Tel: 342 4538
Fax: 342 4539

1187 Pretorius Street,
Hatfield

Surinam
Tel: 344 3910

Represented by the
Netherlands Consul

Swaziland (High Commission)
Tel: 342 5782
Fax: 342 5682

Infotech Building, 1090
Arcadia Street, Arcadia

Sweden (Embassy)
Tel: 321 1050
Fax: 326 6677

Old Mutual Building, 167
Andries Street

Switzerland (Embassy)
Tel: 43 6707
Fax: 43 6771

818 George Avenue, Arcadia

Tanzania, United Republic of (High Commission)
Tel: 342 4371
Fax: 43 4383

George Avenue, Arcadia

Thailand (Embassy)
Tel: 342 4600
Fax: 342 4805

840 Church Street, cnr
Eastwood, Arcadia

Tunisia (Embassy)
Tel: 342 6282
Fax: 342 6284

850 Church Street, Arcadia

Turkey (Embassy)
Tel: 342 6053
Fax: 342 6052

1067 Church Street, Arcadia

Uganda (High Commission)
Tel: 342 6031
Fax: 342 6206

Infotech Building, 1090
Arcadia Street, Hatfield

Ukraine (Embassy)
Tel: 46 1946
Fax: 46 1944

398 Marais Street, Brooklyn

United Arab Emirates (Embassy)
Tel: 342 7736
Fax: 342 7738

980 Park Street, Arcadia

United Kingdom of Great Britain and Northern Ireland
High Commission
Tel: 43 3121
Fax: 43 3207

255 Hill Street, Arcadia

United States of America
(Embassy)
Tel: 342 1048
Fax: 342 2299

877 Pretorius Street, Arcadia

Uruguay (Embassy)
Tel: 43 2829
Fax: 43 2833

MIB House, 1119 Burnett Street, Hatfield

Vatican City
Tel: 344 3815

800 Pretorius Street, Arcadia

Venezuela (Embassy)
Tel: 342 0471
Fax: 342 0480

Hatfield Gables South, Hilda Street, Hatfield

Yugoslavia (Office of Interest)
Tel: 46 5626
Fax: 46 6003

163 Marais Street, Brooklyn

Zaire (Embassy)
Tel: 344 1478
Fax: 344 1510

423 Kirkness Street, Sunnyside

Zambia (High Commission)
Tel: 342 1541
Fax: 342 4963

Sanlam Centre, 353 Festival Street, Hatfield

Zimbabwe (High Commission)
Tel: 342 5125
Fax: 342 5126

798 Merton Street, Arcadia

For foreign visitors the location and telephone number of the South African Department of Foreign Affairs is also of importance:

Department of Foreign Affairs
Union Buildings, Government Avenue
Tel: 351 1000

Hospitals, clinics and medical practitioners

Hospitals are listed under 'H' in the telephone directory. In the event of an emergency patients may telephone or go directly to the casualty department. Medical practitioners are listed in the telephone directory under 'Medical' and dentists under 'Dentists'. Doctors and dentists are, however, available on a 24 hour basis at the following medical centres and hospi-

Medical facilities

tals. This list of hospitals and clinics is not complete and more entries will be found in the telephone directory under the categories indicated.

College Medicross Centre
Tel: 341 1500
    Cnr Mears & Rissik Streets
    Sunnyside

Constantia Park Medicross Centre
Tel: 998 5552
    Duvernoy Street, Constantia Park

Eugene Marais Hospital
Tel: 335 2661
    Fred Nicholson Street

Faerie Glen Hospital
Tel: 348 8811
    Cnr Atterbury Rd & Oberon Ave, Faerie Glen

Gezina Medicross Centre
Tel: 335 7790
    Gezinastad Centre, Michael Brink St, Gezina

Jacaranda Hospital
Tel: 343 2360
    213 Middelberg Street, Muckleneuk, off Walker Street

Little Company of Mary Hospital
Tel: 346 1080
    George Storrar Drive, Groenkloof
    (24 hour casualties)

Medforum General & Heart Hospital
Tel: 317 6700
    412 Schoeman Street

Moot Algemene Hospitaal
Tel: 330 0324
    18th Avenue, Rietfontein

Pretoria Academic Hospital
Tel: 329 1111

> Doctor Savage Road, Pretoria
> (Provincial Hospital – 24 hour
> casualties)

Pretoria East Hospital
Tel: 998 9090

> Menlyn Drive extension,
> Moreleta Park

Pretoria Eye Institute
Tel: 343 5873

> 630 Schoeman Street,
> Arcadia

**Pretoria North Medicross
Centre**
Tel: 565 6091

> 291 Burger Street, Pretoria
> North

Pretoria West Hospital
Tel: 386 5111

> Trans Oranje Road, Pretoria
> West
> (Provincial Hospital – 24 hour
> casualties)

**Pretoria West Medicross
Centre**
Tel: 327 5131

> Church Street, Pretoria West

Pretoria Urological Hospital
Tel: 342 9510

> Cnr Pretorius & Grosvenor
> Streets

Silverton Medicross Centre
Tel: 804 4356

> 310 Pretoria Street, Silverton

Starcare Muelmed Hospital
Tel: 44 2362/341 3540

> 577 Pretorius Street, Arcadia
> (24 hour casualties)

Unitas Hospital
Tel: 664 1100

> 39 Clifton Drive, Lyttelton

Wilgers Hospital
Tel: 807 0019

> Denneboom Drive, The
> Willows, off Lynnwood Road

Zuid-Afrikaans Hospitaal
Tel: 343 0300

> 255 Bourke Street,
> Muckleneuk

*Information Ambassadors at the
Union Buildings*

Pedestrian mall, Church Street

Safety first – a word of warning

Police service

In case of an **emergency** the Flying Squad can be contacted at the 24 hour number **10111**.

The **Central Police Station** is situated on the corner of Pretorius and Bosman Streets. The telephone number is **343 4233**. A list of police stations in Pretoria can be found at the back of the Pretoria Telephone Directory in the section Government Departments, Pretoria, under SA Police Service and the subheading Station Commanders. In the interest of tourist safety a special police patrol unit has been instituted in the central part of the city. Policemen on patrol wear very visible orange-and-white chevron-striped vests with a huge information **i** front and back and inter alia 'Information Ambassador' written on the lower chevron stripes.

General safety and security

As in many cities, it is unfortunately true that not all areas are equally safe, and some neighbourhoods may be downright dangerous. However, most of the large shopping malls work very hard at creating a safe environment, and the Police Service are visible at some of the trouble spots.

Consult your hotel management or host about places you want to visit, especially when you are single or a lonely couple. Be alert and aware of the people around you at all times, do not get drawn into meaningless conversations, and be particularly suspicious when you are approached by three or four young, casually dressed people. Shout loudly for help when necessary!

Streetmarket.
Be security conscious
where people congregate.

Downtown taxis

As in any large city, be alert and
streetwise on crowded sidewalks.

Sponsors

"Keedo"   Oil on canvas   1,2 x 1,3 m
Collection Dr and Mrs B Schutte, Cape Town

Marie Vermeulen Breedt

To view the artist's work contact tel (011) 964 1137 fax (011) 964 2123

SHERE VIEW
GUEST LODGE
Accomodation
Conferences & Functions

Shere View is set against a hillside on the eastern boundaries of Pretoria. Easy access from Lynnwood Road and Hans Strijdom Road. The Lodge is surrounded by indigenous bushveld and subtropical gardens with water features, offering a beautiful bird life and sunset views.

Luxurious accommodation
- 30 en suite double rooms with satellite TV, video and telephone.
- Mini-bar fridges with refreshments in the rooms.
- Coffee/tea maker in each room
- Laundry service

Conferences and business
- Ideal for managers' meetings, planning sessions, staff training and seminars
- Conference facilities for up to 50 delegates
- Ideal for buisiness breakfasts
- Observation room with one-way mirrors and recording equipment
- Telephone and fax facilities

Functions and weddings
- Ideal for functions, banquets and weddings
- Different menus

Recreation
- Swimming pool
- Licensed ladies' bar
- Barbecue and braai facilities
- Golf and horse riding can be arranged

Transport
- Transfers to and from Johannesburg International Airport (35 minutes)
- Trips to tourist attractions can be arranged
- Transport to shopping centres, banks and restaurants
- Doctor and hospital services

Reservations

Tel:	(012) 809 0096/809 0003
Fax:	(012) 809 0177
Cell:	082 892 7354
	083 310 2625
Int:	+27 12 809 0096

248

ENGADINI
Landscaping cc
CK 95 39589/23   Member of SALI

Tel: (012) 807 2688 Fax: (012) 807 2576

The Art of Landscaping

Landscaping services:
Industrial
Domestic
Office
Townhouses
Water features
Landscaping plans
Interior landscaping
Interior decorating
Environmental planning

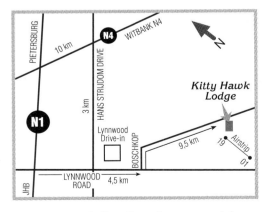

250

Charnan Laser Wars

Healthier new skin:
for 20- to 40-year-olds

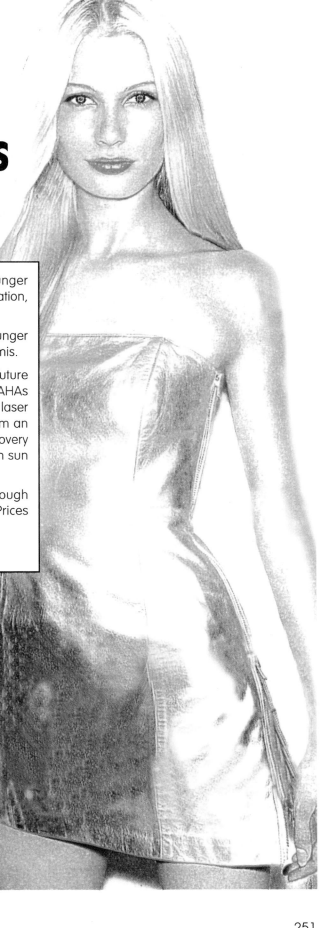

The latest invention, the Erbium Face Saver, is ideal for younger women with sun damage, fine lines and sun-induced pigmentation, including freckles and sun spots.

It's not for the severely wrinkled woman. It makes skin look younger and healhtier, diminishing fine lines and thickening the epidermis.

Making the epidermis thicker will actually help the skin fight future UV rays and damage, unlike other resurfacing methods like AHAs and Retin-A, which heighten skin's sensitivity. Similar to the CO_2 laser treatment, but much less intense, patients can walk away from an Erbium Face Saver treatment without pain and virtually no recovery time at all. The laser can be controlled according to how much sun damage a patient has.

Laser fans will usually go in for a Face Saver fix yearly, although some die-hards may undergo the treatment three-monthly. Prices vary according to the degree of sun damage.

Phone: +27 12 663 1041/2/3

charnan
MEDICAL GROUP

649 Malmesbury St • Wingate Park • Pretoria
Tel 345 4046

Phil Minnaar
Sculptor

Bouwer Broers: the beginning

This family business was founded in 1950 by Nic Bouwer and his brother Petrus. After 49 years this business is still owned by the family, Johan and Hennie Bouwer.

Bouwer Broers is well known over the city and the whole country for their bicycles, fishing tackle, camping equipment and tents.

Over the decades Bouwer Broers became a landmark in Voortrekker Road in Pretoria.

Die Werf offers:

- Traditional food from our country kitchen on open decks in nature during the summer, and next to cosy fireplaces in winter.
- Enjoy our fine selection of estate and cooperative cellar wines in the Taphuis (ladies bar) or in our rustic wine cellar.
- We cater for wedding receptions and other functions. Our chapel seating 100 guests makes weddings a one-stop occasion.

Some people simply live in Pretoria – others visit DIE WERF

PO Box 74055
Lynnwood Ridge
0040
Tel: 991 1809
Fax: 991 0674

Visit **DIE WERF** and experience South African tradition, style and hospitality. **DIE WERF**, with its restaurant, guest rooms, ladies bar and indaba room for smaller conferences, is situated amongst shady indigenous trees on the border of Faerie Glen to the east of Pretoria. This typical old farm yard is only 15 km from the city centre and 35 km from Johannesburg International Airport. Die Werf is within easy reach of the main routes, Johannesburg/Pietersburg N1 and Pretoria/Witbank N4.

Enjoy our traditional dishes to the accompaniment of birdsong.

We are proud of our wine cellar.

Ocean Basket

Shop 34
Brooklyn Square

Tel: (012) 46 1103

257

Heartbeat of Pretoria's CBD

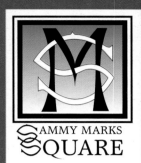

SAMMY MARKS SQUARE

PARK STREET Chagall's R·E·S·T·A·U·R·A·N·T

Tel: 342 1200
Fax: 342 1227
e-mail: chagalls@chagalls.co.za

The Park Street Chagall's has a rich tradition and has been well known to discerning diners for nearly two decades. Having recently moved to new premises in Park Street Hatfield the brightly coloured walls and beautiful shaded patio area creates a less formal and lovely relaxed atmosphere. This is where you still rub shoulders with the familiar and prominent faces in the capital.

Sammy Marks Square is the largest retail centre in the heart of Pretoria's CBD. The centre with its unusual architectural combination of modern and historical elements is superbly located in the most heavily pedestrianised area of the city and offers a wonderful array of speciality stores.

The old world charm of the restored Sammy Marks and Kynoch Buildings are integrated with the piazza and spacious, bright malls to create a warm people-friendly ambience. The unique Sammy Marks building is an example of neo-Dutch architecture and is the only remaining example of its kind of architecture in Gauteng. The Kynoch Building was built between 1875 and 1884 which makes it the oldest existing retail building in Pretoria and the only preserved example of urban architecture before 1886.

Sammy Marks Square focuses on shopping convenience and therefore offers all the basic stores for one-stop shopping. The centre also houses the City Council's library, health department offices, mayoral suite, conference centre and secure basement parking for 870 cars.

Stroll around and discover the many facets of Sammy Marks Square. You will discover it's as exciting, innovative and versatile as you are.

"Punda Malia Family"   Oil on canvas   1,2 x 1,3 m

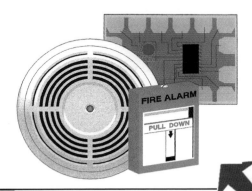

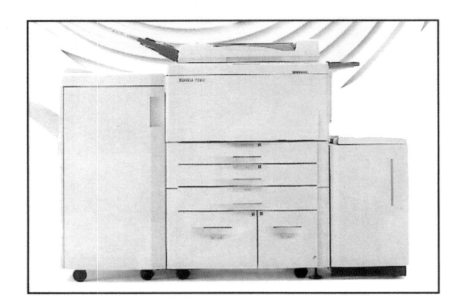

Espada Ranch

Tel: (012) 811 0024
(012) 811 0518
Fax: (011) 811 0503
Int: +27 12 911 0024

PO Box 72041
Lynnwood Ridge
Republic of South Africa
0040

**Weddings
Conferences**

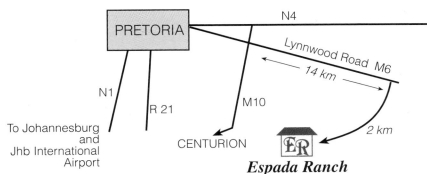

N4

Lynnwood Road M6

14 km

PRETORIA

N1

R 21

M10

2 km

To Johannesburg
and
Jhb International
Airport

CENTURION

Espada Ranch

**Training &
Conference Centre**

Plot 189 Tiegerpoort

UITKYKVLEISMARK

- For more that 30 years Uitkyk has been and still is your friendly butcher.

- We supply our top-grade meat at wholesale prices to all our discerning buyers.

- We cut and pack to your requirements.

- Have you tried our famous boerewors?

- Discuss your braai party plans with us.

- We aim to render outstanding service while you enjoy a friendly buying experience.

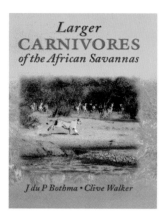

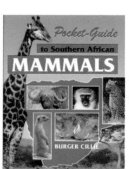
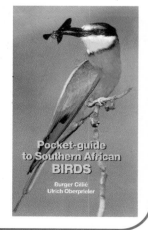

Index